MOJAVE DESERT
WILDFLOWERS

Help Us Keep This Guide Up to Date

Every effort has been made by the authors and editors to make this guide as accurate and useful as possible. However, many things can change after a guide is published—regulations change, facilities come under new management, and so forth.

We would love to hear from you concerning your experiences with this guide and how you feel it could be improved and kept up to date. While we may not be able to respond to all comments and suggestions, we'll take them to heart, and we'll also make certain to share them with the authors. Please send your comments and suggestions to falconeditorial@rowman.com.

Thanks for your input!

MOJAVE DESERT
WILDFLOWERS

A Field Guide to Wildflowers, Trees, and Shrubs of the Mojave
Desert, Including the Mojave National Preserve, Death
Valley National Park, and Joshua Tree National Park

Third Edition

PAM MACKAY THOMAS
AND TIMOTHY THOMAS

FALCONGUIDES

ESSEX, CONNECTICUT

FALCONGUIDES®

An imprint of Globe Pequot, the trade division of The Rowman & Littlefield Publishing Group, Inc.
4501 Forbes Blvd., Ste. 200
Lanham, MD 20706
www.rowman.com

Falcon and FalconGuides are registered trademarks and Make Adventure Your Story is a trademark of The Rowman & Littlefield Publishing Group, Inc.

Distributed by NATIONAL BOOK NETWORK

Photos by Pam MacKay Thomas and Timothy Thomas

Maps by The Rowman & Littlefield Publishing Group, Inc.

British Library Cataloguing in Publication Information available

Library of Congress Cataloging-in-Publication Data

Names: MacKay Thomas, Pam, 1954- author. | Thomas, Tim (Botanist), author.
Title: Mojave Desert wildflowers : a field guide to wildflowers, trees, and shrubs of the Mojave Desert, including the Mojave National Preserve, Death Valley National Park, and Joshua Tree National Park / Pam MacKay Thomas and Timothy Thomas.
Description: Third edition. | Essex, Connecticut : FalconGuides, [2024] | Includes bibliographical references and index.
Identifiers: LCCN 2024005876 (print) | LCCN 2024005877 (ebook) | ISBN 9781493064809 (paperback) | ISBN 9781493064816 (ebook)
Subjects: LCSH: Wild flowers—Mojave Desert—Identification. | Wild flowers—California—Mojave National Preserve—Identification. | Wild flowers—California—Joshua Tree National Park—Identification. | Wild flowers—Death Valley National Park (Calif. and Nev.)—Identification. | Wild flowers—Mojave Desert—Pictorial works. | Wild flowers—California—Mojave National Preserve—Pictorial works. | Wild flowers—California—Joshua Tree National Park—Pictorial works. | Wild flowers—Death Valley National Park (Calif. and Nev.)—Pictorial works. | LCGFT: Field guides.
Classification: LCC QK149 .M234 2024 (print) | LCC QK149 (ebook) | DDC 582.1309794/95—dc23/eng/20240213
LC record available at https://lccn.loc.gov/2024005876
LC ebook record available at https://lccn.loc.gov/2024005877

IN LOVING MEMORY OF OUR MOTHERS,
DOLORES AND NORMA

CONTENTS

PREFACE

It has been more than twenty years since the publication of the first edition of *Mojave Desert Wildflowers*, and over ten years since the second edition. This edition is different for several reasons. A major change, which you may have noticed on the cover, is that Pam MacKay is now Pam MacKay Thomas, and now there are two authors! We married in 2016, and since Tim contributed so much to the first and second editions without the recognition of authorship, we decided this acknowledgment was long overdue.

This edition features quite a few species that were not included in the first or second editions. One of the reasons for this is that we had a fantastic year for wildflowers in the spring of 2023, and a super-bloom also occurred in 2019. It was wonderful to see so many species that seem rare because they only come up in high rainfall years, and since we have acquired better cameras and lenses, we have been able to upgrade and replace many photos of common species as well. In the beginning of the 2023 blooming season, temperatures were colder than normal, and blooming was delayed. Once it warmed up, it seemed like everything was blooming at the same time and at opposite ends of the desert. We then enjoyed multiple field days and many camping trips. We took thousands of images and edited them down to our favorites, many of which you will find in these pages.

We have included in this edition a new and improved section on the genus *Cryptantha*. In the previous editions, we had photos of the variable seed surface features to help identify species, but we realize that most people are not likely to carry a microscope into the field! We now have a section that features photos of 13 species, and they are all distinct enough to tell apart with the naked eye. There is also a discussion of the new nomenclature that goes along with this group, as the genus *Cryptantha* has recently been broken down into several genera. There is also a new section on the tiny but fascinating and adorable *Nemacladus* flowers; this is a genus not previously addressed in the first or second editions. Additional sections with multiple featured species, some of which were not included in previous editions, include *Euphorbia*, *Pectocarya*, *Chaenactis*, *Atriplex*, and *Brickellia*.

As expected, more research has resulted in more name changes, and quite a few species are now considered to be in different families; these changes are also reflected in this new edition. For those interested in the changing taxonomy, you will find a list of plant name synonyms in an appendix toward the back of this edition.

This edition is also unique in that it is the first time that we took every photo in the book and did not rely on the photos taken by others. In previous editions we relied on a map from the DoD Mojave Desert Ecosystem Program, but we constructed a new map for this book. While we appreciate our great photographers and map provider for the first two editions, we decided that it was time to focus on making this *our* book. Even if you already have the first or second edition, or both, we encourage you to get this new unique and improved third edition. As each edition features some species that the others do not have, all three together give pretty good coverage of the plants you are likely to encounter in the Mojave Desert.

As with previous editions, writing the comments for each plant was fun and educational for us! In this third edition as well, each species has various snippets of information; some comments are on the medical and industrial chemistries of the plants, some address insect interactions, while others include little tidbits about the people that first found and described the plant. Some entries discuss Native American usage of the plant, and others may consider how the plant got its name. We hope the book is useful and that you enjoy it. What are we waiting for? Let's go botanizing, in the field or from the armchair!

ACKNOWLEDGMENTS

We are so thankful to all the people who bought one or both of the previous editions of this book, not only for the purchase, but also for the many positive comments we have received over the years from professional botanists, amateurs, and those who just love to visit and explore this great desert. It is encouraging to know that you have found the book useful and have enjoyed it!

We very much appreciate our local fellow plant enthusiasts, especially Tom Egan and Wendy Walker, who spent countless hours finding out where plants were in bloom this spring and posting photos on Facebook and other social media. We got many clues on where to focus our plant searches by following their posts. The posts of Duncan Bell and Naomi Fraga of the California Botanic Garden were also very helpful in this regard. We especially want to thank RT Hawke, as he always finds the best local blooming sites and tells us where to look, especially for plants that are rare and special. Stationed in the middle of the Mojave Desert at the UC Riverside research station in the Granite Mountains, Jim André has contributed enormously to the known distribution and documentation of the Mojave Desert flora. While trying to prove that we had discovered a new location for several plants, we searched the records in the Jepson eFlora or iNaturalist, only to find that Jim had already been there and found those plants! Kudos, Jim.

As with the previous editions, we also want to thank the researchers, young and old, who are making new discoveries about plant systematics, species distributions, plant biochemistry and physiology, and species interactions. Their efforts enabled us to better understand species relationships, update scientific names, and provide interesting new materials to incorporate into species accounts in this edition. The newly published *California Desert Plants*, by Rundel, Gustafson, and Kauffmann, came out in such a timely manner. It summarizes much of the current knowledge about desert plant physiology and ecology, adaptations to desert environments, vegetation types, and other wonderful tidbits of information, some of which we used in writing this edition. We highly recommend that you purchase their excellent book as well!

Many thanks to Dave LeGere at Rowman & Littlefield for editing this edition. We appreciate his patience and willingness to deal with our many questions. We are also indebted to all those who contributed to the previous editions of this book, including our editors and those who provided technical assistance and support, including Andy Sanders,

ACKNOWLEDGMENTS

Elizabeth Lawlor, Don Buchanon, Larry Reese, Gordon Pratt, and others. Although we have replaced all the photographs previously provided by other photographers, we acknowledge that there would not be a third edition without their initial contributions. These previous photographers include Stephen Ingram, John Reid, RT Hawke, Thomas Elder III, Michael Honer, and Wendell Minnich; we are indebted to all of them. We are also grateful to many friends and family members, who provided encouragement and support, and to our grandchildren, who understood that we had to forgo more frequent visits in order to complete this manuscript by the due date.

INTRODUCTION

Mojave Desert Geography and Climate

The Mojave Desert is the smallest North American desert, occupying less than 50,000 square miles between the Sonoran Desert to the south and Great Basin Desert to the north. The southern border runs along the northern edge of the Transverse Ranges, through the middle of Joshua Tree National Park in the Little San Bernardino Mountains, and crossing the Colorado River around Lake Havasu City. The Garlock and San Andreas Faults, the Tehachapi Mountains, and the eastern Sierra Nevada define the western border. On the north the Mojave extends into the Owens, Eureka, Saline, and Death Valleys in California;

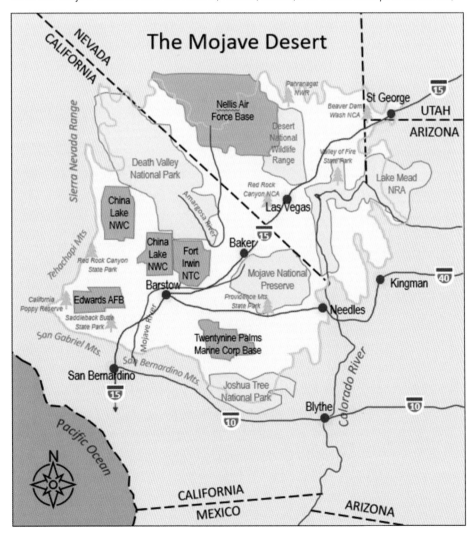

The Mojave Desert

in Nevada the Mojave Desert includes most of Clark County, with fingers extending north into Nye and Lincoln Counties into a small corner of Washington County in southwestern Utah near St. George. The Mojave also occupies the northwestern portion of Arizona to Kingman in Mohave County, with an extension into the lower Grand Canyon area. The map provides a generalized regional view of the area covered in this book.

This area is considered a desert because there is very little precipitation accompanied by significant water loss due to evaporation; in fact, the Mojave is the driest of the North American deserts. The mountains along the southern and western desert borders block many of the moisture-bearing clouds carried by westerly winds from the coast. This "rain shadow" limits the amount of precipitation that reaches the desert. Lowland areas of the western Mojave average about 5 inches of precipitation per year, while the drier areas in the eastern Mojave average only 2 inches per year. Death Valley's average is less than 2 inches per year. In some years less than ½ inch of rain occurs. When it does rain, prevailing dry air masses and winds quickly facilitate evaporation from the soil surface. Most of the rain in the western Mojave occurs during the winter months, whereas the eastern Mojave has a greater chance of receiving summer monsoon rains; many areas east of Twentynine Palms receive more than half of the annual precipitation in the summer months.

The presence or absence of atmospheric water and cloud cover has a tremendous influence on temperature. Water efficiently absorbs and releases heat, so moisture in the atmosphere tends to buffer temperatures. Since the Mojave Desert has low atmospheric moisture and cloud cover, it is a land of temperature extremes; it is very hot in summer and cold in winter. Winter storms may bring snow to the higher elevations of the Mojave. On these rare occasions the snow normally melts within a very short time.

Mojave Desert Topography and Geology

Complex geologic processes have formed the varied topography and soil types in the Mojave Desert, creating many different microhabitats that contribute to the plant diversity present today. The movements of tectonic plates have resulted in the formation of the numerous north–south mountain ranges and valleys in the eastern and northern Mojave Desert and Great Basin. This landscape is called horst-and-graben, where "horst" refers to the moun-tainous uplifted or tilted blocks, and "graben" means "grave," referring to the sunken valleys between the mountain ranges; it is also referred to as a "basin and range" landscape. The lowest graben is Death Valley, with over 550 square miles below sea level, including Bad-water, the lowest spot in the nation, with an elevation of 282 feet below sea level. Some of

A view from Badwater in Death Valley, the lowest elevation in the nation, looking at Telescope Peak at 11,049' in the Panamint Range

the uplifted mountains are quite high, such as Telescope Peak in the Panamint Range (elevation 11,049 feet), which overlooks Badwater to the east. In contrast, the western Mojave is an expansive plain with low, rounded hills known as the Antelope Valley.

Volcanic activity has occurred in what is now the Mojave since at least the Mesozoic, the age of the dinosaurs. Evidence of more recent volcanic activity can be found at Black Mountain in the central Mojave, and lava flows at Cima happened as recently as 12,000 years ago. **Lava flows** and **cinder cones** are visible at Lavic, Amboy, and Pisgah, and in the far northern Mojave and Owens Valley. Volcanic activity in the Mojave is also evident from the presence of **hot springs**. These develop where faults have allowed water that has been heated by magma to come to the surface. The soils around hot springs are often salt-encrusted; these are places where only the most salt-tolerant halophytic plants can grow.

Runoff waters from mountains in and bordering the Mojave Desert have no route to the ocean, so the interior drainage collects in low valleys; an exception is the far northeastern fringe of the desert drained by the Colorado River. Throughout the peak glacial periods of the Pleistocene, the increased precipitation and the melting of glaciers caused so much water to accumulate in these low spots that a large proportion of the Mojave was covered by a series of scattered lakes. The gigantic Lake Manly, which covered what is now Death

A lava flow can be seen behind a creosote bush at Pisgah

Cinder cones in the northern Mojave Desert

Valley, was over 600 feet deep and 90 miles long. There were numerous smaller lakes, including Lake Searles, Lake Panamint, China Lake, and just north of the Mojave Desert, Owens Lake. Lake Mannix stretched along the Mojave River from Barstow to the Cave Mountain area. Lake Thompson occurred in the Antelope Valley; the old lake bed remains include the Buckhorn, Rosamond, and Rogers Dry Lakes.

With the retreat of the glaciers and drying of the climate, these lakes have dried up and are now called **playas**. The ancient shorelines of many of these relic lakes are visible

Ancient shorelines of Lake Manly are visible as strand lines on a slope in Death Valley National Park

as strand lines on adjacent hillsides. During wetter periods, runoff laden with salts and minerals reaches these playas, but because of heavy sedimentation and clay deposits in the underlying soil, the runoff water tends to pool on top. This water eventually evaporates, leaving the salts and minerals deposited on the playa surface. Some playas are high in salts that behave like common baking soda, causing self-rising soil that puffs up and forms an upper crust; these are called **wet playas**. An example is Soda Lake near Baker. Other playas (called **dry playas**) retain clay-like properties, forming large cracks in the mud as the water evaporates, such as at El Mirage Dry Lake in the western Mojave. The high salt content usually prevents plants from growing on the surface in the center of either playa type, but salt-tolerant (halophytic) plants often occupy margins.

Precipitation runoff, especially during the Pleistocene, has eroded and moved enormous amounts of material from mountains in and around the desert to the valleys below, resulting in deposits called alluvium. These deposits are at least 4,000 feet deep in the Antelope Valley, decreasing in depth going eastward. The sloping accumulations of alluvial debris that form skirts at the bases of mountains are called **alluvial fans**, or **bajadas** where fans coalesce. The particle sizes of the deposited materials are larger and coarser on the upper fans and finer-textured below. In valleys, the fine-textured particles have capillarity, meaning that water is drawn upward. It readily evaporates from the soil surface, leaving salts in the soil that affect vegetation.

Wet playas often have clumps of self-rising soil

Dry playa covered with cracked mud at Dry Lake Valley in Nevada

Bajada of merging alluvial fans in the Last Chance Mountains

Mojave Desert Soils and Rock Surfaces

Topsoil formation is poor in most areas of the Mojave. This upper soil layer, which contains most mineral nutrients, is usually less than 6 inches deep; in fertile farmlands it can be several feet deep. Topsoil development is very slow. Low water availability results in sparse vegetation, so there is not a lot of organic debris from which topsoil can form, and lack of water and cold winter temperatures inhibit the growth of microbes that decompose organic debris. Many plant species need a deep topsoil layer and cannot grow in the desert for this reason.

Cryptobiotic soil crusts form when strands of nitrogen-fixing cyanobacteria hold soil particles together, forming a stable matrix where algae, lichens, and mosses can infiltrate. This crust prevents the strong desert winds from blowing away the soil, especially the smaller particles, so the soil can hold more mineral nutrients. These crusts may be the only source of nitrogen for plants in many desert areas. They are necessary for the establishment of some species, yet they also function as a barrier to other seeds. The seeds of the invasive red brome (*Bromus rubens*) are unable to penetrate crusts, which can explain why this plant is prevalent in disturbed areas where the crusts have been broken. Off-highway vehicles, grazing, and other types of soil disturbance are destructive to cryptobiotic crusts, which are essential to proper arid land ecosystem functioning and dust suppression.

Caliche, a hardened, impenetrable subsurface layer of accumulated calcium carbonates bound to gravel, clay, and other materials, is common throughout the Mojave. As water and salts are drawn to the soil surface by evaporation, these materials that are left behind below the surface harden into a crust that can be a few inches to a few feet thick. Water does not soak through this layer, and it is difficult for plant roots to penetrate.

Carbonate outcrops (limestone, dolomite, and marble) are scattered throughout the mountains of the Mojave Desert and on low, north-facing slopes of the Transverse Ranges. The chemical makeup of these carbonate soils is a stressful environment for plants, yet some species are able to tolerate it. Many of our rare and endemic Mojave Desert species are found on these soils.

Desert varnish is the dark reddish-brown or black coating seen on the outer surfaces of rocks and boulders in many parts of the Mojave. It is made up of manganese or iron oxides, it is only several hundred microns thick, and it takes thousands of years to develop. Several theories for its formation have been proposed, one of which involves the absorption and slow oxidation of atmospheric iron and manganese by bacteria that live on the rock surfaces. The effects of desert varnish on plant growth are unclear, although there are some desert plants that seem to be found mostly in areas where desert varnish exists, growing in the spaces between the rocks.

Desert pavement is a relatively flat terrain covered with tightly packed or interlocking pebble- to cobble-sized rocks that form a mosaic. Beneath the cobbles is a unique soil layer composed of a few centimeters of silts and clays with small air pockets. The fine-grained materials have been deposited and accumulated over millenia; these create a

Desert pavement covered by desert varnish

layer between the surface cobbles and underlying rocky substrate. Desert varnish is nearly always present on these surfaces, further sealing against water penetration and making these surfaces a difficult place for seeds to germinate and roots to establish.

Past Vegetation of the Mojave

Pack-rat (*Neotoma lepida*) homes (middens) give us a glimpse of what species were present since the last glacial maximum, about 18,000 to 20,000 years ago. Their nests are built in crevices, caves, and under dense vegetation. The pack rat makes improvements by dragging in sticks, green plant parts, animal droppings, bones, and just about whatever else is available. As pack rats die, new generations of pack rats continue to build nests at the same site, adding materials to the older nests; in some places this has gone on for millennia. The abundant urine that is added to the nest components tends to crystallize, solidify, and preserve the remains of woody plant species used in nest construction, so that they are still identifiable millennia later. These remains from numerous middens have been identified, quantified, and radiocarbon-dated to give a picture of what the vegetation was like during the last 18,000 years in the Mojave Desert and in other areas where middens are found.

About 16,000 to 12,000 years ago, the glaciers began to retreat, and from 12,000 to 10,000 years ago, there was a warming trend, marking the beginning of the modern

A pack-rat nest in rocks in the eastern Mojave Desert

interglacial age called the Holocene. In the middle Holocene there was a drying and warming trend, called the xerothermic, that favored more xeric (dry-adapted) species. Pack-rat midden data from various sites in the Mojave Desert paint different pictures of vegetation change in response to these climate changes. This is not surprising, since topography, latitude, and climate varied from site to site. However, there are general trends that will be described here.

During the last glacial period, pinyon and juniper woodlands were much more widespread, occurring at much lower elevations than at present, sometimes even on the desert floor in moist areas. However, now there remain only small, isolated pockets of woodland, which are restricted to the middle and upper elevations of scattered mountain ranges. On the lowest and very driest sites, steppe species, such as big sagebrush (*Artemisia tridentata*) and winter fat (*Krascheninnikovia lanata*) were present. As the climate changed to the hotter and drier conditions of the xerothermic, the woodlands retreated to higher altitudes and latitudes, and steppe species also migrated northward and upward to moister, cooler areas. With this decline in woodland and steppe species at low elevations came a corresponding increase in heat-loving species, such as white bur-sage (*Ambrosia dumosa*), pygmy-cedar (*Peucephyllum schottii*), honey-sweet (*Tidestromia oblongifolia*), and creosote bush (*Larrea tridentata*) in the lowlands. Creosote bush arrived very early after the glacial retreat in some locations, evidently migrating north from the Sonoran Desert. The King Clone Creosote near Lucerne Valley is estimated to be over 11,000 years old and is one of the oldest living plants on Earth. At the end of the middle Holocene, there was a temporary increase in precipitation, allowing the immigration of more mesic (water-requiring) species such as Mormon tea (*Ephedra* species), rhatany (*Krameria* species), and desert almond (*Prunus fasciculata*), which contribute to the species richness present today.

Past Human Uses of Mojave Desert Plants

Ethnobotanical information, given in the comments section for numerous plants in this book, explains how plants were used by specific tribes that occupied different areas of the Mojave Desert in historical times. Groups with larger populations were restricted to areas with permanent water at rivers and springs, such as the Mojave people, who lived along the Colorado River from the area of Needles to Lake Mead. This was one of the largest concentrations of people in the Southwest at the beginning of Spanish exploration. They were farmers and fishermen. The trade route the Mojave people took from the Colorado

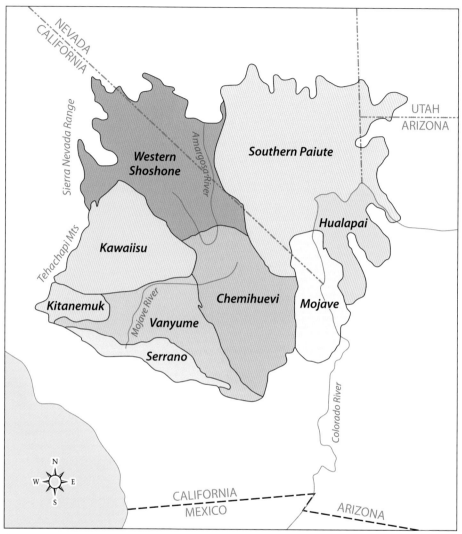

Approximate territories of Native American peoples of the Mojave Desert at the time of European contact

River to the coast, passing through the Vanyume population in the vicinity of present-day Victorville, eventually became the Mojave Road. Throughout most of the desert, water and food items were not as plentiful, so populations of most of these groups were small. These were primarily hunter-gatherers, relying mostly on plant foods and supplementing their diets with meat when it was available. Because of the seasonal availability of resources, they had annual migration patterns, occupying lowlands in winter months and higher elevations in summer.

Early Botanical Exploration of the Mojave Desert

This section gives information about some of the bold, adventurous individuals who explored and collected plants in the Mojave Desert during the past two to three centuries. Many of the early collectors sent plant specimens to university botanists, especially John Torrey (1796–1873) of Princeton and Asa Gray (1810–1888) of Harvard, who often named plants in honor of the collector. It is impossible to include all the collectors on this list, especially those who have made important contributions in the last fifty years. You will find more information in the comments section for many of the species accounts.

Annie Montague Alexander (1867–1950) and her friend **Louise Kellogg** (1879–1967) collected museum specimens of more than 800 plants, as well as many animals and fossils, throughout the northern and eastern Mojave between 1939 and 1941. Annie funded research for Joseph Grinnell, John C. Merriam, and other well-known scientists, and she was a benefactress of the University of California at Berkeley Museum of Paleontology.

William Whitman Bailey (1845–1915) studied botany under Asa Gray of Harvard and later became a botany professor at Brown. He was a botanist on the 1867–1868 US Geological Exploration of the 40th Parallel, and he made vast collections in southern Nevada.

Ira Waddell Clokey (1878–1950) collected throughout southern Nevada, culminating in the production of a noteworthy flora of the Spring Mountains (Mount Charleston) in the 1930s.

Frederick Vernon Coville (1867–1937) was the chief of botany for the US Department of Agriculture, an instructor at Cornell University, and curator of the National Herbarium before and after it was transferred to the Smithsonian. He made extensive plant collections on the Death Valley expedition of 1891.

Mary DeDecker (1909–2000) made botanical explorations throughout the northern Mojave Desert and Owens Valley. She collected nearly 6,500 specimens, many of which she sent to Philip A. Munz when he was working on *A California Flora*. She started the Owens Valley Committee to protect Owens Valley water from the Los Angeles Department of Water and Power; she founded the Bristlecone Chapter of the California Native Plant Society; and she wrote *Flora of the Northern Mojave Desert*.

John Charles Frémont (1813–1890) worked with the US Topographical Corps on surveys in the eastern United States. In the 1840s he was appointed to lead three expeditions to map routes to the West, including one in 1844 that took him from the Tehachapi Mountains, across the Mojave Desert in southern California, and northeast through southern

Nevada. Although he was not a botanist, he made many important collections, one of which was the pinyon pine he found near Cajon Pass. Numerous plant species are named for Frémont.

Father Francisco Garcés (1738–1781) was a Franciscan priest who was the first white man to journey through the Mojave Desert. He followed what is now known as the Mojave Road, passing through Piute Creek, the Providence Mountains, the New York Mountains, and Soda Springs. He encountered the Vanyume at the Mojave River in 1776, near the present-day Oro Grande, and reported on their use of native plants.

M. French Gilman (1871–1944) was a longtime caretaker and naturalist at Death Valley. He made numerous plant collections and ornithological observations.

George H. Goddard (1817–1906) was a cartographer from Great Britain. He served as a naturalist to assist Lieutenant Tredwell Moore on an expedition to eastern California in the 1850s to find a route for a railway that would pass over the Sierra Nevada Range. He made the first map of Death Valley, and he collected hundreds of botanical specimens from that region.

Joseph Christmas Ives (1828–1868) participated in the Whipple expedition and was then assigned to explore the Colorado River. He made botanical collections around present-day Lake Mead and into the Grand Canyon. He erroneously predicted that white settlers would leave that area alone, as it resembled the "gates of hell."

Edmund Carroll Jaeger (1887–1983) was head of the zoology department at Riverside City College from the 1920s to the 1950s. He made botanical collections throughout the Mojave and Colorado Deserts, finding new species and documenting species ranges. He authored *The California Desert*, *Desert Wild Flowers*, *Desert Wildlife*, *A Naturalist's Death Valley*, and *Deserts of North America*. He made the first botanical collections in the Clark Mountains and an important report of plants from the Spring Mountains. Numerous Mojave Desert plants are named in his honor.

Willis Linn Jepson (1867–1946) collected throughout the Mojave Desert in the early 1900s, including Victorville, Barstow, Stoddard Wells, the Ord Mountains, the Panamint and Funeral Mountains, and along the Colorado River. He founded the California Botanical Society and wrote *Trees of California*, *Manual of the Flowering Plants of California*, and the unfinished, multivolume *Flora of California*.

Marcus Eugene Jones (1852–1934) was a self-educated mining engineer and botanist who worked for a Salt Lake City railroad company. He collected plants throughout the West, including the Mojave Desert and San Bernardino Mountains. He questioned the authority of Asa Gray and other prominent botanists by publishing *Contributions to Western Botany*, making it possible for western botanists to publish on their own.

Clinton Hart Merriam (1855–1942) was the head of the Division of Ornithology and Mammalogy for the US Department of Agriculture. One of the first of his many biological surveys of the West was the department's Death Valley expedition in the 1890s. He developed the life zone concept to explain distributions of plants with the purpose of determining the suitability of land for farming.

Philip A. Munz (1892–1974) collected throughout the Mojave Desert, often with other important botanists, including Marcus E. Jones and John C. Roos. He wrote *A California Flora*, in collaboration with David D. Keck, and *A Flora of Southern California*, as well as several popular wildflower books, including the 1963 UC Press volume, *California Desert Wildflowers*.

Aven Nelson (1859–1952) was a professor of botany and college president at the University of Wyoming. He was primarily interested in the flora of the Rocky Mountains but collected extensively throughout the western states, including parts of the Mojave Desert.

Edward Palmer (1831–1911) was born in England but spent most of his life collecting over 10,000 species of plants in the Americas. In 1891 he led an expedition across California through Death Valley, and he collected extensively in southwestern Utah. Many plant species are named in his honor.

Samuel Bonsall Parish (1838–1928) and **William Fletcher Parish** (1840–1918) were brothers from San Bernardino, California. They made extensive botanical-collection trips throughout the local mountains and deserts, including the Mojave. Samuel was in contact with many of the leading botanists, and many species were named for him.

Charles Christopher Parry (1823–1890) worked for the Pacific Railroad and Mexican Boundary Surveys and made many plant collection trips to the deserts and mountains of the American Southwest. He discovered numerous new species, and quite a few are named in his honor.

Carl Albert Purpus (1853–1941) was a German-born horticulturalist who made extensive collection trips to many parts of the United States and Central America. From 1895 to 1899 he explored southern and western Nevada, northern and western Arizona, western Utah, and the northeastern portion of the Mojave Desert in California. He was an approved collector for the University of California at Berkeley Herbarium, although he was not paid. He supported himself by selling seeds and unusual plants that he collected to German horticulturalists.

Sereno Watson (1826–1892) was a camp cook who was appointed as plant collector when William Bailey left the Clarence King expedition of the 40th Parallel. He later was one of the botanists on the 1860–1864 Josiah D. Whitney California Geological Survey, where he collected and described many species across Utah, Nevada, and the eastern Sierra Nevada Range.

George M. Wheeler (1842–1905) conducted surveys in the 1870s for the US Corps of Engineers. The first large survey documented geological, botanical, zoological, and archaeological information on vast areas of southern Nevada, southwestern Utah, and eastern California, including the Mojave Desert. He received such acclaim for the first survey that Congress decided to fund a second survey through Death Valley to the Colorado River.

Lt. Amiel Weeks Whipple (1817–1863) commanded the Pacific Railroad Survey of the 35th Parallel. He made numerous important botanical collections through the Mojave Desert with the survey surgeon and botanist **Dr. John Milton Bigelow** (1804–1878). The survey route was that of the historic Mojave Road and later the famous Route 66, but it was not the ultimate location of the transcontinental railway.

Carl B. Wolf (1905–1974) collected in Kern County and the northwestern Mojave Desert. He was a botanist at the Rancho Santa Ana Botanic Garden and author of several works on oaks and cypress.

Present Vegetation of the Mojave

Although the Mojave Desert does not sustain lush vegetation, the rich topographic variation supports high species diversity, with more than 2,600 species of plants (this excludes elevations above 7,500 feet in the Panamint, Clark, Kingston, Spring, and Sheep Ranges). Some of the most common plant families in the Mojave include the sunflower family (Asteraceae), the grass family (Poaceae), the pea family (Fabaceae), the mustard family (Brassicaceae), the buckwheat family (Polygonaceae), the goosefoot family (Chenopodiaceae), and what was formerly the figwort family, Scrophulariaceae (most of which is now included in the Plantaginaceae, Phrymaceae, and Orobanchaceae).

About one-fourth of Mojave Desert plant taxa are endemic, meaning they are found nowhere else; those with restricted ranges and/or low abundance are considered to be rare. Almost 10 percent of Mojave Desert plants are considered special-status plants—that is, rare enough to be protected by state or federal listing as threatened or endangered or considered rare by other programs or organizations, such as the California Native Plant Society. This is a far lower proportion of special-status plants than the 35 percent reported in the entire state of California. There may be more, as botanical exploration of the Mojave is not yet complete. Because it can be so hot and dry, and there is so much ground to cover, even the most dedicated botanists tend to stick to the roads while collecting specimens. There are so many Mojave Desert canyons and mountain areas where the flora has not yet been documented. There may be undescribed species left to discover!

Different species have individual ranges of tolerance to environmental conditions, so where plants occur depends on elevation, amount of precipitation, soil type, temperature, slope aspect, and many other variables, including the past history of dispersal. Plants are often found in assemblages of those that have similar tolerances, called vegetation types. The species accounts commonly mention the vegetation type in which a species is found.

Vegetation types are determined by the dominant perennial species, which are those that are often the most abundant, sometimes the most conspicuous, and/or those that occupy the greatest area. In addition, nearly all desert vegetation types have ephemerals, which are annuals that germinate in response to seasonal rain. In the Mojave Desert most of these annuals germinate in late winter and appear in the spring and early summer, but occasionally there is a late-summer-to-fall crop, especially in the eastern Mojave, where monsoon rains are more likely. The sizes of the annuals often vary with the amount of rain and duration of the rainy season; in a dry year a plant can be much smaller, and vice versa. Many of the spring annuals have seed coat compounds that inhibit germination. There must be enough winter rain to completely wash away these compounds before germination can occur. The summer-to-fall annuals also appear in response to rain, but they require high temperatures to germinate, and they must be able to tolerate heat after germination. The species diversity of spring annuals is much greater than that of summer-to-fall annuals.

The vegetation types described below are not discrete but blend into one another across environmental gradients, such as an elevation or moisture gradient. Areas where the vegetation types overlap and blend are called ecotones. In general, the vegetation types are presented in order of increasing elevation, beginning with those vegetation types found in the lowest areas of the Mojave Desert, except for riparian and dry wash vegetation types, which can cover wide elevation ranges.

Alkali sink vegetation generally occurs in the lowest areas of the Mojave, often in ring-like zones surrounding playas at or below 3,000 feet. These are areas where rainwater collects and pools; it doesn't penetrate the soil rapidly due to the presence of a clay or caliche layer under the surface.

The surface water eventually evaporates, but the salts that were washed in with the water accumulate and can often be seen as white patches, or if in very high

Alkali sink with Allenrolfea occidentalis *in Death Valley National Park*

Salt crystals drying at the edge of Cudahy Spring in the Last Chance Canyon of the El Paso Mountains in Red Rock Canyon State Park

concentrations, as large chunks of salt crystals. These salts give the soil a very high pH and they tend to draw water out of roots. Plants that live in alkali sinks have methods to deal with salt; they are called halophytes. Common alkali sink perennials include iodine bush (*Allenrolfea occidentalis*), bush seepweed (*Suaeda nigra*), yerba mansa (*Anemopsis californica*), honey mesquite (*Neltuma odorata*), introduced Russian thistle (*Salsola tragus*), saltgrass (*Distichlis spicata*), and the introduced salt cedar (*Tamarix ramosissima*). Some common annual plants that thrive in alkali sinks and elsewhere include yellow pepperweed (*Lepidium flavum*) and Mojave stinkweed (*Cleomella obtusifolia*).

Saltbush scrub occurs in uplands where soils are dominated by silt and clay, often encircling the extreme halophytic alkali sink zone. Soil salts are present, but they are not as highly concentrated as in the alkali sink. However, it is still too salty to support a creosote bush scrub community, and the soil particle size is too fine to be friendly to root growth of many common desert shrubs. Plants here must still deal with high salt content and they also must tolerate the soil structure. Dominant species of saltbush scrub include saltbushes (*Atriplex* species), which are members of the goosefoot family (Chenopodiaceae). The saltbush species in the Mojave Desert include four-wing saltbush (*Atriplex canescens*), shadscale (*A. confertifolia*), allscale (*A. polycarpa*), desert holly (*A. hymenelytra*), Parry's saltbush (*A. parryi*), Mojave saltbush (*A. spinifera*), and near water or alkali washes or seeps, lens-scale (*A. lentiformis*). Some of these species can also be found in shadscale

Saltbush scrub vegetation at Cuddeback Lake

scrub vegetation that occurs in higher elevations in the northern Mojave and near Death Valley. Saltbush scrub communities, and shadscale scrub as well, also commonly include hop-sage (*Grayia spinosa*), winter fat (*Krascheninnikovia lanata*), and sometimes alkali goldenbush (*Isocoma acradenia*).

Creosote bush scrub covers the bulk of the desert floor and lower alluvial fans and bajadas. Creosote bush (*Larrea tridentata*), which can withstand a broad range of environmental conditions, is the dominant species, not only in the Mojave, but in the Sonoran and Chihuahuan Deserts as well. The shrubs seem evenly spaced with enough distance between so that bare ground is seen between them. This is in part due to substances secreted by creosote roots that inhibit root growth of adjacent plants. In different parts of its range in the Mojave, there are codominant shrubs with smaller ranges of tolerance, so that in different areas you will see different shrub species associated with creosote, such as white bursage (*Ambrosia dumosa*), brittlebush (*Encelia farinosa*, *Encelia actoni*, *Encelia virginensis*), cheesebush (*Ambrosia salsola*), Mojave yucca (*Yucca schidigera*), silver cholla (*Cylindropuntia echinocarpa*), and beavertail (*Opuntia basilaris*). In areas where several of these associate species are present, the vegetation may be classified as **mixed desert scrub**.

Desert dune vegetation often occurs within creosote bush scrub in areas of high sand concentrations. The dunes are not stable; sand is constantly blowing up the windward side and sliding down the leeward side when the angle of the slope gets beyond the angle

Creosote bush scrub vegetation at Bonnie Claire Flat in Nevada

Eureka Dunes in northern Death Valley National Park

Plants stabilizing drifting sand at Stovepipe Wells in Death Valley

of repose. The constant sand movement can prevent root establishment, so the steepest areas near the crests of taller dunes, where sand movement is greatest, lack vegetation. The rapid rate of water percolation through sand further adds to the unfavorable environment for plant establishment, as do the stresses of being buffeted by blowing sand, being subjected to intense solar radiation, and having the low nutrient availability characteristic of sandy soils. However, some plants are able to cling to life a little farther down the dune slope, where sand movement is not so rapid and where some water can be retained beneath the surface, protected from evaporation by layers of sand above. These plants, which help to stabilize the sand, must have deep roots to take advantage of water below the surface, and they must be fast-growing to overcome the problem of being buried or having roots exposed by moving sand. Dominant dune species include honey mesquite (*Neltuma odorata*), desert willow (*Chilopsis linearis*), desert sand-verbena (*Abronia villosa*), bugseed (*Dicoria canescens*), and sandpaper plant (*Petalonyx thurberi*). Grasses can dominate on some dunes, and their fibrous roots also contribute to dune stability. Examples include big galleta (*Hilaria rigida*) and sand ricegrass (*Stipa hymenoides*). Eureka Dune grass (*Swallenia alexandrae*) is only found on Eureka Dunes and is a true psammophyte, a dune-adapted species that does not survive elsewhere. There are ten sand dune complexes within the Mojave Desert, in addition to other areas with drifting, banked sand.

Joshua tree woodland occurs between 2,500 and 4,500 feet, in areas that receive between 6 and 15 inches of rainfall per year. The Joshua tree (*Yucca brevifolia*) is the

Joshua tree woodland with Yucca jaegeriana *in the eastern Mojave Desert*

dominant plant of this vegetation type in the western, southern, and northern Mojave Desert, while the newly recognized Jaeger's Joshua tree (*Yucca jaegeriana*) dominates this vegetation type in the eastern Mojave to Nevada, Arizona, and southwestern Utah. On a map, it appears that *Y. brevifolia* locations are west of the 116°W longitude line, while *Y. jaegeriana* is to the east. Edmund C. Jaeger asserted that if you drew a line around the entire range of the Joshua tree (which now would include both species), you would be drawing a line around the entire Mojave Desert; however, the southeastern limit of *Y. jaegeriana* occurs in Sonoran Desert habitats with saguaro cactus (*Carnegia gigantea*). Common associates of the Joshua tree in the Joshua tree woodland community include Mojave yucca (*Yucca schidigera*), paper-bag bush (*Scutellaria mexicana*), box thorn (*Lycium andersonii, Lycium cooperi*), sage (*Salvia dorrii, Salvia mohavensis*), and buckwheat (*Eriogonum* species).

Blackbush scrub can occur on its own or as an understory of Joshua tree woodland or pinyon-juniper woodland. It has a wide elevational range. The dominant species is blackbush (*Coleogyne ramosissima*), which often occurs in vast, somewhat dense stands, making the landscape appear almost a uniform dark-gray color. The species that are commonly associated with blackbush are mostly found in several vegetation types. These include

Blackbush scrub vegetation in the Mojave National Preserve

Blackbush (Coleogyne ramosissima) *in bloom*

ephedra (*Ephedra nevadensis, Ephedra viridis*), hop-sage (*Grayia spinosa*), turpentine broom (*Thamnosma montana*), horsebrush (*Tetradymia* species), cheesebush (*Ambrosia salsola*), and winter fat (*Krascheninnikovia lanata*).

   Sagebrush scrub is the dominant vegetation type of the Great Basin Desert, but some can be found along the margins of the Mojave, such as in the southern Sierra Nevada foothills, the northern slopes of the Transverse Ranges, and along the slopes of the higher desert mountains in the eastern Mojave Desert. Sagebrush scrub can occur on its own or as an understory of pinyon-juniper woodland. The dominant species is big sagebrush (*Artemisia tridentata* subsp. *tridentata*), and in some places it can form nearly pure stands. Other species that may be present include saltbush (*Atriplex* species), rubber rabbitbrush (*Ericameria nauseosa*), green ephedra (*Ephedra viridis*), hop-sage (*Grayia spinosa*), and bitterbrush (*Purshia glandulosa*). There are also numerous species of grasses, including perennial

Sagebrush scrub vegetation in the eastern Mojave Desert

bunchgrasses. Cheat-grass (*Bromus tectorum*) is a frequent annual invasive that competes with the native grasses and is thought to increase fire frequency.

Pinyon-juniper woodland is found between 4,500 and 8,000 feet in areas that receive 12 to 20 inches of precipitation each year, some of which may be in the form of snow. The summer and winter temperatures in this zone are generally lower than those of the desert floor. The dominant tree is pinyon pine (*Pinus monophylla*), or in some areas of the eastern Mojave, the two-needle pinyon pine (*Pinus edulis*). A codominant is the California juniper (*Juniperus californica*) or in some areas in the eastern Mojave, Utah juniper (*Juniperus osteosperma*). Some locations have both juniper species, while infrequently they are both absent, and occasionally the junipers occur without pinyon pine. Other associates include bitterbrush (*Purshia glandulosa*), Apache plume (*Fallugia paradoxa*), big sagebrush (*Artemisia tridentata*), green ephedra (*Ephedra viridis*), mountain mahogany (*Cercocarpus* species), and buckwheat (*Eriogonum* species). Pinyon-juniper woodland is also a common vegetation type in mountains of the Great Basin.

The vegetation cover is denser than at lower elevations, and it can support fire, although the fire frequency is very low, naturally occurring every 150 to 300 years. When fires do occur, they can be devastating; once burned, it may take up to 100 years or more to recover. Slow-growing pinyon pines need nurse plants to become established, since cold temperatures and frost heaving destabilize the soil and harm fragile roots of seedlings.

Pinyon-juniper woodland at Keystone Canyon in the New York Mountains

Single-leaf pinyon pine (Pinus monophylla) *with female cones*

California juniper (Juniperus californicus) *with female cones*

Desert riparian woodland is only found where there is year-round freshwater above the ground or close to the surface. It occurs along the Colorado River in areas where there are sandy banks rather than rocks and cliffs, along the Virgin River and its tributaries in southwestern Utah, southern Nevada, and northwestern Arizona, and along some stretches of the Mojave, Morongo, and Amargosa Rivers. Some of the rivers have dry stretches with deep parent rock; these areas may get intermittent pulses of water from storms, but this water is ephemeral and does not stay long enough for riparian woodland to develop. Large, deciduous trees are dominant in riparian woodland, especially Frémont cottonwood (*Populus fremontii*), red willow (*Salix laevigata*), Goodding's willow (*Salix gooddingii*), arroyo willow (*Salix lasiolepis*), and sand-bar willow (*Salix exigua*). Arizona ash (*Fraxinus velutina*) is often encountered in riparian areas in the western Mojave, and in the eastern Mojave, single-leaf ash (*Fraxinus anomala*) may be found instead. Small trees may include mule-fat (*Baccharis salicifolia*) and willow baccharis (*Baccharis salicina*).

Desert riparian woodland at Morongo

Cottonwood (Populus fremontii), *a dominant desert riparian tree; photo taken near the Mojave River in Victorville*

Freshwater marshes may occur where water forms surface ponds on a floodplain or is in stagnant pools along a river course. Other marsh vegetation occurs where **artesian springs** push groundwater to the surface. There are at least 400 springs in the Mojave Desert, many with apparent surface water. Others may appear dry, but they are still discharging water that gets taken up immediately by plant roots, and then transpired; these are still ecologically important.

Some desert riparian trees (cottonwood, willow, and ash) may be present at larger marshes and springs; smaller ones or those that appear dry although still discharging water may lack trees altogether. Common non-woody marsh species include cattails (*Typha dominguensis* and *T. latifolia*), bull-rush (*Schoenoplectis acutus*), chair-maker's bull-rush (*S. americanus*), giant reed (*Phragmites australis*), lizard tail (*Anemopsis californica*), and salt-grass (*Distichlis spicata*). Since many isolated springs throughout the Mojave were old home sites, it is also common to find various introduced species that were planted purposely, including elm (*Ulmus pumila*), black locust (*Robinia pseudoacacia*), and various fruit trees.

Since a desert spring may be the only freshwater source for

Seasonally wet stretch of the Amargosa River near Shoshone lacks riparian woodland vegetation

Freshwater marsh at Saratoga Springs in Death Valley National Park

miles, even the smallest springs may be ecologically very important. They are considered to be biodiversity hotspots because of the disproportionate numbers of rare and endemic taxa of both plants and animals they support. This is partly due to their isolated nature, and likely also because they act as refugia for relict species left over from bygone climatic conditions. Ash Meadows is a prime example, with twenty-six endemic taxa. A study of desert springs showed that each was also geologically, ecologically, and hydrologically unique, so if a spring were altered or destroyed, it would be difficult or impossible to find another similar enough to use for mitigation or to find alternative habitat for a particular rare taxon; restoration of a spring's previous condition would also be unachievable.

Mesquite bosques are sometimes found in areas where the water table remains stable but very deep, from 80 feet to 40 feet below the soil surface. This may be due to proximity to a river, in which case the mesquite plants are mingled with other desert riparian woodland plants. In other cases, mesquite can form large stands in areas with no apparent standing water; this may be in an area with an ephemeral or intermittent stream where geologic features have made groundwater perennially available. The dominant species is honey mesquite (*Neltuma odorata*); screwbean mesquite (*Strombocarpa pubescens*) may be present in wetter areas as well. Mesquite bosques are important resources for

Mesquite bosque at Death Valley National Park

many wildlife species, and unfortunately, they are in decline—both in their size and number of occurrences—throughout the western states, due to alterations in hydrology and the introduction of invasive species such as tamarisk (*Tamarix* species).

Desert dry wash vegetation occurs in canyons and drainages with infrequent but severe floods that cause only a temporary elevation in the water table. The plants inhabiting these unstable sites must be able to recolonize the area quickly after a flood and become established before the next major flooding event. Some of the species adapted to this lifestyle include the smoke tree (*Psorothamnus spinosus*) and catclaw (*Senegalia greggii*). The tough seed coats of these members of the pea family need to be abraded (scarified) by tumbling with gravel and sand during a flash flood before the seeds can absorb water and germinate. The seedling must then use its large reserves of stored food (cotyledons) to rapidly grow roots deep enough to tap into groundwater before the next flood occurs. Other species frequently found in dry washes include desert waterweed (*Baccharis sergiloides*), catclaw (*Senegalia greggii*), cheesebush (*Ambrosia salsola*), desert willow (*Chilopsis linearis*), and arrowweed (*Pluchea sericea*).

Scoured desert wash after summer rain in the Rodman Mountains

Plant Adaptations to Desert Climate

The Mojave Desert environment presents many difficulties for plants, including temperature extremes, salty soils, and most of all, lack of water. Plants must open their stomates to take in carbon for photosynthesis, but precious water will be lost in the process, as it evaporates out of the stomate. Also, photosynthesis can take place only within a certain temperature range, and evaporation through open stomates is the only cooling method the plant has available; thus, water loss is the inevitable result of making food and staying cool. Desert plants cannot afford this water loss; there are various lifestyle strategies, structural and anatomical features, and physiological schemes that different species employ to help minimize it. These species adapted to desert environments are called **xerophytes**.

There are three basic xerophyte lifestyle strategies. The **drought escapers** are the annual plants that will germinate only when enough water is available to wash away germination-inhibiting chemicals from their seed coats. They then quickly mature and produce flowers, fruit, and seeds. Their individual lives are over when the drought ensues, but their offspring, in the form of seeds, wait beneath the soil for the next rainy season. **Drought avoiders** have vegetative parts that stay alive during the dry season, but they are inactive. By keeping metabolic processes and aboveground leaf surfaces to a minimum, they can avoid water loss. Such plants can be drought-deciduous, losing leaves in summer to minimize evaporative surfaces during hot, dry seasons. Other successful drought avoiders are perennials with some vegetative parts, such as a bulb, surviving underground during the hot, dry seasons. **Drought endurers** remain alive and metabolically active during drought. These plants must have structural and anatomical features to minimize water loss, and/or they must have physiological adaptations to water and heat stress.

Drought-adaptive structural and anatomical features include hairy leaf surfaces that can trap humidity and waxy or gummy coatings to retard water loss. Small leaves or leaflets minimize leaf surface area from which water can evaporate, and plants with green stems don't need water-evaporating leaves at all, since the stem carries on the photosynthesis. Some desert plants stack multiple layers of photosynthetic cells into small leaves so they can still maximize photosynthesis in a smaller area; in plants of wetter climates, only one such layer is present. Many desert plants have tough, fibrous tissues in their leaves, which prevent wilting when water is lacking. Stomates may be located only on undersurfaces of leaves to minimize the desiccating effects of wind, or the stomates may be sunken into hollows to keep them from direct contact with wind; often there are hairs surrounding the stomates to trap moisture. Some grasses have special cells on the upper surface called bulliform cells that will lose water during drought, allowing the leaves to fold or curl to create a chamber to trap humidity. The roots of some species may go very deep to tap groundwater or spread very far to collect as much surface water as possible in a short amount of time, when it is available. Some species access a nearly constant water supply in this manner; these are called **phreatophytes**.

Some plants have interesting physiological adaptations to drought. **CAM (crassulacean acid metabolism) plants** have a special type of photosynthesis that involves opening stomates only at night, when the temperature is lower, to reduce evaporation. The carbon dioxide needed for photosynthesis enters at night and is stored as an organic acid until morning, when light is available. The organic acid then releases the carbon dioxide to complete the photosynthetic process. CAM plants include many succulents and fleshy taxa. To deal with excess heat, **C4 plants** use an enzyme for photosynthesis that is very efficient at high temperatures; the efficiency and stability of the enzyme used by C3 plants (most other plants) is significantly reduced by heat stress. Most C4 plants have Kranz anatomy, a specialized leaf structure with a layer of large bundle sheath cells surrounding leaf veins. Incoming carbon dioxide reacts with the heat-efficient C4 enzyme to form an organic acid, which is transferred to bundle sheath cells; it then releases the carbon dioxide so it can be used to make glucose. Examples of C4 plants include many native grasses, as well as the competitive, introduced, and invasive grass species. The annuals that come up only following summer rainfall are also mostly C4 species.

Plants that have adaptations to salty conditions are called **halophytes**. Some halophytic species, such as saltgrass (*Distichlis spicata*), can tolerate high salt concentrations by secreting salt from leaves and stems. Other species, such as the iodine bush (*Allenrolfea occidentalis*), can store excess salt in organs and tissues until those parts die and fall off.

Threats to the Mojave Desert Flora

The Mojave Desert ecosystem also faces a suite of threats and challenges from human activities, many of which are exacerbated by slow recovery rates due to extremely arid conditions.

Alternative energy development: The 2016 Desert Renewable Energy Conservation Plan, which set a goal of providing 100 percent carbon-free energy production by 2045, involves the development of almost 11 million acres of California for renewable energy projects. Many of these projects are already up and running and many more are planned. The hope is that these projects will effectively mitigate climate change by decreasing

The Ivanpah Solar Power Facility in the eastern Mojave Desert

carbon emissions, and that they will eventually eliminate the need for fossil fuels for energy production.

Solar energy plants require the initial clearing of native vegetation. Most sites are bladed, which uproots and clears all vegetation, although there are a few sites where only mowing is employed. Regardless of the initial clearing method, all sites require periodic mowing to prevent new growth, making recovery impossible. Although the solar plants are visually quite obvious, so far they only occupy 0.5 percent of the total desert acreage, which is not a huge land footprint. However, most large-scale solar plant types require more land per megawatt-hour generation than do most other types of energy, including coal, oil, nuclear, and gas-generated electricity. The environmental impacts are not confined to the development footprint, as they require 800 to 900 gallons of water per megawatt-hour, and this commodity is scarce in the desert! Cooling water must be pumped from the ground, lowering water tables and altering hydrology; this may negatively affect vast areas of vegetation miles away from the solar facility. Maintenance and cleaning of panels also necessitates heavy water use.

Like solar plants, wind farms also require initial vegetation removal, but the amount of land required for towers, substations, roads, and transmission lines is substantially more than that needed for a solar plant. Desert vegetation will take hundreds of years to recover once the wind farms are decommissioned; water for natural regrowth or purposeful revegetation is simply not available. Other impacts include weed introduction, constant erosion, and high levels of bird and bat mortality. Proponents claim that wind turbines have a very low warming potential for each megawatt-hour generated when compared to fossil fuels; however, this is not taking into account the vast quantities of materials and fossil fuels required to manufacture, transport, and replace parts. There is also the problem of disposal after a unit's approximately 20-year life span; the turbine itself is largely made of recyclable metals, but the enormous blades are made of largely nonrecyclable fiberglass, resin, and plastics.

It is not certain whether alternative energy development will result in lower carbon emissions. One important consideration is the ability of intact desert plants to absorb and sequester large amounts of carbon. In addition to the carbon directly absorbed for photosynthesis, desert plants store vast quantities of carbon through fungal networks that interact with their roots. These fungi secrete a carbon-storing protein called glomalin. These carbon stores can be extensive, as some desert plant root systems can grow to 150 feet deep, and this carbon is held for the long term, as many of the plants, such as creosote and Mojave yucca, have very long lives, up to thousands of years. Plant removal eliminates this highly efficient carbon sequestration system and releases thousands of years' worth of stored carbon back into the atmosphere. How many years of solar and wind energy production will be needed to offset the enormous carbon emission from the release of this stored carbon?

The carbon sequestration potential of desert cryptobiotic soil crusts should also be considered. Some of the main components of soil crusts are lichens, terrestrial algae, and mosses, all photosynthetic; they all act as carbon sinks by absorbing atmospheric carbon. In addition, they increase soil stability, prevent wind and water erosion, help establish roots of germinating seedlings, and provide habitat for soil invertebrates involved in mineral cycling and decomposition. They are also capable of nitrogen fixation, an important process by which atmospheric nitrogen is made available to plant roots. These carbon-sequestering crusts are destroyed when the soil is disturbed, and there is no protocol to effectively replace them. Their removal over large areas would likely make restoration of the desert vegetation nearly impossible.

All of these considerations seem to be missing when presenting the benefits of solar and wind energy development in fragile, arid desert ecosystems. None of our points are intended to argue against alternate energy, but they should be studied and included as part

Carbonate mine near Lucerne Valley, California

of the discussion. Without studies, there are insufficient data to convince us that large-scale destruction of Mojave Desert vegetation, especially in pristine areas, is a fix-all, or even a significant piece of the solution, for global climate change. We suggest that an ecologically sound alternative would be to use subsidies currently going to the solar and wind companies to install rooftop solar on businesses and private residences. At the very least, solar power plants could be placed much closer to energy consumption centers, maybe on abandoned, weedy lots in towns and cities. This would also spare land needed for transmission corridors and prevent energy losses from transmission.

Mining: Vegetation is removed at mine sites for roads, piles of tailings, and quarry pits. These direct and localized effects have caused substantial habitat loss for certain endemic plants. Although many effects of mining are quite localized, there are often off-site effects as well. Eroded soil, runoff water carrying toxic materials, problems with windblown dust, and animal deaths at cyanide-pit gold-extraction mines have all been documented in the Mojave Desert. There is also potential groundwater alteration and water diversion from mining activities.

Off-highway vehicles: When motorcycles, dune-buggies, quad-runners, side-by-sides, and four-wheel-drive vehicles stay on designated routes and in designated open areas, the impacts are mostly limited to these sites. However, when drivers don't stay on designated routes or areas, it expands damage from soil compaction, erosion, disruption of cryptobiotic soil crusts, altered hydrology, and reduced soil-percolation rates, as well as causing significant reductions in vegetation cover. Scars from off-highway-vehicle tracks are expected to persist for many years, as vegetation recovery rates are very slow in arid environments.

Military activities: Military bases occupy extensive areas of the Mojave Desert. Intense damage has occurred from military training exercises, tanks and vehicles, small arms fire, and bombing. The recent expansion of Fort Irwin has the potential to negatively impact some of the federally endangered Lane Mountain milkvetch (*Astragalus jaegerianus*) populations. The vast majority of the known Clokey's cryptantha (*Cryptantha clokeyi*) populations are on China Lake and Fort Irwin, and there is no protection for this species. Desert cymopterus (*Cymopterus deserticola*), also a vulnerable species without legal protection, is found on Edwards Air Force Base, Fort Irwin, and the south end of China Lake. A DoD report of 116 listed and at-risk species occurring on DoD-managed lands in California ranked the desert cymopterus as the species at highest risk. The Department of Defense has conducted surveys to map the distributions of sensitive species in order to avoid or limit training activity impacts in those locations. In spite of potential damage from military training, plants on vast military-controlled areas remain protected from many other human impacts.

Grazing: Public lands in the Mojave Desert have been grazed by sheep and cattle since the 1800s. The numbers of grazing animals are declining; Arizona, Nevada, and Utah do not sponsor grazing on public lands in the Mojave Desert, and there is currently pressure in California to stop this activity. Grazing has been shown to cause a decrease in plant cover and biomass, with effects varying according to season, soil condition, and land-use history. Compaction of soil by trampling results in altered surface and subsurface water flow and decreased water availability to plant roots, as well as a redistribution of soluble mineral nutrients. Trampling and compaction also decrease the cover of cryptobiotic soil crusts, which are important in retention of mineral nutrients and water, preventing wind erosion, sequestering carbon, and thwarting establishment of nonnative grasses. Grazing can lead to altered species composition of some plant communities. Recovery from grazing is slow, since the effects of grazing do not stop immediately when animals are removed; the disturbed soil continues to be eroded by wind and invaded by weedy species, and the effects of compaction may permanently alter water flow.

Wild burros and horses: These nonnative animals have severely damaged sensitive desert habitats, especially riparian areas and springs. They eat large amounts of vegetation, compact the soil and alter hydrology, and foul water sources, sometimes

Sheep grazing on creosote bush scrub vegetation on public lands in the Mojave Desert

Wild burros in the Panamint Valley

to the exclusion of native wildlife. Under the Wild Horse and Burro Act, the Bureau of Land Management has a mandate to provide for these animals that are not native to the Mojave Desert ecosystem. Advocates for burros and horses claim that these are part of our western cultural heritage, but the historic population sizes were much smaller than they are now, and the damage was nowhere near as severe. Although some springs are being fenced to exclude burros, the vegetation recovery rate is slow, and in some places, fences are vandalized, making them ineffective barriers.

Altered water flow and water table down-drafting: When rivers are dammed and water flow is controlled, cottonwoods and other riparian vegetation may decline, as they require the periodic scouring of floods that bring essential nutrients into the system. Hydroelectric power, flood control, and water diversion for agriculture along the Colorado River has posed a threat to riparian vegetation. Aboveground water flow in the Mojave River is not continuous; in some areas the water flows underground, and in some areas it is too deep to support riparian trees. When continuous flow does occur, it is totally under artificial control, as water is purposefully released from the Mojave Forks Dam in the San Bernardino Mountains after large winter storms. A 1995 study of Mojave River riparian vegetation showed that cottonwoods were under stress and dying in a 5-mile stretch, and this was shown to be an indirect result of channelization of water. This effectively lowered the water table in that portion of the river following a 1993 flood, when channel alteration was necessary in order to protect homes and developments along this river.

Like the Mojave, the Amargosa River has intermittent aboveground flow, with the water table too deep in some areas to support riparian trees. Unlike the Mojave, it does not have development or a dam to alter water flow, but at the time of this writing, there is a proposal to do exploratory drilling near Ash Meadows National Wildlife Refuge for lithium, needed for production of electric vehicles to meet the current administration's mandate to have all electric vehicle manufacture by the year 2045. Ash Meadows, a rich marshland along the Amargosa's intermittent flow path, is home to twenty-four plant and animal taxa that occur nowhere else in the world. The project, which would involve drilling thirty holes, each 250 feet to 300 feet deep, would likely alter the Ash Meadows hydrology by affecting the water table, potentially damaging habitat for wildlife and vegetation.

Rabbit Springs, near Lucerne Valley in California, is home to several rare plant species, including Parish's popcorn flower (*Plagiobothrys parishii*), Parish's alkali grass (*Puccinellia parishii*), and the alkali mariposa lily (*Calochortus striatus*). Over twenty-five years of our observations showed that these rare plants were abundant in spring, even in years of sparse rainfall, due to saturated soils and ample standing water. However, in a very wet

*Rabbit Springs in Lucerne Valley with the endemic Parish's popcorn flower (*Plagiobothrys parishii*); photo taken in 2014*

spring in 2023, we observed a highly degraded system with very little saturated soil and no standing water; very few plants were to be found. So far, we have not been able to figure out the cause of the lowered water table in this area, and we acknowledge that this may be due to natural causes, such as an earthquake, as the spring sits atop the Helendale

Fault. However, there is no conservation group or watchdog organization monitoring this small area; there are likely other isolated desert springs where groundwater alteration is happening without public awareness.

Nonnative species invasions: The most common woody invasive in the Mojave Desert is salt cedar (*Tamarix ramosissima*), a native of the eastern Mediterranean region. This highly branched shrub can easily be recognized by its reddish-brown twigs, masses of small, pink, four-parted flowers, and sessile, green, scale-like leaves. Salt cedar outcompetes native riparian vegetation, especially cottonwoods and willows, by being highly tolerant of high salt concentrations and low water availability. Its taproots readily draw deep groundwater, lowering the water table and concentrating salts in the soil, creating a hostile environment for other species. Its dense canopy can exclude seedlings of its competitors and can also cause an increase in fire frequency by creating a continuous fuel load; unfortunately, it resprouts very well after fire. Since it evolved elsewhere, its natural herbivores are not around, so not much eats it.

Eradicating salt cedar is a difficult process. It is labor-intensive to mechanically remove it, and it is useless to try to burn it. A study on the Colorado River showed that salt cedar could not tolerate being flooded for more than seventy days, but the native species Goodding's willow (*Salix gooddingii*) survived the flooding. This suggests that if natural water flow were restored, perhaps the resultant flooding may help suppress salt cedar invasion. However, this would not be feasible along the Colorado River, as flooding would threaten agricultural lands and developments. Dam removal on the Mojave River would threaten homes and businesses and would likely be ineffective, as there is probably not enough water available to cause the sustained flooding necessary to suppress salt cedar. The Amargosa River has also been negatively impacted by salt cedar, but its noncontinuous flow pattern would also not allow for a purposeful, prolonged flooding strategy for eradication. Along the Mojave River the introduced giant reed (*Arundo donax*) and Russian olive (*Elaeagnus angustifolia*) are also frequent invasives, although they do not seem to spread nearly as rapidly as tamarisk.

Invasive annual species also can alter the functioning of Mojave Desert ecosystems. The worst pests are the European grasses, including red brome (*Bromus rubens*), Mediterranean grass (*Schismus barbatus*), and cheat-grass (*Bromus tectorum*). Red-stemmed filaree (*Erodium cicutarium*) is also problematic, as is Sahara mustard (*Brassica tournefortii*). These compete with native annuals through spatial displacement, and they provide much lower nutritional value to herbivores such as the desert tortoise. Some of the invasives, especially

*Invasive tamarisk (*Tamarix ramosissima*) in the Fremont Valley near Red Rock Canyon State Park*

the bromes, have been implicated in increasing fire frequency in desert vegetation, which did not evolve with fire.

Some invasive species booms can be linked to air pollution that deposits nitrogen in desert soils. Red brome, in particular, requires high nitrogen levels. Soil bacteria, fungi, and mycorrhizae (fungi associated with plant roots) could also be affected by nitrogen deposition from air pollution, altering litter decomposition rates and further changing species composition in desert plant communities.

Climate Change and Global Warming

Natural cycles of warming and cooling have occurred several times during the current phase of geologic time known as the Pleistocene or Ice Age. The warming periods separating ice advances are called interglacials; the current interglacial warming event, which started approximately 12,000 years ago, is referred to as the Holocene. After the last full glacial event, temperatures warmed, shifting species ranges northward hundreds to even thousands of miles, according to their specific ecological requirements. These shifts resulted in the temporary assemblages of species that we recognize as the plant communities of today.

There have been significant fluctuations of warming and cooling periods during the Holocene as well; the Xerothermic event of around 7,000 years ago saw temperatures exceeding those of today. The Medieval warming period occurred from around AD 950 to AD 1250 and was followed by the recent Little Ice Age, which lasted from AD 1300 to AD 1880. Permanent recordkeeping for weather began in 1880, when it was cooler and wetter than today. Since then, the hottest summers on record occurred during the Dust Bowl of 1930 to 1936.

During the Xerothermic, many desert plants migrated to coastal areas; for example, the iconic desert beavertail cactus is also known from the hills above Thousand Oaks in Ventura County. Not only do plants migrate directionally, but they also migrate up and down in elevation with varying climate patterns. Prior to the Holocene, pinyon-juniper woodland dominated landscapes at much lower elevations than where we find them today.

Since some climate change models show that there will not be uniform changes in temperature and precipitation everywhere, and the Holocene is marked by much variability and unpredictability, it is uncertain what will happen in the Mojave. If current trends continue, there may be a continuing increase in ocean temperatures; this naturally results in the release of carbon dioxide into the atmosphere. Increasing human populations with technologic and industrial advances have also contributed to an increase in atmospheric carbon dioxide and other greenhouse gases. This increase in carbon dioxide has the potential to increase rates of photosynthesis; models predict that desert vegetation should have a 50 percent increase in primary productivity (amount of photosynthesis per area per year). This was tested in a Department of Energy study in Nevada, in which carbon dioxide–rich air was piped into a tented natural desert area. The result was indeed an increase in biomass compared to the control area, but there was also an accompanying increase in red brome (*Bromus rubens*), an introduced European grass that uses C4 photosynthesis, making it very efficient at high temperatures.

Present Conservation and Management

There are many county and state parks scattered throughout the Mojave Desert. For example, the California Poppy Reserve in the western Mojave is famous for the annual display of poppies and other wildflowers, and there are several Los Angeles County wildflower parks as well. Red Rock Canyon State Park is home to some Mojave Desert endemic plants, and the Mojave Narrows Regional Park, managed by San Bernardino County, is home to a cottonwood gallery forest. Nevada has desert trails in the Valley of Fire State Park and Big Bend of the Colorado State Recreation Area. Utah's Snow Canyon State Park is at the northernmost limit of the Mojave Desert.

At the national level, enormous tracts of ecologically critical land are managed by the military. The National Park Service has developed general management plans for Death Valley and Joshua Tree National Parks, the Lake Mead National Recreation Area, and the Mojave National Preserve. The US Fish and Wildlife Service manages the Desert National Wildlife Refuge and the Ash Meadows National Wildlife Refuge in Nevada. The US Bureau of Land Management oversees the largest proportion of the Mojave Desert in all four states. This agency is required to manage for multiple uses and is responsive to public input. Many user groups have paid lobbies supported by industry, such as mining, grazing, and off-highway-vehicle recreation. However, those who are interested in participating in conservation and education-oriented activities do not have industries to back them; most who get involved in lobbying the management agencies are representatives of the various nonprofit conservation organizations like the California Native Plant Society, the Sierra Club, Defenders of Wildlife, Trust for Public Land, Center for Biological Diversity, and others. It is important to pay attention as a citizen to issues that affect your favorite desert area and to voice your opinion on plans and policies for the management of public lands.

HOW TO USE THIS BOOK

This book groups plants by flower color, and within each color the species accounts appear in alphabetical order by the scientific name of the family. Keep in mind that a book of this size cannot cover all the plants in the Mojave Desert, so you may not find an exact match; however, all editions of this book feature some species unique to the edition, so you may want to own all three! Species descriptions have been simplified by minimizing the number of botanical descriptive terms used. A glossary of these terms is found in the back of this book. Following the introduction you will find illustrations of the parts of a leaf, the variations of leaf shape, and their arrangement and venation; careful observations of these characteristics will help to identify the plants you are examining. Basic diagrams of flower parts for several flower types are also included. We highly recommend you have a 10X hand lens to see some of the delightful details up close! These are often available at stamp-collecting shops, jewelers, and forestry suppliers.

The reader is encouraged to compare plants found in the field to herbarium specimens to confirm identification. A herbarium is a museum collection of dried and pressed plant specimens that are used to study ranges, habitats, taxonomy, and genetics of specific plants and to assess and document species diversity of a region. Numerous major herbaria with Mojave Desert specimens are open to the public, including those at University of Nevada at Las Vegas, University of California at Riverside, and Rancho Santa Ana Botanic Garden in Claremont, California. Smaller collections are available locally at Victor Valley College in Victorville, the Maturango Museum in Ridgecrest, the Desert Studies Center at Soda Springs, and the University of California Granite Mountains Reserve. Collectors are required to obtain permission to collect from local land management agencies and private landowners.

There are several online sites to review plant determinations, including CalPhotos (http://calphotos.berkeley.edu/flora/) and SEINet (https://swbiodiversity.org/seinet/collections/harvestparams.php), an herbarium-based website that shares their digitized collection data with many images of the actual herbarium specimens. It also has a tab for photos of plant species. The Jepson eFlora site has technical keys for all of the California species (https://ucjeps.berkeley.edu/eflora/), and iNaturalist is a site where amateurs and botanists alike can contribute their photos of all things natural (http://www.inaturalist.org/).

How Plants Get Their Names

In 1753, Carl Linnaeus published *Species Plantarum*, in which he described a system to inventory and name species, which, although modified somewhat, is still in use today. This system arranges species into taxa (categories) according to their similarities. The taxa are ranked in seven hierarchical levels. All plants belong to the plant kingdom, which is divided into smaller categories called divisions or phyla (singular *phylum*). All of the members of a phylum are arranged into smaller taxa called classes, classes are subgrouped into orders, orders are subgrouped into families, families are divided into genera (singular *genus*), and genera are made up of individual species. The scientific name (also called Latin name or binomial name) of a plant is a combination of the genus and species names. Corn has the scientific name of *Zea mays*. In this book the scientific name appears in italics under the common name for each plant described.

Scientists need a universal way to communicate to other scientists around the globe about their research. One problem with using common names of species is that the common name is usually not understood in another language. Another problem is that a particular species may have more than one common name, or that the same common name may apply to several species. For example, in this book there are unrelated species that can have the common name of bladderpod. Scientific names solve these problems.

The first botanist who publishes a formal plant description in a scientific journal gives the plant its scientific name. This person, the author, must follow rules outlined in the International Code of Botanical Nomenclature. The author's name is customarily written after the scientific name. The specimen used to make the official description of a species is called the type specimen. Sometimes it is interesting to find out where the type specimen was collected and by whom.

Scientific names of plants are currently being changed at a rapid rate as new information, especially molecular data, reveals similarities and relationships between species that were not previously suspected by external appearance, biochemistry, or internal anatomy. As in the second edition, you will see numerous name changes in this edition of *Mojave Desert Wildflowers*. A smaller proportion of the name changes are due to discovery of a previously applied name, prior to publishing of a current name, in which case the earliest published name must be applied. In any case, when a name is changed, the original author's name may be in parentheses, followed by the author of the new name or combination. An example, Bigelow's linanthus, is written: *Linanthus bigelovii* (Gray) Greene. Gray named this plant *Gilia bigelovii*, but Greene later placed it into the genus *Linanthus*, renaming it. Since the original author's name is still given, one could look up in the archives the original publication with highly detailed, descriptive information that is not present in floras, manuals, or popular field identification books such as you are reading.

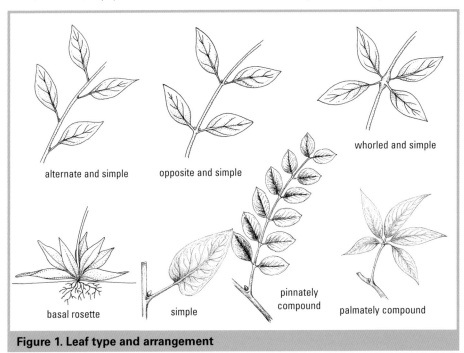

alternate and simple

opposite and simple

whorled and simple

basal rosette

simple

pinnately compound

palmately compound

Figure 1. Leaf type and arrangement

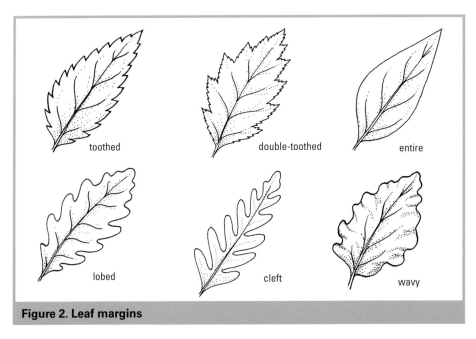

toothed

double-toothed

entire

lobed

cleft

wavy

Figure 2. Leaf margins

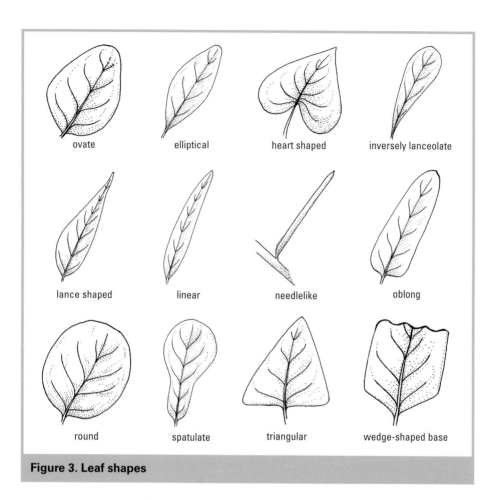

Figure 3. Leaf shapes

ovate   elliptical   heart shaped   inversely lanceolate

lance shaped   linear   needlelike   oblong

round   spatulate   triangular   wedge-shaped base

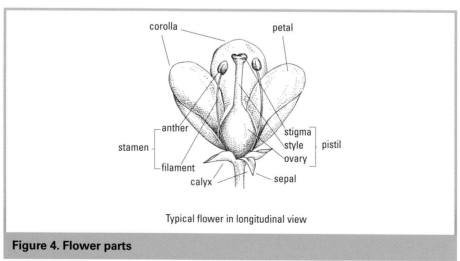

Typical flower in longitudinal view

Figure 4. Flower parts

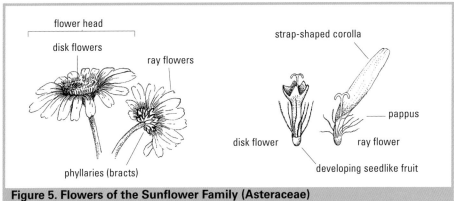

Figure 5. Flowers of the Sunflower Family (Asteraceae)

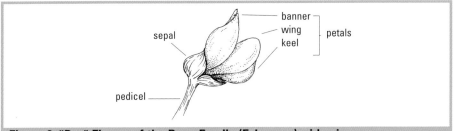

Figure 6. "Pea" Flower of the Bean Family (Fabaceae), side view

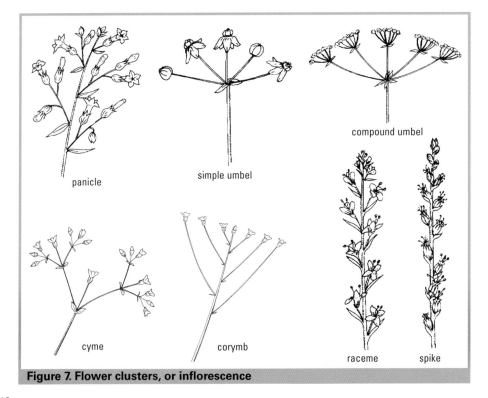

Figure 7. Flower clusters, or inflorescence

BLUE, PURPLE, AND LAVENDER FLOWERS

This section includes flowers ranging from light blue to dark blue and those that are lavender to deep purple. Since pink, rose, and magenta colors grade into lavenders and purples, check that section of the book if you cannot find what you are looking for here. Blue and purplish flower colors are produced by variations of water-soluble pigments known as anthocyanins.

FRINGED ONION
Allium fimbriatum S. Watson var. *fimbriatum*
Onion Family (Alliaceae)

Description: This perennial monocot arises from a reddish-brown bulb. The 4–8"-tall stem bears 1 cylindrical leaf, which is about twice as long as the stem. The purple, 6-parted flowers are borne in an umbel of 6–35 flowers, each on a ¼–¾" pedicel. The tips of the tepals curve outward. The ovary is topped with 6 toothed to deeply cut crests, which can be easily seen with a hand lens.

Bloom Season: April to June

Habitat/Range: Occurs on dry hillsides and flats from 1,000 to 9,000' in the central, western, and northern Mojave Desert, the Transverse Ranges and Tehachapi Range, and California's Coast Ranges to Baja California, Mexico.

Comments: The similar *Allium fimbriatum* var. *mohavense* has white to pink or lavender tepals with purplish veins. It also differs by having up to 60 flowers per umbel, the ovary crests are always deeply cut, and the tepal tips are erect. It is found from 2,300 to 4,600' in the western Mojave Desert and the desert slopes of the southern Sierras.

DESERT CYMOPTERUS

Cymopterus deserticola Brandegee
Carrot Family (Apiaceae)

Description: This 4–6"-tall perennial has finely dissected, 1–2"-long leaves that grow from the root crown on leaf stalks that are the same length as the blades. Purple flowers occur in tight, ball-like clusters, followed by hairy, flattened, ¼" fruits with narrow wings; the fruits are retained in a spherical cluster as they dry.

Bloom Season: April

Habitat/Range: This rare species occurs in creosote bush scrub and Joshua tree woodland from east of Victorville to Kramer Junction in California. More than 50 percent of the known populations and individuals occur on Edwards Air Force Base, and substantial populations have been found at Fort Irwin and China Lake. The Department of Defense manages over 90 percent of the known populations.

Comments: Desert cymopterus is threatened by habitat alteration from historic sheep grazing, urbanization, military activities, and vehicles. With its limited distribution and multiple threats throughout its range, this species meets the requirements for listing as an endangered species, but it is not listed at this time. Yearly surveys of a 140-hectare protected area have shown that the population decreased from 2004 to 2007, not only due to drought but also from periods of unusually high precipitation. Recruitment and resprouting were documented from 2008 to 2011.

HOARY ASTER

Dieteria canescens (Pursh.) Nutt. var. *leucanthemifolia* (Greene) D. R. Morgan & R. L. Hartm.
Sunflower Family (Asteraceae)

Description: This annual or short-lived perennial is less than 4' tall. The short-haired, glandular stems have an open branching pattern, producing an almost bushy effect. The 1–4"-long leaves vary from linear to obovate, and they may have toothed to nearly entire margins. The flowers are produced in ¼–½" heads, each with numerous yellow disk flowers and 8–15 lavender to purplish ray flowers.

Bloom Season: May to June, and also in September to October in years with adequate summer rainfall

Habitat/Range: This variety of hoary aster is found from 3,000 to 6,000' in creosote bush scrub, Joshua tree woodland, and pinyon-juniper woodland in the mountains of the Mojave Desert and the White and Inyo Ranges to Oregon and Utah.

Comments: Look for colorful flower long-horned beetles (Cerambycidae) on the flowers. Some resemble wasps, and many have narrow heads to probe flower parts for pollen and nectar. *D. canescens* var. *minutiflora* has a white flower tube and throat, var. *ambigua* is glandular above, and var. *crenulata* is glandular throughout.

MOJAVE ASTER

Xylorhiza tortifolia (Torrey & A. Gray) E. Greene var. *tortifolia*
Sunflower Family (Asteraceae)

Description: This 1–2'-tall perennial is branched from the woody base. The soft-hairy, elliptical leaves with toothed margins and white midveins are larger near the base of the plant and smaller toward the top of the stem. The stalked, 2½" flower heads have up to 60 light-blue ray flowers surrounding numerous yellow disk flowers, and there are 4–5 rows of 1" phyllaries below.

Bloom Season: March to May and sometimes in October following rainfall, especially in the eastern Mojave

Habitat/Range: Mojave aster is found on rocky desert slopes, canyons, and washes in creosote bush scrub. It is common throughout the Mojave Desert except in the most western areas, and it also occurs in the Sonoran Desert.

Comments: Mojave aster is a food plant for larvae of Neumoegen's checkerspot (*Chlosyne acastus neumoegeni*), one of the more common desert butterflies. The mature larvae are black with gray dots and have 9 rows of black, branching spines. Mojave aster is also a host plant for a fuzzy noctuid moth, *Schinia ligeae*.

DESERT CANDLE

Caulanthus inflatus S. Watson
Mustard Family (Brassicaceae)

Description: This distinctive annual has a leafless, inflated, yellowish-green stem that can grow to 2' tall. Dark-green, oblong, 1–3" leaves clasp the stem at the base of the plant. The conspicuous, dark-purple buds open to reveal ½"-long flowers with 4 crisped, white petals, and the stout, linear fruits are 2–4" long.

Bloom Season: March to May

Habitat/Range: Desert candle is locally common in flat areas between shrubs in creosote bush scrub and Joshua tree woodland below 5,000'. It is found in the western Mojave Desert from Barstow to the southern San Joaquin Valley to western Fresno County in California. It is locally common in areas around Boron and Opal Mountain.

Comments: Native Americans and early settlers boiled the young plants with meat to make a palatable stew. Desert candle has compounds called glucosinolates, or mustard oils; these are the sulfur-containing compounds that give mustard family vegetables their characteristic flavors and odors, and which also yield the healthful benefits, including cancer prevention. The plants, however, are producing them as secondary compounds to avoid being eaten by insects and other herbivores.

SHRUBBY TIQUILIA, WOODY CRINKLEMAT

Tiquilia canescens (DC.) A. T. Richardson var. *canescens*
Ehretia Family (Ehretiaceae)

Description: This low-growing, mat-forming subshrub bears alternate, soft, white-hairy, ovate, ¼–½"-long leaves with entire margins. The bell-shaped, lavender, ¼"-long flowers are produced singly or in small clusters in leaf axils. The style is divided into 2 branches along the entire length, all the way to the ovary. As the ovary matures, it develops 4 grooves that form 4 nutlets in the fruit.

Bloom Season: March to May

Habitat/Range: Found on hillsides and ridges from 1,000 to 5,000' in the southeastern Mojave Desert and in the Sonoran Desert to Texas and northern Mexico.

Comments: This species has been used medicinally for cleansing wounds, treating stomach problems and gonorrhea, and for sweat baths. Cattle and goats do not tend to graze on it, perhaps due to a cyanide-releasing compound called menisdaurin, which is present in *T. plicata* as well. There are 27 *Tiquilia* species in the deserts of North and South America, four of which occur in the Mojave. They do not appear to hybridize, even when growing in close proximity.

FRÉMONT'S MILKVETCH

Astragalus lentiginosus Douglas var. *fremontii* (Gray) Wats.
Pea Family (Fabaceae)

Description: This herbaceous perennial has pinnately divided leaves and typical "pea" flowers with a banner petal, 2 wing petals, and 2 petals fused to form a boat-shaped keel under ¼" long. The hairless, 2-chambered fruits are sessile, strongly inflated, and narrowed abruptly to form an upcurved, triangular beak.

Bloom Season: April to June or July

Habitat/Range: Frémont's milkvetch is common throughout the Mojave to the central Great Basin Desert. It occurs in open sand and gravel habitats between 1,300 and 9,500'.

Comments: Eleven of the 19 California varieties of *A. lentiginosus* occur in the Mojave. Var. *variabilis* is widespread in sandy sites below 5,200' in the southern and western Mojave. It has hairs on the fruit and a gently incurved fruit beak. Var. *albifolius*, with dense white hairs, white petals, and a downcurved beak, occurs in clay flats and alkaline areas in the western Mojave. The rare var. *micans* has silky white hairs, is woody at the base, and is found only on Eureka Dunes.

ARIZONA LUPINE

Lupinus arizonicus (S. Watson) S. Watson
Pea Family (Fabaceae)

Description: This somewhat fleshy, branched, 1–2'-tall annual has palmately divided leaves with 5–10 inversely lanceolate, ½–1½"-long leaflets. Magenta "pea" flowers with yellowish banner spots occur in 2–12"-long clusters, followed by shiny, ½"-long pods. The diagnostic hairs on the back of the banner petal can only be seen on young flowers in bud.

Bloom Season: March to May

Habitat/Range: Common in sandy washes and open areas below 2,000' in creosote bush scrub in both the Mojave and Sonoran Deserts to southern Nevada, Arizona, and northwestern Mexico. It is especially abundant and conspicuous along highways.

Comments: The genus name means "wolf" in Latin. It was mistakenly believed that this plant robbed the soil; however, many pea family members add soil nitrogen with the aid of symbiotic bacteria in root nodules that convert atmospheric nitrogen into ammonia, a form of nitrogen that many plants can use, by a process called nitrogen fixation.

BAJADA LUPINE, ELEGANT LUPINE
Lupinus concinnus J. Agardh
Pea Family (Fabaceae)

Description: This densely hairy, compact, 4–10"-tall annual has palmately divided leaves with 5–9 soft-hairy leaflets. The reddish-purple flowers with white to yellow banner petal spots are spirally arranged into 1–3" clusters on 2–3" stalks. The narrow, hairy, ½"-long pods have 2–4 seeds.

Bloom Season: March to May

Habitat/Range: Bajada lupine occupies dry, sandy soil in open and often disturbed sites such as roadsides and burned areas in many plant communities in southwestern North America to Baja California, Mexico.

Comments: A study of bajada lupine, which is predominantly self-pollinating, showed that 90 percent of its flowers develop into fruits, and 91 percent of the ovules it produces develop into seeds.

YELLOW-EYED LUPINE
Lupinus flavoculatus A. Heller
Pea Family (Fabaceae)

Description: This up-to-8"-tall annual has palmately compound leaves, each with 7–9 leaflets, crowded mostly near the base. The stems, petioles, and lower leaf surfaces are covered with long, spreading hairs, but the upper leaflet surfaces are hairless. The spirally arranged, bright-blue flowers have a yellow to cream banner spot that ages purple. The keel is hairless. The ½"-long fruits with a straight upper suture and 1–2 wrinkled seeds tend to be produced on one side of the inflorescence.

Bloom Season: April to June

Habitat/Range: Found from 2,000 to 7,500' in sandy or gravelly soils in creosote bush scrub and pinyon-juniper woodland in the eastern Mojave Desert and White and Inyo Mountains to Utah and Arizona.

Comments: The genus includes over 199 species, with centers of diversity in North and South America, North Africa, and the Mediterranean. Historically, Egyptians, Greeks, and Romans boiled lupine seeds to remove bitter alkaloids before consumption. "Sweet" varieties, currently cultivated in Europe, lack alkaloids due to a single gene difference. People allergic to peanuts are often allergic to lupines as well.

DESERT LUPINE, SHOCKLEY LUPINE

Lupinus shockleyi S. Watson
Pea Family (Fabaceae)

Description: Desert lupine may have a stem up to 4" long or may appear stemless. The leaves are palmately divided with 7–10 narrow, spoon-shaped leaflets on 1½–5"-long stalks. Upper leaflet surfaces are hairless except at the margins, and the undersurfaces have silky, flattened hairs. The dark-blue-purple flowers with yellow-spotted banner petals, hairless keels, and white-hairy sepals occur in scattered clusters. The upper seams of the pods are wavy with stiff, long hairs, and there are 2 wrinkled seeds in each pod.

Bloom Season: March to May

Habitat/Range: Widespread and fairly common in dry, sandy soils below 6,500' in creosote bush scrub in both the Mojave and Sonoran Deserts.

Comments: *Lupinus shockleyi*, *L. odoratus*, and *L. flavoculatus* share many characteristics, such as non-whorled flowers, persistent cotyledons, hairless keels, and the same flavonoid compound, O-glucosyl flavone. *L. odoratus* differs from the others by having a hairless calyx, an intense violet odor, and deeper-purple flowers. Both *L. odoratus* and *L. flavoculatus* have broad, round banner petals, while those of *L. shockleyi* are pointed. The upper calyx lobe in *L. odoratus* and *L. flavoculatus* is less than half as long as the lower, while in *L. shockleyi* it is longer, covering part of the banner petal. This species was named in honor of William H. Shockley (1855–1925), who was one of the first botanical collectors in the White Mountains of California.

COULTER'S LUPINE

Lupinus sparsiflorus Benth.
Pea Family (Fabaceae)

Description: This semi-erect, branched, up-to-16"-tall annual has palmately compound leaves with 7–11 nearly linear, slightly folded, ½–1¼"-long leaflets with hairs on the upper surfaces near the margins. The ½"-long, purple-blue, pea-like flowers are spirally arranged, each with a white and yellow banner spot that may get flecks of reddish-purple with age. The 1"-long fruit has coarse hairs and holds 4 seeds.

Bloom Season: February to May

Habitat/Range: Found in sandy soils and washes below 4,000' in creosote bush scrub and Joshua tree woodland in California deserts and in coastal sage scrub of cismontane southern California to Utah, Arizona, and northern Mexico.

Comments: Although some lupine species have edible seeds, this species' seeds are high in quinolizidine alkaloid compounds, including lupinine and sparteine. Lupinine, which has a very bitter flavor, is highly toxic to mammals in general and can cause shaking, trembling, and convulsions in humans. Grazing cattle and sheep can get lupinosis, a fatal condition that destroys liver function.

PARRY DALEA, PARRY'S FALSE PRAIRIE-CLOVER

Marina parryi (Torrey & A. Gray) Barneby
Pea Family (Fabaceae)

Description: This slender, sprawling, 8–20"-tall, gland-dotted subshrub has purple stems with gray hairs. The alternate pinnately divided leaves have 13–35 round leaflets. Blue and white "pea" flowers with hairy sepals are produced in loose clusters, followed by small, 1-seeded fruits.

Bloom Season: March to June

Habitat/Range: Parry dalea is found in disturbed habitats such as roadsides and washes and also on rocky slopes below 2,600' in creosote bush scrub in the southeastern Mojave Desert and through the Sonoran Desert to Baja California, Mexico.

Comments: This species is named in honor of Dr. Charles C. Parry (1823–1890). He was a surgeon and botanist on the United States and Mexican boundary survey, which was led by Major W. H. Emory from 1848 to 1855.

BEAVER DAM BREADROOT
Pediomelum castoreum (S. Watson) Rydb.
Pea Family (Fabaceae)

Description: This gland-dotted perennial from a deep, thickened taproot has a rosette of long-petioled, palmately compound basal leaves with 5–6 pointy, oblanceolate leaflets with whitish, flattened hairs. The flower clusters arise from the center of the leaf rosette on erect stalks that are generally much shorter than the leaf petioles. Each purplish, pea-style flower has 9 fused filaments, a swollen upper calyx base, and a banner up to ½" long. The small, oval, 1-seeded, ¼"-long fruit is mostly enclosed in the calyx, except for the protruding beak.

Bloom Season: April to May

Habitat/Range: Found in sandy hills, flats, washes, and roadcuts from the Barstow to Victorville area; also found in Death Valley and the eastern Mojave to Nevada and Arizona. It is a Mojave Desert endemic.

Comments: There are 60 known locations for this species. It is vulnerable throughout its range due to road widening and potential damage by vehicles, and it is on the California Native Plant Society's List 1B.

INDIGO BUSH

Psorothamnus arborescens (A. Gray) Barneby var. *minutifolius* (Parish) Barneby
Pea Family (Fabaceae)

Description: This variety of indigo bush is a spreading, somewhat spiny shrub around 2–3' tall. The pinnately divided leaves have 5–7 lanceolate leaflets that are ¼–½" long. Showy, deep-blue-violet flowers are produced in dense clusters at the branch tips, followed by 2-seeded, gland-dotted fruits that narrow to a long beak.

Bloom Season: April to May

Habitat/Range: Indigo bush is found on flats and in washes up to 3,000' in the northern and central Mojave Desert.

Comments: Isoflavone compounds extracted from the roots are toxic, in vitro, against some protozoa species that cause African sleeping sickness and visceral leishmaniasis. More research is needed to see if these compounds can be used clinically. Mojave indigo bush (*P. arborescens* var. *arborescens*), which is distinguished from var. *minutifolius* by its larger, hairy calyx, occurs in the western Mojave, where there are potential impacts from Fort Irwin military base activities. It is on the California Native Plant Society watch list.

FREMONT'S DALEA
Psorothamnus fremontii (Torr. ex A. Gray) Barneby var. *fremontii*
Pea Family (Fabaceae)

Description: Fremont's dalea is similar to indigo bush in its growth form and habit, but it differs in several details. The leaves are covered in soft, flat, silvery hairs. They are less than ¼" wide and are elliptic to ovate. The fruits have numerous small glands that are often lined up longitudinally.

Bloom Season: April to May

Habitat/Range: Occurs in washes and on flats and slopes below 4,500' throughout the Mojave Desert to southern Utah and northern Arizona.

Comments: Fremont's dalea is named for John Charles Frémont (1813–1890), the first governor of California. He led and directed five transcontinental expeditions, helping to establish trade routes across the new lands of the United States between 1842 and 1854. Unlike other expedition botanists, he was not educated in the field sciences, so he had to be trained quickly prior to his first expedition. He collected some of the more unique plants of the West.

CALTHA-LEAVED PHACELIA
Phacelia calthifolia Brand.
Waterleaf Family (Hydrophyllaceae)

Description: Caltha-leaved phacelia is a spreading to erect, brittle annual with short, stiff, glandular hairs. It grows up to 12" high with few spreading branches. The rounded, 1½" leaves are on petioles of the same length. They have lobed margins and a notch at the base. Coiled inflorescences of purple, bell-shaped flowers are found on branch tips, each flower up to ½" long with unequal stamens and purple pollen. The style is split along ½–¾" of its length from the tip. The fruits are spherical with numerous seed, each having 4–8 cross-furrows.

Bloom Season: March to May

Habitat/Range: Found below 4,000' in sandy soils in creosote bush scrub in the northern and central Mojave Desert to western Nevada.

Comments: The specific name was applied due to the resemblance of the leaves to those of *Caltha*, the marsh marigold, a genus in the buttercup family (Ranunculaceae). Herbarium sheets stain a reddish-brown from the sticky glands covering the plant. Hall and Chandler collected the type specimen from Pleasant Canyon in the Panamint Mountains in Death Valley in 1906.

DESERT CANTERBURY BELL
Phacelia campanularia A. Gray subsp. *vasiformis* G. Gillett.
Waterleaf Family (Hydrophyllaceae)

Description: This erect, glandular-hairy, branched annual can grow to over 2' tall. The deep-green, rounded, alternate leaves, with shallowly lobed and toothed margins, have 1–2"-long blades on 2–8"-long petioles. They are larger near the base, decreasing in size up the stem. Gorgeous deep-blue, 1–1½"-long, funnel-shaped flowers are produced in large, loose cyme-like clusters. The protruding stamens each have a hairless, dilated base. The dry, 2-chambered pods contain many tiny, pitted seeds.

Bloom Season: March to May

Habitat/Range: Found in dry, sandy, and gravelly places in creosote bush scrub below 4,000'. The range of this subspecies extends from the Victorville to Barstow region and Joshua Tree National Park to the Mojave National Preserve.

Comments: Many people develop contact dermatitis after handling *Phacelia* species. The reaction is due to hydroquinone secondary compounds, which plants produce as defense against herbivores. The most glandular species cause the worst problems, and highly sensitive individuals can develop a rash as severe as that caused by poison oak.

NOTCH-LEAVED PHACELIA
Phacelia crenulata Torrey
Waterleaf Family (Hydrophyllaceae)

Description: This glandular, foul-smelling annual is 4–24" tall. The dark-green, 1–5" leaves are pinnately divided or lobed into segments with scalloped margins. Bell-shaped, bluish-purple flowers with white throats and protruding stamens are produced on the upper flattened edges of the coiled flower stalks. The fruits are ovate capsules with 2–4 black, pitted seeds, each with a central ridge that separates 2 longitudinal grooves.

Bloom Season: March to May

Habitat/Range: Notch-leaved phacelia occurs in open areas and rocky washes below 6,000' in creosote bush scrub, Joshua tree woodland, and pinyon-juniper woodland from the Mojave and Sonoran Deserts to the eastern Sierra Nevada, Modoc Plateau, and northwestern Mexico.

Comments: Contact dermatitis may develop after exposure to notch-leaved phacelia. If you have sensitive skin, it is best to avoid contact with this and all other *Phacelia* species. Three varieties of *P. crenulata* are recognized: var. *minutiflora* has a white tube and throat, var. *crenulata* is glandular throughout, while var. *ambigua* has stems that are only glandular above.

LACE-LEAF PHACELIA, FAT-LEAF PHACELIA
Phacelia distans Benth.
Waterleaf Family (Hydrophyllaceae)

Description: This annual has sparse, stiff hairs and small glands, especially on the upper half of the plant. The alternate, short-petioled, 1–4"-long leaves are once or twice pinnately divided with toothed segments. The blue to whitish, 5-parted, bell-shaped flowers are in coiled clusters; the corollas fall off as the fruit develops. Each round, puberulent fruit is on a stalk that is ⅟₁₆–³⁄₁₆" long. There are 2–4 pitted seeds per fruit, each with inner surfaces that are not clearly ridged or grooved.

Bloom Season: March to June

Habitat/Range: Lace-leaf phacelia often occurs in abundance under shrubs in creosote bush scrub, Joshua tree woodland, and pinyon-juniper wood-land. It is very common throughout the Mojave and Sonoran Deserts to northern Mexico.

Comments: Tansy phacelia (*P. tanacetifolia*) is similar to lace-leaf phacelia, but it has fruit stalks that are less than ⅟₁₆" long, ovate, glabrous fruits, and linear calyx lobes vs. the more ovate calyx lobes of *P. distans*. Unlike *P. distans*, the corollas remain attached as the fruits develop. It is found in the western Mojave.

FRÉMONT'S PHACELIA

Phacelia fremontii Torrey
Waterleaf Family (Hydrophyllaceae)

Description: This 8–20" annual usually has small hairs and glands on the upper half of the plant. The some-what succulent, 2–5" leaves are deeply pinnately lobed or divided with rounded segments. The 5-parted, violet, yellow-throated flowers are produced in coiled clusters at the ends of branches, followed by ovate fruits with 10–18 seeds, each with 6–9 crosswise furrows.

Bloom Season: March to June

Habitat/Range: Frémont's phacelia is common in sandy or gravelly soils below 7,500' in the Mojave Desert and elsewhere in California, Arizona, and Utah.

Comments: The corolla color of Frémont's phacelia seems to vary from magenta to violet or blue in different locations. Since soil acidity or alkalinity is known to affect the flower color of some species with anthocy-anin pigments, it would be interesting to find out if soil chemistry is responsible for the color variation in this and other *Phacelia* species, such as round-leaf phacelia.

PARISH'S PHACELIA
Phacelia parishii A. Gray
Waterleaf Family (Hydrophyllaceae)

Description: This 2–6"-tall annual has elliptic to obovate ⅓–1¼"-long, mostly basal leaves, with blades that are longer than the petioles. The flower stalks are hairy and very glandular, and they are not tightly coiled like those of many *Phacelia* species. The lavender, narrowly bell-shaped corollas have yellow tubes and are less than ¼" long. The unequal stamens do not protrude from the flower tube. The oblong to oval, short-hairy fruit contains 20–40 finely pitted seeds.

Bloom Season: April to June

Habitat/Range: Parish's phacelia inhabits alkaline or clay soil around playas from 2,500 to 4,000'. It is known only from Coyote Dry Lake in California and a few scattered locations in northwestern Arizona and southern Nevada. There are historic collections from Rabbit Dry Lake that have yet to be rediscovered.

Comments: Parish's phacelia was presumed extinct in California until rediscovered by Mark Bagley in 1989. Although it is potentially threatened by military vehicle activity on the Mannix Tank Trail, it is not listed as endangered or threatened. *P. pachyphylla*, a similar, more common species, is distinguished by having leaf blades shorter than the leaf stalk, round leaf blades, and fruits with more than 60 seeds, each with 6–11 cross-furrows. The hairs are very distinctive, with large, stalked, black glands.

SPECTER PHACELIA
Phacelia pedicellata A. Gray
Waterleaf Family (Hydrophyllaceae)

Description: Specter phacelia is an erect, densely glandular, thick-stemmed annual that grows to 20" tall. The lower leaves have 3–7 pinnate, rounded or toothed leaflets, while upper leaves are often lobed and wavy-margined. The bell-shaped, blue to pinkish, ¼" flowers are on the upper surfaces of split, hairy, tightly coiled flower stalks. Each fruit has 4 grooved seeds that are pitted on the back and ridged on the inner surface.

Bloom Season: March to May

Habitat/Range: This species occurs in talus slides on partly shaded cliffs along sandy and gravelly gullies and washes below 4,500' in the Mojave and Sonoran Deserts of California to southern Nevada, Arizona, and Baja California, Mexico.

Comments: The species name means "with a pedicel" in Latin, referring to the individual flower stalks. This species is reported to be foul-smelling, although the authors have not found it so.

DEATH VALLEY PHACELIA
Phacelia vallis-mortae J. W. Voss
Waterleaf Family (Hydrophyllaceae)

Description: This straggly, purple-stemmed annual is often found growing among shrubs for support. The pinnately compound leaves, which get up to around 3" long, have toothed or rounded leaflet lobes, but the leaves are often hidden in the supporting shrub. The corolla is funnel-shaped and light lavender to violet, while the sepals are linear, bristly, hairy, and later curve around the tiny, oval, puberulent fruit, which has 4 pitted seeds.

Bloom Season: May to June

Habitat/Range: Found on rocky to sandy soils below 5,500' in the eastern Mojave Desert, northern Sonoran Desert, and Owens Valley to southwestern Utah and northwestern Arizona. It is also found in California's San Joaquin Valley.

Comments: The specimens found in the San Joaquin Valley have darker-veined corollas and may be recognized in the future as *P. vallis-mortae* var. *heliophila*. Death Valley phacelia closely resembles *P. cicutaria* var. *hispida*, which is a taxon from cismontane southern California. Philip Munz collected the type specimen in 1932 at Keane Spring in the Amargosa Mountains of Death Valley.

DESERT LAVENDER
Condea emoryi (Torr.) Harley & J. F. B. Pastore
Mint Family (Lamiaceae)

Description: This 3–9'-tall shrub has erect to spreading gray branches and twigs with dense, stellate hairs. The opposite, ovate, ½–1"-long leaves on ¼" petioles have a minty odor when crushed. The fragrant, lavender, 2-lipped, ¼"-long flowers are produced in bracted clusters.

Bloom Season: March to May

Habitat/Range: Desert lavender occurs in sandy canyons and washes below 3,000' in the eastern and southern Mojave Desert, but it is more common in the Sonoran Desert to Arizona and northwest Mexico.

Comments: Data from fossilized pack-rat middens show that desert lavender moved into the southernmost Mojave Desert during the warming trend of the Middle Holocene. Current cooler temperatures likely prevent it from expanding its range. Smaller, densely hairy leaves are produced during hot, dry summer months when less water is available, while larger, sparsely hairy leaves are present when more water is available. Stems often swell, turn black, and die due to a rust fungus (*Puccinia distorta*).

THISTLE SAGE
Salvia carduacea Benth.
Mint Family (Lamiaceae)

Description: Erect, 1–3' stems arise from a basal rosette of 1–4" pinnately lobed and toothed leaves of this beautiful, white-woolly annual. Spiny bracts subtend 1–4 round clusters of intricate flowers along the stem. The petals are lavender with fringed, 2-cleft upper lips. The lower lateral petal lobes are irregularly toothed, and the lower central lobe is fringed and fan-shaped. The protruding stamens have anther sacs of a striking orange-red color.

Bloom Season: March to May

Habitat/Range: Thistle sage is locally common in sandy to gravelly soils below 4,500' in creosote bush scrub and Joshua tree woodland in the western Mojave Desert. Its range extends from just east of the San Francisco Bay area to northern Baja California, Mexico.

Comments: The genus name, *Salvia*, is derived from the Latin word for healing and wellness, since many of the sages have medicinal value. The species name literally means "thistle-like." The common name of sage was given to *Salvia* species because of its purported power to make one wise.

CHIA

Salvia columbariae Benth.
Mint Family (Lamiaceae)

Description: This 4–20"-tall annual has a basal rosette of 1–4"-long, bristly, bumpy-textured leaves that are once or twice pinnately lobed. The square, erect flowering stalks bear 1–3 dense, round clusters of blue, 2-lipped, ½"-long flowers with protruding stamens, and each flower cluster has rounded, bristle-tipped bracts beneath.

Bloom Season: March to June

Habitat/Range: Chia is a common species in dry, open, and disturbed areas below 8,200' in the Mojave Desert to Nevada, Utah, and Arizona. It is found in many other plant communities throughout much of California to Mexico.

Comments: Unlike desert sage and thistle sage, chia is capable of self-pollination. Native Americans beat the nutritious chia seeds from dried plants into baskets, ground them into meal, and mixed them with water to form a nutritious mush. They also placed whole or ground seeds in the eye to ease soreness. This sounds painful, but a mucilaginous hydrogel forms when the seed coat is in contact with moisture (do *not* try this at home). Commercial chia seeds are from the Mexican perennial, *S. hispanica.*

DESERT SAGE, GRAY BALL SAGE

Salvia dorrii (Kellogg) Abrams var. *pilosa* (A. Gray) J. L. Strachan & Rev.
Mint Family (Lamiaceae)

Description: This low, rounded shrub is usually 1–2' high. Its distinctive blue-gray color and opposite, entire, spoon-shaped leaves make it easy to identify. Blue, 2-lipped flowers occur in tight, 1–2" ball-like clusters up the stems. Beneath each cluster is a whorl of hairy, magenta bracts.

Bloom Season: May to July

Habitat/Range: Desert sage is found on alluvial slopes and in washes from 2,500 to 8,500' in Joshua tree woodland and pinyon-juniper woodland. Its range includes the desert slopes of the San Bernardino and San Gabriel Mountains and scattered locations throughout the Mojave Desert to Lassen County, California.

Comments: In this species and in thistle sage (*S. carduacea*), the flowers are protandrous, which means the anthers open to release pollen before the stigma lobes separate to be able to receive pollen. By the time the stigma lobes are receptive, nearly all the pollen is gone. This keeps flowers from pollinating themselves, ensuring outcrossing. *Salvia dorrii* var. *dorrii* in the northern Mojave Desert has hairless or scaly bracts and calyces, distinguishing it from var. *pilosa.*

67

DEATH VALLEY SAGE
Salvia funerea M. E. Jones
Mint Family (Lamiaceae)

Description: This intricately branched shrub grows to 3' high. Its overall white appearance is due to woolly hairs covering the stems and leaves. The opposite, ovate, sessile leaves are ¼–1" long and often have 2–4 spiny lateral teeth. The deep-purple, 2-lipped, ½"-long flowers are in 1–3" leafy spikes in leaf axils and are partially hidden by tufts of wool.

Bloom Season: March to May

Habitat/Range: This uncommon plant is associated with limestone soils in dry washes and narrow canyons in Inyo County, California, in the mountains surrounding Death Valley to just southeast of Death Valley National Park, and in the mountains in the vicinity of Pahrump, Nevada. Its southernmost known location is disjunct, in the mountains surrounding Ludlow.

Comments: Although there are potential threats from limestone mining, the largest populations of Death Valley sage are protected within Death Valley National Park.

MOJAVE SAGE
Salvia mohavensis E. Greene
Mint Family (Lamiaceae)

Description: This rounded shrub has opposite, ovate, ½–1"-long leaves with a puckered texture, dark-green color, and small, rounded teeth on the margins. Head-like whorls of pale-blue flowers occur singly at stem tips, with white ovate bracts beneath them. Each 2-lipped flower is around ½" long with long, protruding stamens.

Bloom Season: April to June

Habitat/Range: Mojave sage is found on dry walls of canyons and washes and in steep, rocky areas from 1,000 to 5,000' in creosote bush scrub and Joshua tree woodland throughout the Mojave Desert, except for the western portion, east through western Arizona, and south to the Sierra Pinacate of northwestern Sonora, Mexico.

Comments: Pack-rat midden data show that this species occupied areas of what is currently the Chihuahuan Desert, in woodlands of southeastern Arizona, at other times during the past 40,000 years when the continental glaciers of the Pleistocene were active.

BLADDER SAGE, PAPER-BAG BUSH
Scutellaria mexicana (Torr.) A. J. Paton
Mint Family (Lamiaceae)

Description: This 1½–3' shrub has opposite branches that form right angles to the main stem. Younger stems are fine-hairy and light green, and they turn grayish-brown with age. The opposite, deciduous, entire, up-to-½"-long leaves are present only when water is available. Each flower has a hooded, white to light-purple upper lip enclosing 2 pairs of stamens and the style. The purple lower lip is 3-lobed. The rose- to maroon-colored calyx becomes inflated and papery in fruit, enclosing 4 nutlets, a characteristic of the mint family.

Bloom Season: March to June

Habitat/Range: Paper-bag bush is found on sandy and gravelly slopes, canyons, and washes below 5,000' in creosote bush scrub and Joshua tree woodland. It is widespread and common throughout much of the Mojave Desert to Inyo County, California. It also occurs in the Sonoran Desert to New Mexico and Texas, and to Baja California and Sonora, Mexico.

Comments: The flower structure enables bees to pollinate without carrying any of the pollen to the hive or bee larvae, as the anthers and stigmas come in contact with the back of the bee only, not the legs. This plant was previously named *Salazaria Mexicana*, named in honor of José Salazar, a Mexican representative and officer on the Mexican Boundary Survey. The Latin *scutella* means "helmet"; it refers to the helmet shape of the calyx.

SCALY-STEMMED SAND PLANT, DESERT CHRISTMAS TREE
Pholisma arenarium Hook
Lennoa Family (Lennoaceae)

Description: This fleshy herb has no chlorophyll and is parasitic on roots of several shrub species. The aboveground portions of the whitish stem are 4–8" tall, and the ½"-long leaves are whitish-brown and scaly. The narrow, funnel-shaped flowers are in a spike-like cluster on the top swollen stem portions, and the petals are purple with white margins.

Bloom Season: April to July, and in October following summer rain

Habitat/Range: Occurs mostly in sandy soils at elevations below 6,000' in creosote bush scrub and Joshua tree woodland in the Mojave, where its host plants include yerba santa (*Eriodictyon trichocalyx*), California croton (*Croton californicus*), goldenbush and rabbitbrush (*Ericameria* species), cheesebush (*Ambrosia salsola*), and white bur-sage (*Ambrosia dumosa*). It is also on steep limestone bedrock on the northeastern-facing slopes of the San Bernardino Mountains. Also occurs in the Colorado Desert and coastal California from San Luis Obispo County to Baja California, Mexico.

Comments: The fleshy portion of the root is said to be edible. Sand food (*P. sonorae*) is a related plant of the Algodones Dunes in the Sonoran Desert. The roots of its host plant are more than 5' deep, but the tiny seeds don't store enough food to germinate on the surface and penetrate that far underground. Ants and rodents may store the seeds in their burrows, bringing them closer to their host.

FLAX
Linum lewisii Pursh
Flax Family (Linaceae)

Description: Entire, linear, ½–1"-long leaves occur along the length of the 6–30", wand-like stems of this perennial. The blue, 5-parted flowers occur in 1-sided, leafy, stalked clusters, and the petals are very quick to wither and fall. The fruit is a round, ¼"-long capsule with 10 gelatinous seeds.

Bloom Season: May to September

Habitat/Range: Although usually considered a species of higher elevations, flax is locally common in pinyon-juniper woodland in the eastern Mojave Desert. Flax has a widespread distribution in the West from northern Mexico to Alaska.

Comments: Flax had a variety of uses in Western Shoshone culture. They boiled plant parts to make eyewash, boiled stems for a tea to relieve gas, applied crushed leaves to swollen body parts, and made string from the fibers. Other species are widely used today for linen, flaxseed oil, and linseed oil. Low yields were encountered in a recent study to explore the potential use of *L. lewisii* as a commercial crop; genetic improvement is needed before it would be economically feasible.

PURPLE MAT
Nama demissum A. Gray var. *demissum*
Nama Family (Namaceae)

Description: The slender, glandular-hairy, 1–8"-long stems of this spreading, prostrate annual have a forked branching pattern. Narrow, sessile, spoon-shaped leaves appear in dense clusters at the stem tips. The funnel-shaped, purple to rose flowers occur singly in the branch axils and are numerous at leafy stem tips.

Bloom Season: April to May

Habitat/Range: Purple mat is widespread and common in sandy or gravelly soils in creosote bush scrub below 4,000' from Inyo County south to Imperial County in California and east to Arizona.

Comments: The rare *N. demissum* var. *covillei*, which occurs around Death Valley, has winged leaf petioles and gray-hairy leaves. The Kawaiisu made an edible mush of purple mat seeds by pounding them in a mortar. There are 45 species of *Nama* in the United States and tropical Americas; one species, *N. sandwicense*, is from Hawaii.

COOPER'S BROOM-RAPE

Aphyllon cooperi A. Gray
Broom-Rape Family (Orobanchaceae)

Description: This 4–12"-tall, purplish-brown root parasite has stout, fleshy, sticky-hairy stems that are unbranched above the ground. Small, overlapping, scale-like leaves cover the lower stem. The upper stem terminates in a dense, spike-like cluster of lavender to yellowish flowers, which are somewhat hidden by bracts. Each flower is ¾–1½" long, with a 3-lobed lower lip and an erect, 2-lobed upper lip.

Bloom Season: March to May

Habitat/Range: Occurs in flat, sandy areas and washes below 4,000' in all deserts of southern California to Utah, Arizona, New Mexico, Texas, and south to Sinaloa, Durango, and Baja California, Mexico.

Comments: This plant's hosts are mostly in the sunflower family, including burrobush (*Ambrosia dumosa*), cheesebush (*Ambrosia salsola*), and brittlebush (*Encelia* sp.). It has also been reported as a parasite of creosote bush and on roots of cultivated tomato plants.

PANAMINT PENSTEMON

Penstemon fruticiformis Cov. var. *fruticiformis*
Plantain Family (Plantaginaceae)

Description: This hairless, 1–2'-tall shrub is highly branched and usually wider than it is tall. The thick, entire, narrow leaves are 1–2½" long and often folded lengthwise. The 2-lipped, glandular, 1"-long flowers have a cream-colored tube and lavender limb with purple nectar guides.

Bloom Season: May to June

Habitat/Range: Panamint penstemon can be found in dry, rocky canyons and gravelly washes from 3,500 to 7,000' in creosote bush scrub, Joshua tree woodland, and pinyon-juniper woodland in the Panamint, Argus, and Inyo Mountains of the northern Mojave Desert.

Comments: The type locality of Panamint penstemon is from Wild Rose Canyon in the Panamint Mountains, where it is abundant. The rare Death Valley beardtongue (*P. fruticiformis* var. *amargosae*), which is known from the Kingston, Nopah, and Spring Mountains, is rare in California and threatened in Nevada.

MONO PENSTEMON
Penstemon monoensis A. Heller
Plantain Family (Plantaginaceae)

Description: This erect, up-to-12"-tall perennial herb has opposite, clasping, lanceolate, up-to-5"-long leaves with toothed or wavy margins. They appear grayish due to a coating of short, reflexed hairs. Glandular, spike-like clusters at the tops of stems produce tubular, ½–¾" flowers that expand into two lips, the 2-lobed upper lip purple to reddish on the inner surfaces, while the 3 lobes of the lower lip are lavender to pink. The anthers split open along their full length, and the yellow-haired staminode does not protrude from the tube.

Bloom Season: April to May

Habitat/Range: Found in sand or on gravel slopes and in washes in Joshua tree woodland, pinyon-juniper woodland, and sagebrush scrub in the northern Mojave Desert, the White and Inyo Mountains, and the desert slopes of the southern Sierra Nevada Range.

Comments: Penstemons with blue flowers and a lower lip that serves as a landing platform tend to attract bees, while those with elongated, tubular, red flowers and high nectar production are hummingbird-pollinated. Bee pollination is believed to be the ancestral trait from which hummingbird pollination evolved, and this happened numerous times within this genus.

THOMPSON'S BEARDTONGUE
Penstemon thompsoniae (A. Gray) Rydb.
Plantain Family (Plantaginaceae)

Description: The spreading, flattened stems of this low-growing, matted perennial have grayish, reflexed hairs and opposite, ovate leaves to just over ¾" long. The blue, two-lipped, ½–¾"-long flowers are borne in leaf axils, and they have some glandular hairs on the outside. The floor inside is pale yellow and hairy, and the staminode has dense, orange to yellow hairs.

Bloom Season: May to June

Habitat/Range: Grows on alkaline limestone soils up to 5,000' in the New York and Clark Mountains to Utah and Arizona.

Comments: This species was named for Ellen Louella Powell Thompson (1843–1911), a botanist and sister of John Wesley Powell. She and her husband, Almon Harris Thompson, explored the Escalante Wilderness.

PERENNIAL ERIASTRUM, GIANT WOOLLYSTAR

Eriastrum densifolium H. Mason subsp. *mohavense* (T. T. Craig) H. Mason

Phlox Family (Polemoniaceae)

Description: Erect, branched, 6–18"-tall stems arise from the woody base of this grayish-white, woolly perennial. The alternate, ¾–2"-long, pinnately lobed and toothed leaves are somewhat recurved. Dense heads of pale-blue flowers with protruding anthers are produced on the stem tips, and each ½"-long flower has a slender tube that abruptly expands into 5 flattened lobes.

Bloom Season: June to October

Habitat/Range: Occupies dry slopes and sandy areas from 2,500 to 8,500' in Joshua tree woodland and pinyon-juniper woodland in the western Mojave Desert. Other subspecies occur in adjacent areas of southern California to Baja California, Mexico.

Comments: There are 18 species of *Eriastrum* in western North America. Two additional subspecies of *E. densifolium* can be found along the western edge of the Mojave Desert, including subsp. *elongatum*, in which leaves are not recurved, and subsp. *densifolium*, which has larger flowers.

DESERT WOOLLYSTAR

Eriastrum eremicum (Jeps.) H. Mason subsp. *eremicum*

Phlox Family (Polemoniaceae)

Description: This 2–12"-tall annual bears alternate, entire to pinnately toothed leaves with linear segments and short, spiny tips. The ½–¾"-long, bilaterally symmetrical flowers are clustered in heads and are subtended by numerous spine-tipped bracts congested with loose, white, woolly hairs. Each flower has 5 lavender to light blue petals united into a tube below, with open, flaring lobes. The corolla throat is short and yellowish. The 5 protruding, unequal stamens are bent toward the lower corolla lobe.

Bloom Season: April to June

Habitat/Range: Occurs below 4,000' in openings with sandy soil in the Mojave and Sonoran Deserts to Utah and Arizona.

Comments: Similar annual *Eriastrum* species in the Mojave include *E. sappharinum* subsp. *ambiguum* of the western desert foothills, with intense-blue, nearly bilateral flowers with yellow throats and protruding stamens, and *E. pluriflorum* subsp. *albifaux* of western desert fringes, with a radial, yellow- to white-tubed corolla and protruding stamens inserted between the corolla lobes instead of in the tube. *E. diffusum* var. *diffusum* of the eastern deserts has non-protruding, unequally inserted stamens and a ¼"-long corolla with short lobes, and *E. sparsiflorum* along western desert margins is tall, slender, and glandular with pale-blue to pink or cream, ¼–½"-long flowers with equal, non-protruding stamens.

DAVY'S BROAD-FLOWERED GILIA
Gilia latiflora (A. Gray) A. Gray subsp. *davyi* (Milliken) A. D. Grant & V. E. Grant
Phlox Family (Polemoniaceae)

Description: The basal rosette leaves of this 4–12"-tall annual are toothed or lobed and have cobwebby hairs. A few short, tapered leaves may clasp the hairless stem. Loose clusters of 1"-long lavender flowers are produced on the upper stems. The tube and lower part of the throat are a deep-purple color, while the upper throat is white with gold blotches. The 3-parted lavender style and stamens are exserted and the pollen is blue. The 3-chambered capsule is longer than the calyx.

Bloom Season: April to May

Habitat/Range: Broad-flowered gilia is common in deep, sandy soils in creosote bush scrub and Joshua tree woodland in the central and western Mojave Desert.

Comments: In *Gilia latiflora* subsp. *latiflora*, the purple color is in the tube only, while the throat is yellow below and white above. It occurs on desert slopes of the San Bernardino and San Gabriel Mountains. *G. latiflora* subsp. *elongata*, which occurs north of Barstow to the El Paso Mountains, has stems with cobwebby hairs near the base and corollas up to 1½" long.

LILAC SUNBONNET

Langloisia setosissima (Torr. & A. Gray) Greene subsp. *punctata* (Coville) Timbrook
Phlox Family (Polemoniaceae)

Description: This 1–3"-tall, tufted annual has alternate leaves with 3–5 bristle-tipped teeth at the widened apex and clusters of 2–3 bristles at the base. The 5-parted, radial, bell-shaped flowers have ½–1"-long, purple to white or pink corollas with numerous purple markings and 2 yellow to reddish spots in the middle of each lobe. The flowers also have protruding stamens and bristle-tipped calyx lobes. The fruit is a 3-sided capsule with angled seeds.

Bloom Season: March to June

Habitat/Range: Lilac sunbonnet is common in washes, flats, and slopes with gravelly or sandy soil below 5,500' in the Mojave Desert to the eastern Sierra foothills, the Great Basin, Idaho, and Nevada.

Comments: Large bee flies (Bombyliidae) are known to visit these flowers. The genus *Langloisia* was separated from the similar genus *Loeseliastrum* in part by having radial symmetry, equal-length stamens, branched hairs, and white to blue pollen vs. yellow pollen in *Loeseliastrum*.

BRISTLY LANGLOISIA

Langloisia setosissima (Torr. & A. Gray) Greene subsp. *setosissima*
Phlox Family (Polemoniaceae)

Description: The leaves of this bristly, tufted, 1–3"-tall annual are similar to those of lilac sunbonnet. The flowers, however, differ in having ½"-long, lavender to blue petals without spots, although sometimes purple streaking is present. The filaments are less than ⅛" long.

Bloom Season: January to June

Habitat/Range: Found in sand and gravels below 6,000' in the eastern and northern Mojave Desert; also occurs in the Sonoran Desert to Nevada, Arizona, and just barely into northwestern Mexico.

Comments: The ashy-white bee fly (*Pantarbes*) has been observed as the most frequent bristly langloisia pollinator, probing the flower with its ¼"-long proboscis, acquiring pollen on its belly, and moving rapidly between plants and flowers. The genus *Langloisia* was named after the French-born Louisiana botanist and clergyman, Rev. A. B. Langlois (1832–1900). He collected numerous vascular plants and described several species of Louisiana lichens.

MOJAVE LINANTHUS
Leptosiphon breviculus (A. Gray) J. M. Porter & L. A. Johnson
Phlox Family (Polemoniaceae)

Description: This slender, erect, 4–10"-tall annual has opposite, palmate leaves with 3–5 linear lobes. Flowers are produced in dense, compact clusters. Each flower has a deeply cleft, ¼"-long calyx with membranes connecting the lobes for over half of their length, and a slender, maroon, ½–1"-long corolla tube that spreads abruptly into 5 flattened pink, blue, or white lobes. The style is 3-parted, and the stamens are short, with the anthers positioned at or just beyond the opening of the throat.

Bloom Season: May to August

Habitat/Range: Mojave linanthus is found in dry, open areas below 7,800' in Joshua tree woodland, pinyon-juniper woodland, and yellow pine forest on north slopes of the San Bernardino, San Gabriel, and Liebre Ranges. It also occurs in the south-central Mojave Desert north to the Ord and Calico Mountains.

Comments: Mojave linanthus is often seen blanketing recently burned areas. In a pollination study, the most commonly observed visitor of Mojave linanthus flowers was a bee fly, *Bombylius lancifer.* It collected pollen on the base of its proboscis and on its face.

PARRY'S LINANTHUS
Linanthus parryae (A. Gray) E. Greene
Phlox Family (Polemoniaceae)

Description: Tufted clusters of Parry's linanthus are only 2–3" tall. The opposite, crowded leaves have 3–7 linear, palmate segments. The funnel-shaped, 5-parted flowers come in blue and white, and both colors can occur within the same population.

Bloom Season: March to May

Habitat/Range: This species occupies sandy flats below 3,500' in creosote bush scrub and Joshua tree woodland from the western Mojave Desert to Mono County. It also grows in southern California's inner coastal ranges north to Monterey County.

Comments: A single gene locus determines flower color in this species. Some populations are either predominantly blue or predominantly white, while others have varying amounts of both colors. A natural selection process appears to be involved, in which blue flowers have an advantage in dry years, producing more seeds, but in wet years, the reverse is true.

DESERT LARKSPUR

Delphinium parishii A. Gray subsp. *parishii*
Buttercup Family (Ranunculaceae)

Description: This erect, 6–24"-tall perennial arises from woody roots. The triangular basal leaves have 3–5 linear to oblong lobes, and they wilt by blooming time. The stem leaves have up to 20 lobes, each under ¼" wide at the widest point. The fuzzy, light-blue to azure-blue flowers with tubular nectar spurs are produced in a long, branched cluster at the tops of the stems. The fruit is made up of 3 segments and contains winged seeds. Seed coat cells have wavy margins visible with a hand lens.

Bloom Season: April to June

Habitat/Range: Desert larkspur occurs in gravelly areas below 7,500' in creosote bush scrub, Joshua tree woodland, and pinyon-juniper woodland in the Mojave and Sonoran Deserts to Mono County, California, and southwestern Arizona.

Comments: The Kawaiisu mixed dried, ground roots into a paste for swellings. Most larkspurs are very toxic to humans and livestock due to their production of norditerpenoid alkaloid compounds. High-elevation *Delphinium* species produce more alkaloids early in the season, and the levels decrease as the season progresses. Although the lowland *Delphinium* species are generally less toxic, they retain the same level of toxicity throughout the growing season.

TURPENTINE BROOM

Thamnosma montana Torrey & Frémont
Rue Family (Rutaceae)

Description: This yellowish-green, 1–2'-tall shrub is related to citrus. The tiny leaves fall off early, so its glandular stems appear leafless most of the year. The ½"-long flowers are deep purple with a somewhat leathery texture. The rounded, 2-lobed fruits resemble tiny greenish-yellow grapefruits; check them out with a hand lens. All parts of the plant yield an oily compound with a pungent odor.

Bloom Season: March to May

Habitat/Range: Common on dry slopes below 5,500' in creosote bush scrub, Joshua tree woodland, and pinyon-juniper woodland throughout the Mojave Desert. It rims the northern Sonoran Desert in Arizona and extends to Baja California and northwestern Sonora, Mexico.

Comments: The Kawaiisu and Western Shoshone believed this plant would keep snakes away and make trouble for their enemies. The Southern Paiute used a tea brewed from it as a laxative, but they said it could also make one crazy for a while. Smoking the bark was said to induce sleep.

RABBIT THORN

Lycium pallidum Miers var. *oligospermum* C. L. Hitchc.
Nightshade Family (Solanaceae)

Description: This thorny, hairless, 3–6'-tall shrub has oblong, alternate, ½–2"-long leaves. The drooping, narrowly bell-shaped, 5-parted flowers are produced on ½" stalks. The calyx lobes are at least half as long as the calyx tube, and the ½"-long, lavender to white corolla has purplish veins. The fruit is a ¼–½" round, hard, greenish-purple berry with 5–7 seeds.

Bloom Season: March to April

Habitat/Range: Rabbit thorn is found on rocky hillsides and washes below 2,500' in creosote bush scrub. It occurs from around Barstow, California, to Death Valley, and it has also been found in the northern Sonoran Desert.

Comments: Asian box thorn relatives *L. barbarum* and *L. chinense* are the "goji berries" of Chinese herbal lore. The recent discovery of goji's high-antioxidant value has increased the popularity of goji products in the health-food market. Like other members of the nightshade family, they contain atropine, but not at toxic levels.

LOBED GROUND CHERRY
Physalis lobata Torr.
Nightshade Family (Solanaceae)

Description: Lobed ground cherry is a spreading perennial herb up to 20" tall. The lanceolate to ovate leaves are tapered to the base and are up to nearly 3" long. Each flower has a very short tube of 5 fused, purple petals that flare into a semi-flat, nearly 1"-wide, wheel-shaped limb. The anthers are bright yellow. The calyx dries and expands to form a sac-like structure that encloses the berry-like fruit as it develops.

Bloom Season: September to January

Habitat/Range: Found in granitic soils along the edges of dry lakes up to 2,600' in the southeastern Mojave Desert and the northeastern Sonoran Desert to Kansas, Texas, and northern Mexico.

Comments: The genus *Physalis* includes over 80 species. Most are from Mexico, and others occur in Central and South America and throughout Eurasia to Japan. The tomatillo, *Physalis ixocarpa*, is from Mexico. The genus name is derived from the Greek word *physallis*, meaning "bladder," and referring to the inflated calyx.

DESERT HYACINTH
Dipterostemon capitatus (Benth.) Rydb. subsp. *capitatus*
Brodiaea Family (Themidaceae)

Description: This perennial grows from an underground corm coated with brown, fibrous tissue. There are 2–3 linear, keeled, 4–16"-long leaves that grow from the base. The erect, over-9"-tall stem bears a dense cluster of 2–16 blue-lavender flowers with 6, ½–1"-long tepals, which form a tube in the lower half. The individual flower stalks are shorter than the purple or purple-striped bracts found below the flower cluster.

Bloom Season: February to June

Habitat/Range: This subspecies of desert hyacinth inhabits open areas below 8,200' in many plant communities, especially in the western Mojave Desert and in much of California, north to Washington, and south to Baja California, Mexico. There are a few records in the western Sonoran Desert, near the Colorado River.

Comments: The bulb-like corm of desert hyacinth was collected by the Native Americans and early European explorers as a food called "grass-nuts." *Dipterostemon capitatus* subsp. *pauciflorus* has clusters of 2–5 flowers with widely spreading tepals, and the flowers are on stalks that are longer than the whitish to purplish, striped bracts below, distinguishing it from subsp. *capitatus*. It occupies much of the range of subsp. *capitatus* in California, but it is more frequent in the central and eastern Mojave Desert and Sonoran Desert to southern Arizona, southern Utah, and Nevada.

GOODDING'S VERBENA, SOUTHWESTERN VERBENA
Verbena gooddingii Briq.
Vervain Family (Verbenaceae)

Description: This 8–18"-tall perennial has several erect or spreading branches from the base. The opposite, ½–1½"-long, hairy leaves are divided into 3 segments, which are each pinnately divided again and coarsely toothed. The flowers are produced in rounded, showy, spike-like clusters with ⅓"-long bracts. Each flower has a 5-ribbed calyx with spreading, often flattened hairs and a blue to light-purple, tubular corolla with radial symmetry. The 4–5 abruptly spreading corolla lobes are shallowly notched.

Bloom Season: April to June

Habitat/Range: This species grows in dry, sandy canyons and rocky slopes from 4,000 to 6,500' in Joshua tree woodland and pinyon-juniper woodland in the eastern Mojave Desert to Sonora, Mexico.

Comments: A hexane compound extracted from this plant showed anticancer activity against the HeLa cell line, the famous culture of breast-cancer cells discussed in the best-selling book *The Immortal Life of Henrietta Lacks*. This genus was named for Leslie Newton Goodding (1880–1967), one of the first botanists to collect in southern Arizona.

PINK, ROSE, AND MAGENTA FLOWERS

These colors are produced by water-soluble anthocyanin pigments, which can vary according to the acidity or alkalinity inside the cells. Pinks and magentas may grade into lavenders, purples, and blues. Be sure to check the "Blue, Purple, and Lavender Flowers" chapter if you cannot find your plant here.

WESTERN SEA PURSLANE
Sesuvium verrucosum Raf.
Fig-Marigold Family (Aizoaceae)

Description: This hairless iceplant relative has fleshy, opposite, narrowly spoon-shaped leaves with thin, membranous edges on the petiole bases. The flowers, which occur singly in leaf axils, have 5 spreading, pointed, horned sepals that are magenta to pinkish on the inside, but thick and green on the outside; there are no petals. The ovary has 3–5 chambers, and the number of style branches matches the number of chambers. The number of stamens can vary.

Bloom Season: April to November

Habitat/Range: Occasionally found in alkali seeps and on the edges of seasonal alkali wetlands in the Mojave Desert and in many plant communities throughout California to Oregon, Kansas, central Mexico, and South America.

Comments: View the bumpy, glistening foliage surface with a hand lens to see the bladder cells that store water and salts. In the related iceplant, compounds such as betacyanin and flavonoids are produced and stored in bladder cells in response to light. Mutant iceplants that lack bladder cells were found to have decreased pod production and lowered seed weights, suggesting that these cells are important for photosynthesis.

TWINING MILKWEED
Funastrum hirtellum (A. Gray) Schltr.
Dogbane Family (Apocynaceae)

Description: This twining, grayish-green, milky-sapped perennial has opposite, narrow, 1–1½"-long leaves that taper at the base. The pale-pink to greenish-white flowers are produced in umbels in the leaf axils. Each 5-parted ⅛–¼" flower has a ring of white tissue on the inside base of the corolla, and white, oval, filament appendages that are attached to the ring. The tan, tapering, 1½–2"-long fruit has flattened, tufted, ¼"-long seeds.

Bloom Season: March to May

Habitat/Range: Twining milkweed is found clambering over shrubs and draped over trees at the edges of washes below 2,000' in the eastern Mojave Desert and in the Sonoran and Chihuahuan Deserts, as well as in southwestern California.

Comments: This is one of the food plants for the striated queen butterfly (*Danaus gilippus strigosus*), a relative of the monarch butterfly. It breeds mostly in the Colorado Desert but can be found as far north as Mono County, California. The similar climbing milkweed (*F. cyanchoides* var. *hartwegii*) has arrowhead-shaped leaf bases, fruits up to 4" long, and pink to purplish flowers with white, oval, filament appendages unattached to the ring.

HOLE-IN-THE-SAND PLANT
Nicolletia occidentalis A. Gray
Sunflower Family (Asteraceae)

Description: This hairless, 4–12"-tall perennial arises from deep, twisted, woody roots. It has succulent, bluish-gray foliage with translucent glands and a very pungent odor. The alternate, pinnate, 1–2"-long leaves are divided into bristle-tipped, linear segments. Each flower head has 1 row of 8–12 gland-tipped, ½"-long phyllaries. The disk flowers are yellow with purple tips, while the ray flower color varies from pink to purple, salmon, or almost orange.

Bloom Season: April to June

Habitat/Range: Occurs in very sandy soils in creosote bush scrub and Joshua tree woodland, especially in washes out of the north slopes of the San Bernardino and Little San Bernardino Mountains to northeastern Kern County and the Panamint Valley in southern Inyo County. Its range extends to northern Baja California, Mexico.

Comments: Members of this marigold tribe of the sunflower family produce many secondary compounds, including terpenes, flavonoids, and oils, some of which repel insects and kill fungi, bacteria, and roundworms. This genus was named for the French astronomer, geographer, geologist, and mathematician J. N. Nicollet (1786–1843), who was hired by the US government to explore areas west of the Mississippi River.

DESERT NEEDLES
Palafoxia arida B. Turner & M. Morris var. *arida*
Sunflower Family (Asteraceae)

Description: This erect, rough-textured, 1–2'-tall annual has branched stems and alternate, entire, linear leaves that are 1–4" long. The cylindrical flower heads are produced in branched, flat-topped clusters. Each head has 10–20 light-pink to white, 1"-long disk flowers with protruding, dark-pink styles, subtended by numerous linear, pointed, ½–¾"-long phyllaries. The upper portions of the plants are glandular.

Bloom Season: March to May

Habitat/Range: Desert needles are widespread in sandy areas below 3,000' in creosote bush scrub and alkali sinks in the eastern and southern Mojave Desert, throughout the Sonoran Desert, and along the coastal areas of Sonora and Baja California, Mexico.

Comments: The similar but larger giant Spanish needles (*P. arida* var. *gigantea*) occur in the Algodones Dunes of the Colorado Desert south to Sonora, Mexico. It is threatened by off-highway vehicles and is designated a California species of concern.

ARROW-WEED
Pluchea sericea (Nutt.) Coville
Sunflower Family (Asteraceae)

Description: This erect, evergreen, up-to-15'-tall willow-like shrub has simple, alternate, sessile, silvery-hairy leaves with entire margins. It spreads by rhizomes and can form heavy thickets. The dense flower heads, which are arranged in cymes, have numerous pink to rose, ¼"-long disk flowers subtended by a hemispheric involucre with 3–6 rows of hairy phyllaries. A row of several slender bristles comprises the pappus.

Bloom Season: March to July; sometimes year-round

Habitat/Range: Scattered in dunes, sandy flats, and riparian regions such as springs, stream-banks, dry lake beds, and washes below 3,000' throughout the Mojave and Sonoran Deserts and cismontane southern California to Utah, Texas, and northwestern Mexico.

Comments: Native Americans made arrows from the stalks and used the plant for hut thatching and medicines, including an eyewash and diarrhea treatment. Arrow-weed extracts have been shown to repel and kill whiteflies, which are destructive pests of vegetable crops, including cucumber, grape, beans, citrus, potatoes, and more.

SMALL WIRE LETTUCE
Stephanomeria exigua Nutt.
Sunflower Family (Asteraceae)

Description: This erect, 4–80"-tall annual has many spreading branches. Basal and cauline leaves are pinnately lobed and decrease in length up the stem, but basal leaves wither by the time the flowers appear. Flower heads are solitary or in small clusters along branches at the nodes. Each head has 5–11 pink to whitish, strap-like flowers subtended by 5, ¼"-tall phyllaries with some small bractlets below. The cylindric, 5-angled akenes have a pappus of white or beige bristles.

Bloom Season: May to August

Habitat/Range: Small wire lettuce is widespread in arid regions in many plant communities of the western United States.

Comments: Members of this chicory tribe of the sunflower family produce latex, a compound group that includes rubber, in special cells or tubes called laticifers. Latex production also occurs in the milkweed family (Asclepiadaceae), spurge family (Euphorbiaceae), and the fig family (Moraceae), to which the commercial rubber tree belongs. Noctuid flower moth larvae (*Schinia scarlatina*) have been noted to visit plants in this genus.

PARRY'S STEPHANOMERIA, PARRY ROCK-PINK

Stephanomeria parryi A. Gray
Sunflower Family (Asteraceae)

Description: This somewhat fleshy, 8–16"-tall perennial has bluish, hairless stems filled with milky sap. The thick leaves are 1–3" long with teeth that point toward the base. The flowers are produced in open clusters of heads on short stalks. Each head has 10–14 pink to whitish, strap-like flowers that are ½–¾" long. The phyllaries occur in 2 rows, the inner over ½" long, and the outer much shorter. The pappus bristles are united at the bases into groups of 2 or 3, and they are a dirty-looking brownish or yellowish color.

Bloom Season: May to June

Habitat/Range: Parry's stephanomeria is found in dry, open soil from 2,000 to 7,000' in creosote bush scrub and Joshua tree woodland from the western Mojave Desert to Mono County, California, to Utah and Arizona.

Comments: Charles Christopher Parry (1823–1890) worked for the Pacific Railroad and Mexican Boundary Surveys and made many plant collection trips to the deserts and mountains of the American Southwest. He discovered numerous new species, and quite a few Mojave Desert taxa are named in his honor, including but not limited to *Stephanomeria parryi*, *Nolina parryi*, *Marina parryi*, *Linanthus parryi*, *Atriplex parryi*, and *Penstemon parryi*.

DESERT WILLOW

Chilopsis linearis (Cav.) Sweet subsp. *arcuata* (Fosberg) Henrickson
Bignonia Family (Bignoniaceae)

Description: This deciduous, 6–18'-tall shrub has alternate, slightly curved, lanceolate, 4–6"-long leaves. The fragrant, lavender to pink flowers have 2-lipped, inflated corollas with purple markings. The fruit is a narrow, 6–12"-long capsule, which splits apart to release numerous thin, flattened seeds with tufts of hair at both ends.

Bloom Season: May to September

Habitat/Range: This common desert shrub occupies washes and other habitats below 5,000' where subsurface water is found. It occurs throughout the central and eastern Mojave Desert and the Sonoran Desert to Texas and Mexico.

Comments: Although not a true willow, its leaves resemble those of true willows (*Salix* species). It is dependent on subsurface water and can grow roots as deep as 50'. It loses its leaves when temperatures drop to 41 degrees F or with the onset of drought. It cannot self-pollinate, and the stigma folds shut after being touched. It is commonly cultivated, and the dried flowers are brewed to make cough syrup in northern Mexico. It is purported to have antifungal properties.

BEAUTIFUL ROCK-CRESS

Boechera pulchra (S. Watson) W. A. Weber
Mustard Family (Brassicaceae)

Description: The erect stems and linear basal and cauline leaves of this perennial arise from a woody base. Rose-magenta flowers, with 4 petals, 4 sepals, and 6 stamens, are borne in loose terminal clusters. The stems and sepals are covered with short, white, stellate hairs. The mature, short-hairy, 1½–3"-long fruit is reflexed and more or less flattened against the stem, and the winged seeds are in 2 rows within the fruit.

Bloom Season: March to June

Habitat/Range: Often on gravelly and rocky soils from 1,500 to 8,000' on desert-facing slopes of the Transverse Ranges and in the mountains of the Mojave Desert through the Owens Valley to Nevada; also throughout cismontane southern California to Baja California, Mexico.

Comments: Similar species include *B. glauco-valvula*, which has white to pink flowers and wider fruits, and *B. perennans*, with spreading, non-reflexed fruit and oblanceolate, toothed basal leaves. Both have glabrous fruits. *Boechera* plants infected with rust fungi (*Puccinia*) produce fake yellow flowers made of modified leaves that mimic the shape, color, and even the odor of unrelated flowers growing in the same area in order to attract insects to distribute their fungal spores.

HEDGE-HOG CACTUS, CALICO CACTUS

Echinocereus engelmannii (Engelm.) Lem.
Cactus Family (Cactaceae)

Description: The erect, cylindrical, 8–12"-tall stems, each with 5–13 prominent ribs, usually occur in groups of 5–15, forming a 2–3'-diameter mound. The straight spines are of multiple colors, including yellow, pink, gray, and black. The flowers, which occur singly at the tops of stems and close at night, come in shades of magenta, lavender, or purple. The inner flower segments are sharp-pointed, and the anthers are yellow. The round, sweet, edible, 1"-diameter fruits with fat-rich seeds turn red when ripe, attracting birds and rodents.

Bloom Season: April to May

Habitat/Range: Hedge-hog cactus occurs in gravelly soil below 7,500' in creosote bush scrub, Joshua tree woodland, and pinyon-juniper woodland in the Mojave, Sonoran, and southern Great Basin Deserts.

Comments: This plant has CAM photosynthesis, opening its stomates only at night to conserve water.

NIPPLE CACTUS

Mammillaria tetrancistra Engelm.
Cactus Family (Cactaceae)

Description: This 3–10"-tall, 1½–3"-wide, cylindri-cal cactus has dense, whitish radial spines and 3–4 curved, ¾–1"-long central spines, 1 or more with dark, hooked tips. Short-lived, white- to rose-colored flowers with central lavender stripes and fringed outer petals are produced in a circular pattern at the tops of stems. The stigmas are yellowish, and the red, cylindrical fruits are ½–1¼" long.

Bloom Season: April

Habitat/Range: Nipple cactus is found on dry, sandy soil pockets on rocky desert hillsides and upper alluvial slopes below 4,000' in the Mojave Desert, from the Panamint Mountains in the north-ern Mojave Desert and throughout the Sonoran Desert to western Arizona and northwestern Sonora and Baja California, Mexico.

Comments: Nipple cactus and its relatives respond to drought with contractile roots that pull the plant down into the soil, making it very inconspicuous until it becomes rehydrated. The similar *Coryphan-tha vivipara* var. *rosea* has more than 8 central spines, stems from 3–6" diameter, and magenta flowers with ascending, white to pale-magenta stigma lobes. It also lacks hooked spines. It is rare on limestone in the eastern Mojave Desert in California, but it is more widespread in Nevada and Arizona.

BEAVERTAIL CACTUS

Opuntia basilaris Engelm. & Bigel. var. *basilaris*
Cactus Family (Cactaceae)

Description: Beavertail cactus has clumps of flat, bluish-gray to purplish, transversely wrinkled pads that are generally 3–8" long and 2–5" wide. The plants appear to be spineless, but clusters of short bristles (glochids) cause a painful surprise if this plant is handled. Rose to magenta, 1–1½"-long flowers with dark-red-purple filaments and white stigmas are produced along the upper edges of the pads. The dry, tan fruits are 1–1½" long.

Bloom Season: March to June

Habitat/Range: Beavertail cactus is very common on dry slopes below 6,000' in creosote bush scrub, Joshua tree woodland, and pinyon-juniper wood-land throughout the Mojave and Sonoran Deserts to Sonora, Mexico.

Comments: Fossilized pack-rat middens record beavertail cactus in Death Valley 19,500 years ago. Native Americans used the pulp on cuts and wounds to promote healing and alleviate pain. Fruits were de-spined by brushing with twigs, baked in a stone-lined pit until soft, and then eaten. The rare short-joint beavertail (*O. basilaris* var. *brachyclada*) is distinguished by having short, club-shaped segments. It occurs from 4,000 to 7,500' on desert slopes of the Transverse Ranges and is threatened by residential development and off-highway vehicles.

PINEAPPLE CACTUS, DEVIL CLAW
Sclerocactus polyancistrus (Engelm. & J. M. Bigelow) Britton & Rose
Cactus Family (Cactaceae)

Description: The cylindric, unbranched stems of this 12–16"-tall cactus occur mostly singly, rarely in clusters, and they have 13–17 well-developed, vertical ribs. It is densely covered with variable-colored spines that may be over 4" long; these vary in cross section from flat to nearly round, and many are hooked. The spicy-smelling, magenta flowers have 15–30 inner tepals and 5–10 outer tepals with greenish-purple mid-stripes. The stamens have cream-colored anthers and greenish-yellow filaments.

Bloom Season: April to June

Habitat/Range: Occurs between 2,500 and 6,500' on gravelly and carbonate soils in creosote bush scrub and pinyon-juniper woodland in the southwestern Great Basin Desert near Tonopah in western Nevada and in the central Mojave Desert around Barstow, Ridgecrest, and Opal Mountain.

Comments: A 15-year study showed that mortality at elevations above 5,000' is most often due to the cerambycid cactus borer beetle (*Moneilema semipunctaum*), while at lower elevations, the woodrat (*Neotoma lepida*) is the chief predator. It is also threatened by horticultural collection, although it doesn't grow well in captivity. Limestone mining near Victorville has also impacted this species. It is on the California Native Plant Society's List 4, a watch list of species that could easily become vulnerable to extinction.

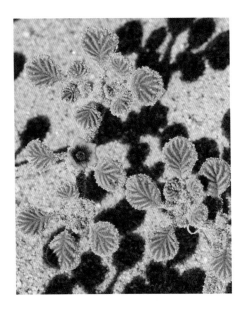

FAN-LEAF TIQUILIA

Tiquilia plicata (Torrey) A. T. Richardson
Ehretia Family (Ehretiaceae)

Description: This low, creeping, evergreen perennial spreads by means of a woody rhizome. The 4–16" stems have opposite branches with small, glandular hairs. The round to ovate leaves are about ¼" long, silvery-hairy, and distinctively fan-folded (plicate). The 5-parted, bell-shaped, lavender, ¼"-long flowers are produced in leaf axils.

Bloom Season: April to June

Habitat/Range: Fan-leaf tiquilia grows in sandy soil and dunes below 3,000' in creosote bush scrub in the eastern Mojave Desert and the Colorado Desert to Baja California, Mexico.

Comments: Two similar species occur in the Mojave Desert, neither of which have prominent leaf folds. *Tiquilia nuttallii*, an annual without a rhizome or glandular hairs, occurs from the Mojave Desert to Washington and Wyoming. *T. canescens* is a perennial herb with alternate branches. It occurs in the mountains of the eastern Mojave.

SILK DALEA

Dalea mollissima (Rydb.) Munz
Pea Family (Fabaceae)

Description: The sprawling, 4–12"-long stems of silk dalea are covered with fine, soft hairs. The pinnately divided leaves have 8–12 round to oblong, ¼"-long leaflets with gland-dots along the wavy margins. The pink to white "pea" flowers are produced in dense, 1"-long spikes. The shaggy-haired, ¼"-long calyx is the same length as the corolla or longer, and the calyx lobes are longer than the calyx tube.

Bloom Season: March to June

Habitat/Range: Silk dalea is common throughout the Mojave and Sonoran Deserts in coarse or gravelly flats and washes in creosote bush scrub below 3,000'.

Comments: A similar annual species, hairy prairie clover (*D. mollis*) does not have wavy leaf margins, the calyx is usually less than ¼" long, and the corolla is longer than the calyx. It generally occupies lower, sandier sites than silk dalea, and its range extends to Mexico. This genus was named for the English physician and apothecary, Samuel Dale (1659–1739), who published on such widely diverse topics as philosophy, pharmacology, and botany.

RED-STEMMED FILAREE, CRANESBILL

Erodium cicutarium (L.) Aiton
Geranium Family (Geraniaceae)

Description: This introduced annual develops a basal rosette of twice-divided leaves. Slender, decumbent, 4–20" stems grow from the rosette to bear clusters of 5-parted, ¼"-long, rose to lavender flowers. The distinctive fruit has 5 loosely fused, ¼"-long lobes at the base, each with a 1–1½" extension that forms the long fruit beak. These 1-seeded lobes split apart, and as they dry, their beak extensions coil. This results in a twisting action that digs the seeds into the soil.

Bloom Season: February to May in the Mojave Desert and nearly year-round in other parts of southern California

Habitat/Range: Red-stemmed filaree is common in dry, open areas below 6,000'. It can be found just about anywhere in California, and it also occurs throughout the United States. It is especially abundant in disturbed sites and along roadsides and can turn entire fields a pink-lavender color when in full bloom.

Comments: Pieces of red-stemmed filaree have been identified from adobe bricks manufactured in 1771 to build the Spanish mission at Jolon in San Luis Obispo County, providing evidence that this Mediterranean species was established in California by that time. Identification of pollen in layered mud deposits in the Central Valley confirmed the arrival of this species in the 1700s. The genus name is derived from the Greek word for heron, *erodios*, since the fruit shape resembles a heron's bill.

WHITE RHATANY
Krameria bicolor S. Watson
Rhatany Family (Krameriaceae)

Description: This shrub resembles the low, densely branched growth form of Pima rhatany (*K. erecta*) in its vegetative state; however, it has spiny branch tips. The dull grayish color of branches and leaves reflects that it is a partial root parasite of creosote bush. The flower buds are curved upward, and the 5 magenta sepals are highly reflexed. The flag petals are purplish on the upper portion and greenish-yellow below, while the lower petals are modified into bumpy, purple, oil-producing glands that are quite visible, even without a hand lens. The purplish stamens are curved upward. The spherical fruits have spines that are barbed only at the tip.

Bloom Season: April to May

Habitat/Range: Occurs throughout the Mojave Desert and in the Sonorna and Chihuahuan Deserts to central Mexico, preferring lower slopes and valleys with sandy soils, often with creosote bush.

Comments: Some groups of Native Americans ate the tiny seeds of white and Pima rhatany plants, and a dye made from the roots was used in basketry. The oils produced by the lower, modified petals are collected by bees in the genus *Centris*. They mix the oils with pollen and feed it to their larvae.

PIMA RHATANY
Krameria erecta Shultes
Rhatany Family (Krameriaceae)

Description: This spreading, 1–3'-tall shrub with blunt stem tips looks like a jumble of dead branches in disarray when not in bloom. The stems and simple, alternate, linear, sessile, up-to-½"-long leaves often have silky hairs and are a dull, grayish-green or reddish-brown color; lacking much chlorophyll, it absorbs some of its food and water from the roots of other plants. The bilaterally symmetrical, ¼"-long flowers are produced on ½"-long, leafy-bracted stalks. Each has 5 cupped, magenta sepals and 3 upper, erect, clawed flag petals, each with a purplish blade and a yellowish base. The 2 lower petals are modified into oil-secreting glands. The 4 yellowish stamens are curved upward. The unique bumpy, teardrop-shaped fruit is matted with whitish hairs and has maroon-colored spines with downward-pointing barbs along the upper half.

Bloom Season: March to May

Habitat/Range: Pima rhatany is found on dry, rocky ridges below 5,000' in the central, eastern, and southern Mojave Desert, as well as the Sonoran and Chihuahuan Deserts to Texas and northern Mexico.

Comments: This genus was named for Johann Georg Kramer (1684–1744), an Austrian botanist and physician. Both white rhatany and Pima rhatany will flower in response to summer and/or winter rains.

ALKALI MARIPOSA LILY
Calochortus striatus Parish
Lily Family (Liliaceae)

Description: This elegant perennial has linear, 4–8"-long leaves that wither early. The flowers occur singly or in clusters of 1–5 on long, slender stems with ½–1" bracts below. Each 3-parted, bell-shaped, ¾–1¼"-long flower has lavender, pink, or white toothed petals with purple veins. The fruit is a narrow, erect, angled, 2"-long capsule.

Bloom Season: April to June

Habitat/Range: Occurs in springs and alkali seeps from 2,500 to 4,500' in the westernmost Mojave Desert and along the desert slopes of the Transverse Ranges to Joshua Tree National Park. Populations are most concentrated in the southwestern portion of Edwards Air Force Base. Its range extends to the foothills of the Sierra Nevada in Kern and Tulare Counties in California to western Nevada at Ash Meadows.

Comments: This rare species is threatened by down-drafting of water tables from nearby development. It is a California species of concern and is on the watch list in Nevada.

DESERT FIVE-SPOT
Eremalche rotundifolia (A. Gray) E. Greene
Mallow Family (Malvaceae)

Description: The erect, rough-hairy, 4–16"-tall stems of this spectacular annual bear dark-green, round, scalloped, 1–2"-long leaves on 1–4" stalks. The globe-shaped flowers have 5 separate, pink, ¾–1¼"-long petals, each with a dark-purplish blotch on the inside.

Bloom Season: March to May

Habitat/Range: Desert five-spot occurs in creosote bush scrub below 3,600' in the eastern and northern Mojave Desert and west to the Barstow, California, region. It is locally common in Death Valley. It also occurs in the Sonoran Desert, including throughout Anza Borrego Desert State Park and along the very western border of Arizona south to northern Mexico.

Comments: Look for the larvae of the large white-skipper butterfly (*Heliopetes ericetorum*), which feed on desert five-spot in the spring. They have white hairs and green stripes on a yellowish-green background. The adult butterflies are on the wing from April to October.

SAND-CRESS
Calyptridium monandrum Nutt.
Miner's Lettuce Family (Montiaceae)

Description: The 2–7"-long, branched stems of this unusual, fleshy annual spread flat against the ground. The narrow, succulent, ¼–¾"leaves form a basal rosette, while the sparse stem leaves are smaller. The tiny flowers occur in short, flattened spikes on curved stalks. Each flower has 2 white-margined sepals and 3 white petals. The fruit is a flattened, ¼"-long capsule with 5–10 tiny, shiny, black seeds.

Bloom Season: March to June

Habitat/Range: Sand-cress is widely scattered in sandy open areas throughout the Mojave Desert and along desert edges, especially along the desert foothills of the Transverse Ranges. It is also common in coastal and inland valley areas of California to Sonora, Mexico.

Comments: Sand-cress is known to be a fire follower and will sometimes be seen in great abundance on desert slopes of the mountains for the first few years after a burn. The genus name is derived from the Greek word *kaluptra*, for covering; it refers to the way the petals close over the capsules.

DESERT SAND-VERBENA

Abronia villosa S. Watson var. *villosa*
Four O'Clock Family (Nyctaginaceae)

Description: Desert sand-verbena is a sticky, hairy, trailing annual with branched 4–20" stems. The ½–1½"-long leaves are triangular to round, opposite, and unequal at the base. The rounded, head-like flower clusters are on 1–3" stalks and have 15–35 pink, ½"-long flowers and lanceolate bracts below. The triangular, ¼"-long fruit has 3–4 wings, raised veins, and a hardened beak at the tip.

Bloom Season: March to June

Habitat/Range: This species is common in low, sandy valleys below 3,000' in creosote bush scrub, from the Mojave and Sonoran Deserts to northwestern Mexico.

Comments: Native Americans used the leaves and flowers as a poultice to reduce swellings and stop pain from burns. The related *A. turbinata* has white to pink flowers, thickened fruit wings, and glabrous leaves. It is scattered across the Mojave Desert north to the Great Basin Desert. A study of several *Abronia* species showed that the roots of desert species have more fibrous tissue than those species found at higher elevations; this probably makes the desert species better adapted to remaining stable in shifting desert sands.

WINDMILLS

Allionia incarnata L.
Four O'Clock Family (Nyctaginaceae)

Description: This short-lived perennial has trailing, slender, glandular stems with forked branches. The opposite, unequal leaves are darker green on the upper surface and lighter below. The rose-colored, funnel-shaped, ½"-long flowers are produced singly on ¼–1" stalks, and each has 3 partly fused, hairy bracts beneath. The entire flower is up to 1" wide, and the stamens are exserted. The oblong, compressed fruit has lengthwise glands and incurved margins, and it is less than ¼" long.

Bloom Season: March to September

Habitat/Range: Windmills occur in creosote bush scrub below 4,500' in the eastern and southern Mojave Desert and in the Sonoran Desert to Colorado, Texas, Mexico, and South America.

Comments: This genus was named in honor of Charles Allioni (1728–1804), a botanist and friend of Carl Linnaeus. *Allionia incarnata* var. *incarnata* has smaller flowers and includes non-exserted stamens. In the desert members of the four o'clock family, heat-efficient C4 photosynthesis is present in all species of *Allionia* and *Boerhavia*.

SPIDERLING

Boerhavia triquetra S. Watson var. *intermedia* (M. E. Jones) Spellenb.
Four O'Clock Family (Nyctaginaceae)

Description: This annual is less than 24" tall, with slender stems that have sticky areas between the nodes. The opposite, entire, ½–1¼"-long leaves are narrowly lanceolate with brownish dots. The tiny, bell-shaped flowers are pale pink to white, arranged in a small umbel, and the truncate-tipped, club-shaped fruit has wrinkles between the 3–5 sharp, longitudinal ribs.

Bloom Season: September to December

Habitat/Range: Spiderling is found in sandy washes and gravelly open areas below 5,500' in creosote bush scrub and Joshua tree woodland in the southern Mojave Desert and the Sonoran Desert to Baja California, Mexico, and in the Chihuahuan Desert of New Mexico, Texas, and central Mexico.

Comments: The similar Wright's boerhavia (*B. wrightii*) has glandular stems, a spike-like inflorescence, large, persistent bracts below the reddish flowers, dome-tipped fruits, and wider leaves than spiderling. This genus was named for Herman Boerhaave (1668–1738), a botany professor in the Netherlands. Members of this genus are found throughout the tropics and subtropics. The extract of a Eurasian relative, *B. diffusa*, has long been used in India to treat a wide variety of diseases, including asthma, cough, colic, hemorrhage, anemia, hemorrhoids, and cancer.

WISHBONE BUSH

Mirabilis laevis (Benth.) Curran
Four O'Clock Family (Nyctaginaceae)

Description: The forked, 6–24"-long stems of this trailing perennial are sometimes woody at the base. The ovate, glandular-hairy leaves are ½–1" long and are opposite on short petioles. The bell-shaped, pink to purple-red, ½"-long flowers generally open during the morning hours, but often close in the afternoon heat or wind. Each flower has a whorl of 5 partly fused bracts beneath.

Bloom Season: March to June

Habitat/Range: Wishbone bush is very common in dry, rocky, or sandy areas and washes below 3,000'. It is found along the western edges of the Mojave Desert to Baja California, Mexico.

Comments: Varieties of *M. laevis* are somewhat difficult to distinguish and their ranges overlap. Var. *crassifolia*, predominantly found in cismontane California, has darker pink to purple-red flowers. Vars. *retrosa* and *villosa*, both found in desert and cismontane regions, have white to light-pink flowers and are generally found in rocky areas. The fruits of var. *retrosa* have 5–10 visible lines, while var. *villosa* tends not to display these lines, and the hairs of var. *retrosa* are bent backward.

GIANT FOUR O'CLOCK

Mirabilis multiflora (Torr.) A. Gray var. *glandulosa*
(Standley) J. F. Macrb.
Four O'Clock Family (Nyctaginaceae)

Description: This sprawling perennial has opposite, round to ovate leaves that are often glandular
and hairy when young, becoming hairless with
age. The funnel-shaped, 2½"-long magenta
flowers occur in groups of 6 in a cup formed by 5
partly fused bracts. The ¼–½" elliptic fruits are
somewhat warty and gelatinous when wet.

Bloom Season: April to August

Habitat/Range: This somewhat rare variety of
giant four o'clock is found in the northern Mojave
Desert in Inyo County, California, west to Colorado.

Comments: The more common *M. multiflora* var.
pubescens is distinguished from var. *glandulosa*
by its smooth, 10-ribbed fruits that do not become
gelatinous when wet. It occurs in the eastern
Mojave Desert and Sonoran Desert to northwestern Mexico. These varieties are sometimes
difficult to distinguish in areas where their ranges
overlap.

PURPLE OWL'S CLOVER

Castilleja exserta subsp. *venusta* (A. Heller)
Chuang & Heckard
Broom-Rape Family (Orobanchaceae)

Description: The erect, 4–18"-tall stems of purple
owl's clover are reddish and hairy, with ½–2"-
long, narrow, linear, lobed leaves. The flowers are
produced in a dense, 1–10"-long, spike-like cluster
with 1" linear, lobed, purple-tipped bracts. The
½–1"-long calyx is split partway down the front,
sides, and back, and the magenta, hairy, bilateral
corolla, which is slightly longer than the calyx, has
a hooked beak and orange-yellow lower lip.

Bloom Season: March to May

Habitat/Range: This subspecies is found in sandy
soils and washes in creosote bush scrub and
Joshua tree woodland from 2,000 to 3,000' in the
western and central Mojave Desert. Purple owl's
clover can be locally common in years with good
rainfall, covering vast, open areas.

Comments: The more widespread *C. exerta* subsp.
exerta occurs in grasslands in the western states
to northwest Mexico. It differs from subsp. *venusta*
by having a white to light-yellow lower lip. The
owl's clovers and the paintbrushes are all species
of *Castilleja*; however, owl's clovers are annuals,
while paintbrushes are nearly all perennials.

BIGELOW'S MONKEYFLOWER
Diplacus bigelovii (A. Gray) G. L. Nesom var. *bigelovii*
Lopseed Family (Phrymaceae)

Description: This erect, 2–4"-tall, glandular-hairy annual has sessile, entire, obovate, 1–1½"-long leaves that abruptly narrow to a sharp, pointed tip. Two magenta, 2-lipped, 1–1¼"-long flowers are produced per node, each with hairy, yellow, purple-dotted throats and hairy anthers. The calyx lobes are unequal and spreading, and the 2 unequal stigma lobes have a fringe of short hairs.

Bloom Season: March to June

Habitat/Range: Bigelow's monkeyflower is common on slopes and along washes below 7,500' in creosote bush scrub, Joshua tree woodland, pinyon-juniper woodland, and sagebrush scrub in the Mojave Desert to Mono County, California.

Comments: In *D. bigelovii* var. *bigelovii*, the distance between leaf nodes decreases up the stem, while in var. *cuspidatus* the leaves are more equally spaced and abruptly sharp-pointed. Frémont's monkeyflower (*D. fremontii*), of the southern Mojave, is distinguished from Bigelow's monkeyflower by its narrowly elliptic leaves, equal calyx lobes, single flower per node, and smaller flowers that lack hairs inside. The 2-parted stigma of a monkeyflower fold together when touched, preventing self-pollination and ensuring outcrossing.

DEATH VALLEY MONKEYFLOWER, ROCK MIDGET
Diplacus rupicola (Cov. & A. L. Grant) G. L. Nesom and N. S. Fraga
Lopseed Family (Phrymaceae)

Description: This delicate, appealing perennial is covered with fine hairs, some of them glandular. It can grow up to 6" tall, but it can begin flowering when less than 1" tall. It branches from the base and takes on a somewhat tufted appearance, with ovate, entire leaves that are about 1–3" long. The 2-lipped, rose to light-pink, 1–1¼"-long corolla has glandular hairs inside the tube, and each lobe has a purple spot at the base. The ⅝"-long calyx has ridges, and the fruit is a 2-chambered, ⅛"-long, curved capsule.

Bloom Season: March to May

Habitat/Range: Death Valley monkeyflower grows in cracks and crevices of limestone from 1,000 to 5,000' in mountains of the northern Mojave Desert, including the Cottonwood, Grapevine, Last Chance, Funeral, and northern Panamint Ranges. It also grows in Titus Canyon in the Grapevine Mountains.

Comments: This uncommon species is on the California Native Plant Society's watch list. There are no immediate threats, since most of the populations are within Death Valley National Park, growing on limestone cliffs.

TWINING SNAPDRAGON, ROVING SAILOR

Maurandella antirrhiniflora (Humb. & Bonpl. Ex Willd.) Rothm.
Plantain Family (Plantaginaceae)

Description: This hairless vine has alternate, entire, triangular leaves with palmate veins and smooth margins. The magenta flowers are on winged, ascending, ½–2"-long pedicels. Each flower has 5 fused petals forming a somewhat flattened, pouched tube that opens into two lips, the upper with 2 petal lobes and the lower with 3 lobes. The lower lip base bulges and is covered with yellow hairs and magenta markings. The stamens have yellow hairs at the bases and do not protrude from the flower tube. The fruit is a round, ¼–½" capsule with tiny seeds.

Bloom Season: February to December

Habitat/Range: Found on soils with silica, limestone, and gypsum on flats, in canyons, and on rocky slopes up to 8,000' on the east slopes of the Providence Mountains, the Lake Mead National Recreation Area, the lower Grand Canyon, and various other areas in the eastern Mojave Desert to Arizona, New Mexico, and Texas, and southern Mexico.

Comments: The genus name honors Catalina Pancratia Maurandy, wife and colleague of an 18th-century Spanish botany professor and botanic garden director.

WHITE-MARGINED BEARDTONGUE

Penstemon albomarginatus M. E. Jones
Plantain Family (Plantaginaceae)

Description: The hairless stems of this herbaceous perennial arise from a 1–4' taproot that is sunk deep into sandy soil. The ½–1¼"-long, glossy, pale-green leaves have entire margins and white edges, giving this plant its common name. The tubular, 2-lipped, pink to lavender flowers have spreading lobes and purple nectar guides, and the floor of the throat is hairy.

Bloom Season: March to May

Habitat/Range: This Mojave Desert endemic occurs in deep sand on flats, at bases of mountains, and in wash bottoms at elevations from 2,000 to 3,000'. There are 20 known sites in California in an approximate 20-mile radius from Pisgah. In Nevada, there are 25 collection locations extending northwest from Primm and 25 observations from the Amargosa Valley. There are also 15 known locations around the town of Yucca, Arizona.

Comments: This species is threatened by off-highway recreational and military vehicles, by alternative energy development on public land, and by residential development on private land in Arizona. It is a federal species of concern.

CLEVELAND'S BEARDTONGUE

Penstemon clevelandii A. Gray var. *mohavensis* (D. D. Keck) McMinn

Plantain Family (Plantaginaceae)

Description: This perennial, 12–28"-tall herb has numerous erect stems. It is mostly hairless, except for the flowers and pedicels. The opposite, sessile, somewhat wedge-shaped, light-bluish-green leaves arch downward and have pointed tips and sharp teeth on the margins. The pink to magenta flowers are produced in clusters of 2–8 on somewhat hairy, maroon-tinged pedicels. Each flower is glandular-hairy and up to 1" long and tubular, opening into 2 lips, the upper with 2 petal lobes and the lower 3-lobed. The staminode, which does not protrude from the flower tube, is densely hairy.

Bloom Season: March to May

Habitat/Range: Found amid rocks and in crevices below 5,000' in creosote bush scrub and pinyon-juniper woodland in the mountains of the southern Mojave Desert, mostly in Joshua Tree National Park and the Sheephole Mountains northwest of the park. There is a historic location in the Granite Mountains and a recent discovery (represented by this photo) in the Sidewinder Mountains, both locations just east of Victorville.

Comments: This species was named for Daniel Cleveland (1838–1929), a prominent lawyer from San Diego who collected local plant and animal specimens. He founded the San Diego Society of Natural History, which later became the San Diego Natural History Museum. He sent numerous specimens to Dr. Asa Gray of Harvard, who, in turn, named some species after him.

PALMER'S PENSTEMON

Penstemon palmeri A. Gray var. *palmeri*

Plantain Family (Plantaginaceae)

Description: This conspicuous, erect, grayish perennial is 2–6' tall with oblong, toothed basal leaves on long stalks. The clasping upper leaves have almost entire margins, and the uppermost pairs are united across the stem by their bases. The 2-lipped, 1–1½"-long flowers are lilac to pink and white, with darker nectar guides extending into the abruptly inflated throat. The fifth, sterile stamen (staminode) has yellow, shaggy hairs.

Bloom Season: April to June

Habitat/Range: Palmer's penstemon occurs on roadsides and in canyon floors and washes from 3,500 to 7,500' in creosote bush scrub, Joshua tree woodland, and pinyon-juniper woodland. It is found in the mountains of the eastern Mojave Desert.

Comments: The genus name means "fifth stamen," referring to the sterile staminode, a stamen without an anther. This species was named in honor of Edward Palmer (1831–1911), a Department of Agriculture botanist who made numerous collection expeditions to Mexico, South America, and the western United States. More than 200 plants have been named for him.

PETIOLATE BEARDTONGUE
Penstemon petiolatus Brandegee
Plantain Family (Plantaginaceae)

Description: This perennial has 2–10" stems with 2–4 pairs of opposite, ovate, bluish-green leaves that are up to 1¼" long, up to ¾" wide, and that have toothed margins. The deep-pink flowers are borne in clusters on maroon-tinged, short-hairy peduncles. Each flower is up to ¾" long and has a glandular, maroon calyx, violet nectar guides, and sparse, glandular hairs on the outside of the slightly expanded tube. The tube flares into 2 lips. The fruit is a capsule around ¼" long.

Bloom Season: May to June

Habitat/Range: Found on limestone rocks and crevices in desert scrubs and juniper woodlands from 3,000 to 5,500' in the Mojave Desert outside of California, from the Charleston and Sheep Ranges in Nevada to the Beaver Dam Mountains in Utah.

Comments: Plants of this taxon have previously been misnamed as *Penstemon calcareous* by Marcus Jones, who published the name in 1908. However T. S. Brandegee originally described this species as *P. petiolatus* in 1899. In the naming of plants, the first published name takes precedence, so the name *P. calcareous* was dropped.

MOJAVE BEARDTONGUE
Penstemon pseudospectabilis M. E. Jones subsp.
pseudospectabilis
Plantain Family (Plantaginaceae)

Description: This stunning perennial grows up to 36" high. Several erect, often pinkish-gray stems bear triangular to ovate, 1½–3½"-long, bluish glaucous leaves with serrated margins. The 1"-long, magenta flowers are spreading to slightly reflexed in a loose, terminal, glandular panicle, and each flower has a bulge in the tube toward the throat.

Bloom Season: March to May

Habitat/Range: Sandy or gravelly washes and canyon bottoms in upland creosote scrub and pinyon-juniper woodland habitats up to 4,500' from the eastern Mojave into the Sonoran Desert. *P. pseudospectabilis* subsp. *conatus*, which has a glabrous panicle, is found in Arizona and New Mexico.

Comments: This species is often used in native plant gardens. It may be confused with *P. palmeri*, which has similar but thicker leaves and can also be distinguished by its larger, fragrant, lighter-pink, and more bulbous-looking flowers.

BROAD-LEAVED GILIA

Aliciella latifolia (S. Watson) J. M. Porter subsp.
latifolia
Phlox Family (Polemoniaceae)

Description: This fetid-smelling annual has
simple, broad, leathery, ovate to round, 1–3"-long
leaves with toothed margins. The 4–12"-tall stem
can be simple or branched, supporting a cluster
of numerous narrow, funnel-shaped flowers. The
corolla is pale pink to tan on the outside and bright
pink to red on the inside, and the stamens, which
are of unequal lengths, barely protrude from the
flower tube. The ¼"-long capsule has 3 compartments and many reddish-brown seeds.

Bloom Season: March to May

Habitat/Range: Fairly common in washes and on
rocky hillsides below 2,000' in creosote bush scrub,
especially in areas where desert varnish is evident.
It has been collected in the eastern, northern, and
western Mojave Desert and from the western
edges of the Sonoran Desert.

Comments: The genus was named for Alice
Eastwood (1859–1953), a self-taught botanist who
eventually became the head of the botany department and curator of the herbarium at the California
Academy of Sciences in San Francisco. She had
the forethought to separate type specimens from
the regular herbarium collections, and she was
thus able to rescue them following the San Francisco earthquake.

DESERT CALICO

Loeseliastrum matthewsii (A. Gray) S. Timbrook
Phlox Family (Polemoniaceae)

Description: Desert calico is a rounded, tufted,
1–6"-tall annual with white stems. The alternate,
½–1½"-long leaves have bristle-tipped teeth. The
most common background color of the 2-lipped,
½–1"-long flowers is rose purple, but they also
come in yellow or white. The erect upper lip has
a white spot and arched maroon lines, while the
lower lip has 3 teeth or notches. The 3-parted style
and the stamens protrude from the corolla tube.

Bloom Season: April to June

Habitat/Range: Desert calico is locally abundant in sandy and gravelly soils below 5,000' in
creosote bush scrub and Joshua tree woodland in
the Mojave, Great Basin, and Sonoran Deserts to
Sonora, Mexico.

Comments: Asa Gray named this species in honor
of Dr. Washington Matthews (1843–1905), a
physician at the US Army post in Owens Valley,
where he vaccinated hundreds of Owens Valley
Paiute against smallpox. He was an ethnographer
and linguist who was known for his publications
of Native American peoples, including Navajo,
Hidatsa, Mandan, and Arikara, and he also studied
the Modoc language.

CALIFORNIA FAGONBUSH
Fagonia laevis Standl.
Caltrop Family (Zygophyllaceae)

Description: This mound-shaped subshrub with rough stems and spreading, intricate, angled branches has opposite, waxy, palmately compound leaves with 3 sharp-pointed, lanceolate, ⅛–⅜"-long leaflets and spiny, curved stipules; they are on petioles that are longer than the leaves. The star-shaped flowers, which are solitary in leaf axils, are less than ½" across and have 5 separate, pinkish-purple, clawed petals that fall off readily. The fruit is a tiny, smooth, ovoid, 5-lobed capsule with some small, glandular hairs.

Bloom Season: March to May and November to January

Habitat/Range: Found primarily on rocky and sandy slopes and washes up to 2,000' in the eastern and southern Mojave Desert into southwestern Utah and in the Sonoran Desert into northwestern Mexico.

Comments: *Fagonia pachyacantha*, of the southernmost Mojave and Sonoran Deserts, can be distinguished by its longer, wider, more ovate leaflets, somewhat larger flowers, and straight stipules. The genus is named for the French physician and botanist Guy-Crescent Fagon (1638–1718) who was the director of the Royal Gardens. He also was the head physician for Louis XIV, who died under his care.

RED AND ORANGE FLOWERS

In this section you will find flowers ranging from deep maroon to red, orange, and orange-yellow. Red and orange flower colors are produced by fat-soluble carotene compounds, such as the beta-carotenes you need in your diet. Reddish colors can also be due to the presence of water-soluble anthocyanin pigments located in the large central vacuole of plant cells. Red flowers often attract birds as pollinators, especially if they offer a large nectar reward.

BUCKHORN CHOLLA, STAGHORN CHOLLA
Cylindropuntia acanthocarpa (Engelm. & J. M. Bigelow) F. M. Knuth var. *acanthocarpa*
Cactus Family (Cactaceae)

Description: One trunk-like stem forks repeatedly to form this 3–6'-tall, spreading, tree-like cactus. The cylindrical joints are 6–12" long with conspicuous, ½–1¼"-long protrusions (tubercles) that are flattened sideways and are more than twice as long as they are broad. Each areole has 12–21 brownish spines with tan sheaths. The 2"-wide flowers have numerous orange to yellow tepals and purple to reddish filaments with dull-yellow anthers. The bumpy, spiny, 1–1¼"-long fruit contains tan seeds.

Bloom Season: May to June

Habitat/Range: Occurs on sandy and gravelly slopes and flats from 2,000 to 4,000' in creosote bush scrub and Joshua tree woodland in the eastern Mojave Desert and Sonoran Desert to Nevada and Arizona.

Comments: Touching the stamens of most cactus flowers causes a thigmotropic response; that is, the stamens move in response to touch to facilitate pollen dispersal by coating the visiting insects with pollen. The similar silver cholla (*Opuntia echinocarpa*) is distinguished by having tubercles that are twice as long as they are broad, and both the tepals and filaments of silver cholla are greenish-yellow.

MOJAVE MOUND CACTUS
Echinocereus mojavensis (Engelm. & J. M. Bigelow) Rümpler
Cactus Family (Cactaceae)

Description: This cactus forms large, circular mounds of rounded, light-green, 10–12-ribbed, 4–16"-tall stems. Some mounds can be as big as 9' across! The reddish or yellowish young spines appear on the stem tops, while lower, older, gray spines arise from areoles with cobwebby hairs. Narrow, 2"-long flowers with scarlet tepals, yellow to pinkish filaments, pink to light-purple anthers, and green stigmas are produced singly at areoles, followed by 1"-long, oblong, reddish fruits with black seeds.

Bloom Season: April to June

Habitat/Range: Found among rocks on slopes in creosote bush scrub, Joshua tree woodland, and pinyon-juniper woodland, often on limestone, from the Inyo and White Mountains south to Riverside County, California, and east to Utah, Arizona, Colorado, and New Mexico.

Comments: Southwest natives used the pulp extensively in cooking, making it into candy and breads, roasting it as a vegetable, and preparing preserves from the fruit. The flowers remain open at night, while the flowers of the hedge-hog cactus (*E. engelmannii*) close at night. Some botanists recognize var. *melanacanthus*, with shorter flowers and 1–3 spreading central spines. It is found in Joshua Tree National Park, Cushenberry Canyon in the San Bernardino Mountains, Clark Mountain, and the Granite Mountains in the Mojave National Preserve.

SCARLET MILKVETCH, SCARLET LOCOWEED
Astragalus coccineus Brandegee
Pea Family (Fabaceae)

Description: This clumped perennial is covered with dense, white hairs, giving the entire plant a silvery cast. The 2–5" leaves are pinnately divided into 7–15 leaflets with pointed tips. The shimmering grayish foliage contrasts beautifully with the intense scarlet "pea" flowers, which are produced in clusters of 3–10. The curved, compressed, 1–1½"-long fruits have 1 compartment, and they are covered with long, silky hairs.

Bloom Season: March to June

Habitat/Range: Scarlet milkvetch occupies gravelly and rocky soils from 2,000 to 7,000' in pinyon-juniper woodland in mountains of the northern and eastern Mojave Desert to northern Baja California, Mexico.

Comments: The foliage of Newberry milkvetch (*A. newberryi*) resembles that of scarlet milkvetch, but the Newberry milkvetch flowers are pink and the fruits are only ½–1" long. Edmund C. Jaeger (1887–1983), who wrote many natural history books about the southwestern deserts, considered *A. coccineus* to be "the handsomest *Astragalus* of the desert."

MARIPOSA LILY

Calochortus kennedyi Porter var. *kennedyi*
Lily Family (Liliaceae)

Description: This 4–8"-tall perennial has linear, channeled, up-to-8"-long leaves that coil on the ground before the flowering stalk appears. Each plant usually produces 1–2 open, bell-shaped flowers with 3 vermilion petals, each 1–2" long with purplish spots and round, fringed glands at the base. The anthers are purple. The lanceolate, striped, 1–3"-long fruit has 3 compartments, each with 2 rows of seeds.

Bloom Season: April to June

Habitat/Range: Found between 2,000 and 6,500' in creosote bush scrub, Joshua tree woodland, and pinyon-juniper woodland in the mountains of the Mojave Desert and western Nevada through central Arizona to the Rincon Mountains. Mariposa lilies can appear with surprising density in years with heavy rainfall, making the landscape ablaze with color.

Comments: Mariposa lilies from east of the Panamint Mountains tend to have flowers that are lighter orange than those of the western and southern Mojave Desert. In the Mojave Desert, yellow-flowered mariposa lilies from the Providence, Inyo, White, and Clark Mountains are *C. kennedyi* var. *munzii*; scattered populations also occur east through Arizona.

PLAINS FLAX

Linum puberulum (Engelm.) A. Heller
Flax Family (Linaceae)

Description: The grayish to yellowish-green stems and leaves of this 2–10"-tall annual are densely covered with fine, short hairs. The linear to lanceolate, sessile leaves are up to 1¼" long and alternate, although the basal leaves may be opposite. Flowers are produced on tips of branches, each flower with 5 yellow to orange, ½"-long, obovate petals with red, maroon-veined bands at the base. The 5 sepals are each around ¼" long with gland-tipped teeth along the margins.

Bloom Season: May to July

Habitat/Range: Plains flax is found in sandy to rocky soils from 3,000 to 6,000' in the mountains of the eastern Mojave Desert to Wyoming, Nebraska, Texas, and northern Mexico.

Comments: Early uses include heartburn treatment and eye medication, and the flower pigment has been used to make paint. *Linum* is a worldwide genus with about 180 species from temperate and subtropical regions.

DESERT MALLOW, APRICOT MALLOW

Sphaeralcea ambigua A. Gray var. *ambigua*
Mallow Family (Malvaceae)

Description: This perennial subshrub is densely covered with short, stellate, cream-colored hairs. The thick, alternate, 3-lobed leaves are 1–2" long and wide with somewhat scalloped margins. The flowers have 5 separate orange-red petals and numerous stamens that are fused by the filaments. The dry, rounded fruit is composed of 9–13 bumpy segments, each with 2 seeds.

Bloom Season: March to June

Habitat/Range: Desert mallow occurs on sandy flats, rocky slopes, and canyons below 4,000' in creosote bush scrub and Joshua tree woodland. It is quite common in the deserts of southwestern North America.

Comments: In a recent Mojave Desert study in which researchers tested the ability of different vegetation types to resist invasion by Mediterranean grass and red brome, a monoculture of desert mallow was the most effective, reducing the biomass of invasive grass species by 91 percent. Native North Americans used desert mallow to treat bruises, mouth sores, and coughs, and to promote hair growth.

DESERT PAINTBRUSH

Castilleja chromosa A. Nelson
Broom-Rape Family (Orobanchaceae)

Description: The grayish-green stems of this herbaceous, 6–18"-tall perennial bear alternate, lanceolate, ½–1½"-long leaves that may be entire or have 1–2 pairs of narrow, spreading lobes. Leaves grade into lobed, scarlet-tipped flower bracts higher up the stem. The tubular, 2-lipped, ¾"-long calyx is dark green with reddish margins, and it is split for approximately a third of its length. The cylindrical, 1"-long corolla has a red-margined upper hood and a dark-green lower lip, which is enclosed by the calyx.

Bloom Season: April to August

Habitat/Range: Occupies dry, brushy, or rocky hillsides from 2,000 to 9,000' in Joshua tree woodland, pinyon-juniper woodland, shadscale scrub, and sagebrush scrub in the Mojave Desert and throughout many western states.

Comments: Some species of *Castilleja* have seeds that sprout only if a suitable host is present, probably in response to a chemical given off by the root. The young seedlings sink root-like projections called haustoria into the host tissues to absorb water and food. Plants grown in the greenhouse without a host are much less vigorous than plants in the field. The genus *Castilleja* was named after Domingo Castillejo (1744–1793), a professor of botany in Cadiz, Spain.

113

CALIFORNIA POPPY

Eschscholzia californica Cham.
Poppy Family (Papaveraceae)

Description: This 6–24" hairless, herbaceous annual or perennial has leaves dissected several times into narrow, somewhat pointed segments. The bright-orange, 4-petaled flowers open from erect buds, pushing the deciduous calyx off in the process. California poppy is distinguished from other poppies by having 2 rims on the receptacle (the torus) at the base of the pistil.

Bloom Season: February to September

Habitat/Range: Occurs in many plant communities throughout California Floristic Province to southern Washington and cismontane regions of Baja California, Mexico. In the Mojave Desert, it is confined to the western regions in grassy, open areas and is especially abundant near Lancaster, California, where the Antelope Valley Poppy Reserve has been established. Plants of the central and eastern Mojave are now recognized as *E. mexicana*. The petals are yellow to deep orange. Its range extends to New Mexico, Texas, Sonora, and the desert regions of Baja California, Mexico.

Comments: This is the California state flower. It was named for J. F. Eschscholtz (1793–1831), a surgeon and naturalist on a Russian expeditionary ship that circumnavigated the globe in the early 1800s. The California poppy has alkaloids (but not opium) that are supposed to treat anxiety, depression, and insomnia; however, there seems to be a dearth of evidence supporting its effectiveness.

MOJAVE MONKEYFLOWER

Diplacus mohavensis (Lemmon) G. L. Nesom
Lopseed Family (Phrymaceae)

Description: This purplish, 1–4" annual has glandular-hairy stems and opposite, elliptical, ½–1"-long leaves. The radial, tubular flowers have an angled, purple, ½"-long calyx with hairs along the veins, and the maroon corolla tube is around ¾" long. The petal lobes abruptly spread out perpendicular to the tube, and the margins of the petal lobes are white to pinkish with a network of maroon veins.

Bloom Season: April to June

Habitat/Range: Mojave monkeyflower grows on gravelly slopes and washes from 2,000 to 3,000' in creosote bush scrub and Joshua tree woodland from northwest Victorville to the Calico Mountains north of Barstow, the Stoddard OHV Recreation Area, and the Newberry and Ord Mountains in California.

Comments: This plant is threatened throughout its range by off-highway vehicles, mining, development, alternative energy development, and grazing. Despite its restricted range and susceptibility, it currently has no legal protection.

UTAH PENSTEMON, UTAH FIRECRACKER
Penstemon utahensis Eastw.
Plantain Family (Plantaginaceae)

Description: This erect, hairless, 1–2'-tall perennial has thick, opposite, entire leaves that are often folded lengthwise. They have clasping bases and are up to 20" long near the base of the plant, decreasing in size up the stem. The 1"-long, red, tubular to funnel-shaped flowers have spreading to somewhat reflexed upper lobes with darker red veins and subtle, lighter-colored nectar guides.

Bloom Season: April to May

Habitat/Range: Utah penstemon is found in rocky places from 4,000 to 5,500' in shadscale scrub, sagebrush scrub, and pinyon-juniper woodland in the New York and Kingston Mountains in California, and in the Spring Mountains of Nevada. Its range extends to southern Utah and northern Arizona.

Comments: This species was used by the Hopi for decoration and as a ceremonial plant. It was described by Alice Eastwood (1859–1953), who retired in 1949 after 56 years as the curator for the Herbarium of the California Academy of Sciences.

ARIZONA FIRECRACKER
Ipomopsis arizonica (Greene) Wherry
Phlox Family (Polemoniaceae)

Description: This erect, 8–18"-tall, short-lived perennial herb has alternate, short-hairy, deeply pinnately lobed leaves up to 2" long. The flowers are produced on short pedicels in clusters of 5–13 on the upper third of the stem. The tubular, nearly 1"-long corolla projects far beyond the tiny, short, glandular-hairy calyx and flares widely into 5 narrow, pointy lobes that are radially arranged. The stamens and style do not protrude from the tube.

Bloom Season: May to October

Habitat/Range: Occurs in open areas with sandy to rocky soil, often in canyons in pinyon-juniper woodland and coniferous forest from 5,000 to 10,000' in the mountains of the eastern Mojave Desert to southern Nevada, northern Arizona, and southeastern Utah.

Comments: Most red, tubular plant species tend to be pollinated by hummingbirds, and often the flowering season closely coincides with hummingbird migration. Native Americans brewed a tea of the leaves to alleviate stomachaches.

RED TRIANGLES
Centrostegia thurberi A. Gray
Buckwheat Family (Polygonaceae)

Description: This 2–8"-high annual, with its basal rosette of 7–10 hairless, tidily arranged, obovate leaves, produces erect, red, hairy stalks with whorled green bracts at the branching points. Two tiny, white to pink flowers are found within each red, cylindric, 3-pointed involucre.

Bloom Season: March to July

Habitat/Range: Found on sandy or gravelly soils below 7,500' in the Mojave Desert through Owens Valley to Utah and Arizona, and into the Sonoran Desert to Mexico; also found in cismontane southern California to the northernmost portion of Baja California, Mexico.

Comments: This species was named in honor of George Thurber (1821–1890), who was the botanist for the Mexican Boundary Survey in the mid-1800s. He was the first to collect *Centrostegia thurberi* and *Pilostyles thurberi* in the eastern California deserts.

CANAIGRE, WILD RHUBARB
Rumex hymenosepalus Torrey
Buckwheat Family (Polygonaceae)

Description: This conspicuous, 2–4'-tall perennial has stout, reddish stems. The fleshy, oblong, 6–24"-long leaves have curled margins and pointed tips. Each petiole clasps the stem, forming a papery sheath called the ochrea. Reddish-pink to maroon, 6-parted flowers are borne in dense, 4–12"-long clusters. The 3 outer flower lobes enlarge and become papery, veiny, and very noticeable in fruit.

Bloom Season: March to May

Habitat/Range: This species is locally common in dry, sandy areas in creosote bush scrub and Joshua tree woodland in the Mojave Desert and western states to Baja California, Mexico.

Comments: The high oxalic content makes this species toxic to humans and livestock, but the leaves can be eaten like spinach if boiled. The Navajo extracted orange dyes for basketry from this plant. Since the roots contain up to 30 percent tannin, canaigre was grown as a commercial tannin source in the Southwest to prevent destruction of oaks, as previously tannin was supplied by oak bark. Two anthocyanin compounds from canaigre, leucodelphinidin and leucopelargonidin, have been shown to have antitumor activity.

WHITE TO CREAM FLOWERS

Since cream colors often grade into yellow, be sure to check the "Yellow Flowers" chapter if you do not find the flower you are searching for here. White and cream-colored flowers appear to have no pigments, but in fact many have water-soluble flavonol compounds. White flowers (and flowers of other colors as well) often have ultraviolet markings that serve as nectar guides to orient visiting insects. White and cream-colored flowers that are open in the evening may be attractive to night-flying moths and sometimes bats.

BANANA YUCCA, FLESHY-FRUITED YUCCA, SPANISH BAYONET
Yucca baccata Torr. var. *baccata*
Century Plant Family (Agavaceae)

Description: This trunkless plant has rosettes of stiff, concave, 20–40"-long leaves with spiny tips and coarse fibers clinging to the margins. The light-bluish-green color is obvious from a distance, distinguishing this from the yellowish-green Mojave yucca. Clusters of flowers are nestled down in the leaves on short, leafless stalks. Each fleshy, waxy flower has 6, 2–4" segments that are cream-colored inside and reddish-brown outside. The fruit is a fleshy, 6"-long capsule.

Bloom Season: April to June

Habitat/Range: Occurs on dry hillsides from 2,000 to 5,000' in Joshua tree woodland and pinyon-juniper woodland in the eastern Mojave Desert to Texas and Colorado.

Comments: The fruits were made into flour or eaten dried. Fibers from leaves of all *Yucca* species were woven into baskets and sandals. The mashed roots have soap-like compounds (saponins) and were used for bathing and ritual shampooing before weddings. Saponins found in *Yucca* species have been touted as a treatment for rheumatoid arthritis and osteoarthritis, but they are potentially toxic. This species has CAM photosynthesis.

DESERT LILY
Hesperocallis undulata A. Gray
Century Plant Family (Agavaceae)

Description: This 1–6'-tall perennial arises from a deep, underground bulb. Narrow, bluish-green leaves up to 20" long form a basal rosette, while smaller leaves may be found up the stem. It's easy to distinguish this plant by the obvious wavy leaf margins. Elongated, showy flower clusters occur at the ends of unbranched stems. Each funnel-shaped flower has long, golden anthers and 6 white, waxy, 1½" segments, each with a silvery-green strand on the back. The fruit is a ½–¾"-long capsule with 3 compartments.

Bloom Season: March to May

Habitat/Range: Desert lilies are found on sandy flats and dunes below 2,500' in creosote bush scrub in the Mojave and Sonoran Deserts to Arizona and northwestern Mexico.

Comments: Desert lily was highly regarded as a food by many of the Native Americans of the Southwest. The bulb has a garlic-like flavor and was eaten raw or baked in a rock-lined pit. The genus name, *Hesperocallis*, literally means "western beauty" in Greek.

JOSHUA TREE

Yucca brevifolia Engelm.
Century Plant Family (Agavaceae)

Description: The straight, fibrous trunk of this monocot can grow to over 30' tall. The trunk grows until insects or its own flowers destroy the growing tip; at this point, branching occurs. The narrow, rigid, 8–14"-long, spine-tipped leaves are coated with a thick, waxy layer and have tiny teeth on the margins. Older leaves reflex downward. Dense, 12–20"-long clusters of cream-colored, 6-parted, 1½–3"-long flowers are produced at branch tips, followed by oblong, 3-chambered, 2–4"-long capsules.

Bloom Season: March to May

Habitat/Range: Occurs between 2,000 and 6,000' throughout the Mojave Desert.

Comments: All *Yuccas* are pollinated by yucca moth species, many very specific in which species they visit. The female moth rolls a ball of pollen, makes a hole in the pistil, deposits her eggs, and tamps the pollen onto the stigma, effectively pollinating the flower. Her larvae consume seeds as the fruit develops, but some seeds escape predation, enabling the plant to sexually reproduce. Botanists now recognize the eastern Joshua tree (*Yucca jaegeriana*) from the eastern Mojave Desert as a distinct species. It has a different species of moth pollinator and is morphologically distinct, with more greenish, narrowly bell-shaped corollas, perianth lobes that curve back, and narrower, somewhat shorter trunks that branch lower to the ground.

MOJAVE YUCCA

Yucca schidigera Roezl ex Ortgies
Century Plant Family (Agavaceae)

Description: Mojave yucca has rosettes of stiff, 1–5'-long, spine-tipped leaves on short, 3–15' trunks. The leaves are unmistakable with their yellowish-green color, shredding marginal fibers, and white bases. The waxy, cream-colored flowers with 6 incurved segments are produced in heavy, branched, 2–4' clusters on leafless stalks. The fruit is a fibrous, 2–3" capsule.

Bloom Season: April to May

Habitat/Range: Mojave yucca occurs on dry, rocky slopes and flats below 5,000' in creosote bush scrub, Joshua tree woodland, and blackbush scrub in the southern and eastern Mojave Desert. It also occurs in the northern Sonoran Desert and mountains and coastal areas of southern California to Baja California, Mexico.

Comments: With its smaller fruits, Mojave yucca was not as important a food source for Native Americans as were other *Yucca* species. The flowers have a pleasant flavor if the soapy-tasting, green ovary is removed. This species was an important source of fibers for sandals and other textiles, and torches were made from the dried leaves. Several varieties of Martin's giant skipper butterfly (*Megathymus coloradensis*) lay eggs on sucker shoots of various *Yucca* species. The larvae bore into the tissues, sometimes breaking rhizomes and separating cloned yuccas.

FRINGED AMARANTH

Amaranthus fimbriatus (Torrey) Benth.
Pigweed Family (Amaranthaceae)

Description: This slender, erect, summer annual has pink to reddish stems and alternate, bright-green, 1–4"-long, linear to narrowly lanceolate leaves on 1"-long stalks. Numerous small, male and female flowers are produced in loose, leafy, axillary, and terminal spike-like clusters. The white to pink sepals are around 1/10" long and fringed at the tips.

Bloom Season: August to November, following summer rainfall

Habitat/Range: Occurs in washes and gravelly or sandy soils below 5,000' in creosote bush scrub and Joshua tree woodland in the central, eastern, and southern Mojave Desert and in the Sonoran Desert to Big Bend, Texas, and Baja California and Sinaloa, Mexico.

Comments: *Amaranthus* species have C4 photosynthesis. Along with its relative, quinoa (*Chenopodium* species), amaranth seeds are popular as a grain substitute; amaranth has up to 30 percent more protein than wheat or oats, a wide variety of minerals, and several B vitamins. Both are gluten-free.

AMSONIA

Amsonia tomentosa Torrey and Frémont
Dogbane Family (Apocynaceae)

Description: This milky-sapped perennial has numerous erect, herbaceous, 6–16"-tall stems that sprout from a woody base. The alternate, green, ovate-lanceolate leaves are ¾–1½" long. White to light-blue, 5-parted, tubular flowers with spreading, pointed lobes are produced in dense clusters at the tops of branches, followed by 1–3"-long, narrow, 2-parted fruits.

Bloom Season: March to May

Habitat/Range: Amsonia occurs in dry soils and canyons from 1,000 to 4,000' in creosote bush scrub, Joshua tree woodland, blackbush scrub, and pinyon-juniper woodland in the mountains of the eastern and southern Mojave Desert, the north-facing slopes of the San Bernardino Mountains, and the Sonoran Desert to Utah and western Texas.

Comments: The Paiute used amsonia stem fibers to make cord, and a laxative was made from the milky juice. A Chinese species, *A. elliptica*, is one source of yohimbine used in treating erectile dysfunction and promoting weight loss. Controlled tests are inconclusive, and side effects include nervousness, irritability, insomnia, diarrhea, heart palpitations, dizziness, increased blood pressure, and anxiety. Yohimbine is also used in veterinary science and animal research, as it rouses animals from sedation.

DESERT MILKWEED

Asclepias erosa Torr.
Dogbane Family (Apocynaceae)

Description: This 18–30"-tall perennial has white-woolly stems and opposite, sessile, lanceolate, leathery, 2–6"-long leaves with veins running parallel to the wavy leaf margins. Numerous ¼" cream to greenish-white flowers are produced in rounded, stalked umbels. The filaments are fused to form a central tube, and the anthers are also fused, forming a head with peculiar attachments called hoods and horns. The dry, brownish, 2–3"-long, reflexed fruits split open lengthwise to release numerous seeds with long hairs.

Bloom Season: May to July

Habitat/Range: Desert milkweed is found on dry slopes and in washes from 500 to 6,000' in creosote bush scrub, Joshua tree woodland, and pinyon-juniper woodland in the Mojave Desert to central Nevada and in the Sonoran Desert to Baja California, Mexico.

Comments: Herbalists and Native Americans employed various species of *Asclepias* as expectorants and purgatives and as remedies for lung problems. The pulp of the roots was used as a poultice on bruises, and seeds were ground and boiled as a remedy for sores and rattlesnake bites. The larvae of the monarch butterfly (*Danaus plexippus*) feed on *Asclepias* species.

NARROW-LEAF MILKWEED, MEXICAN WHORLED MILKWEED

Asclepias fascicularis Decne.
Dogbane Family (Apocynaceae)

Description: This hairless, erect, 20–30"-tall perennial has linear to lanceolate leaves that are 1½–4" long and less than ½" wide. They occur in whorls of 3–6 on the stem and are often folded lengthwise. The small, greenish-white flowers have reflexed petals and elevated hoods with thin, incurved horns. They are produced in rounded umbels at the tops of stems, followed by narrow, erect, ¼–½"-long fruits that split open along 1 suture to release numerous tufted seeds.

Bloom Season: June to August

Habitat/Range: Narrow-leaf milkweed is common around rivers and alkali seeps and springs in the Mojave Desert, as well as in valleys and foothills throughout the western states.

Comments: This species is a food plant for monarch butterflies, which migrate from coastal wintering sites to deserts in the spring. The plant contains toxic compounds called cardiac glycosides that the monarchs store in their tissues, making them toxic to their predators. The Paiute used the fibers of milkweeds to make cloth, rope, and nets. The milky juice, which contains latex, was boiled and sometimes mixed with deer fat to make chewing gum.

121

GRAVEL GHOST, PARACHUTE PLANT

Atrichoseris platyphylla (A. Gray) A. Gray
Sunflower Family (Asteraceae)

Description: Branched, leafless, 1–5'-high stems emerge from the flat basal rosette of this hairless annual. The round to oblong, 1–4"-long, finely toothed basal leaves are grayish-green above and purple on the undersurface. Stem leaves are reduced to triangular scales and are barely noticeable. The 1" flower heads have numerous white, strap-shaped flowers subtended by 2–4 rows of triangular, ¼"-high phyllaries. The flowers have a vanilla odor.

Bloom Season: March to May

Habitat/Range: Gravel ghost occurs in sandy washes and dark, rocky, and clay soils in creosote bush scrub in the eastern and northern Mojave Desert. It is especially common in open areas in Death Valley. It also occurs in the Sonoran Desert to Yuma, Arizona.

Comments: The gravel ghost can trap moisture under its large basal leaves, and reflect the sun's rays with its light-colored upper-leaf surface. It has a lower leaf temperature than the ambient air, and escapes high water loss by growing its basal leaves very early in the season before the very hot temperatures prevail; later in the season its leaves wilt and bolting occurs.

MULE FAT
Baccharis salicifolia (Ruiz & Pav.) Pers. subsp. *salicifolia*
Sunflower Family (Asteraceae)

Description: This sticky, erect, 3–12'-tall shrub has alternate, sessile, linear to lanceolate leaves that are 2–6" long. They are somewhat sticky, with entire or slightly toothed margins, and 3 veins from the base, with the central vein more prominent than the lateral veins. The ¼"-long male and female flower heads are produced in rounded clusters on separate plants, each with numerous dull-white, thread-like flowers and 4–5 rows of red-tinged, lanceolate phyllaries.

Bloom Season: July to November

Habitat/Range: Mule fat is found along streams, seeps, and in canyon bottoms below 3,500' throughout the southwestern United States, including the deserts.

Comments: Mule fat is not a willow, although it grows in the same habitat. Willows have only 1 main vein from the leaf base, not 3, and willows never have the old, dried clusters of phyllaries like those that persist on this shrub through the seasons. The Cahuilla prepared an eyewash by steeping mule fat leaves.

123

Brickellia incana

BRICKELLBUSH
Brickellia species
Sunflower Family (Asteraceae)

Genus Description: These shrubs have alternate or opposite, resin-dotted leaves with 3 main veins. The white to cream, tubular flowers are in cylindrical heads, each subtended by an involucre with several overlapping rows of phyllaries. The receptacle is flat and lacks chaff. The pappus is of 10 or more somewhat plumose bristles, and the hairy, cylindric fruits often have 10 ribs. There are 12 *Brickellia* species known from the Mojave Desert. A few of the more common include **woolly brickellbush** (*B. incana*), a round, 1–3'-tall shrub found in washes and covered with dense, white, woolly hairs. **Pungent brickellbush** (*B. atractyloides* var. *arguta*) from rocky slopes and cliffs has teeth along the leaf margins and flavonoid compounds that show potential for treating cataracts. **California brickellbush** (*B. californica*), found on rocky slopes, has triangular leaf blades and very narrow heads, while **narrow-leaved brickellbush** (*B. oblongifolia* var. *linifolia*), a subshrub found on rocky hillsides, has a woody caudex covered with short, glandular hairs, and has alternate, sessile leaves and solitary heads subtended by unequal rows of pointed, green-striped phyllaries.

Brickellia atractyloides var. *arguta*

Brickellia californica

Brickellia oblogifolia var. *linifolia*

WHITE TACK-STEM
Calycoseris wrighti A. Gray
Sunflower Family (Asteraceae)

Description: The distinctive, tack-shaped glands on the upper portions of the branched stems of this annual are a pale cream or grayish color. The 1½–4"-long leaves are mostly basal and pinnately divided into long, narrow segments. The showy, 1–1½"-wide heads are composed only of numerous white, squared-off, toothed ray flowers, these with some pink-purplish marks on the backs. The heads are subtended by 2 rows of green-ribbed, membranous-edged phyllaries, the outer row short, uneven, and untidy-looking, and the inner row long, nearly linear, and neatly arranged. The tack-shaped glands occur on the phyllaries as well.

Bloom Season: March to May

Habitat/Range: Occurs on desert pavement, flats, and gravelly slopes and washes from the White and Inyo Ranges in the northern Mojave, and throughout the eastern and southern Mojave Desert west to Texas.

Comments: This species was named for William Greenwood Wright (1831–1912), an author of numerous volumes on butterflies and moths. He collected plants in California from 1880 to 1889, including from the top of Mount San Gorgonio in 1882. He also made collections from Alaska and New York.

Chaenactis macrantha

PINCUSHION
Chaenactis species
Sunflower Family (Asteraceae)

Genus Description: Our Mojave Desert pincushions are generally erect, somewhat branched annuals with alternate, pinnately lobed leaves. Flower heads consist of disk flowers, which are white (to cream or pinkish), subtended by a row of distinct phyllaries. Most have protruding anthers. All of the following are found on open gravel flats and slopes.
Pebble pincushion (*C. carphoclinia*) has reddish, cylindrical, bristle-tipped phyllaries and leaves often 3–4 times pinnately lobed. **Fremont pincushion** (*C. fremontii*) is fleshy and hairless by flowering time, with once-pinnate leaves and 1 row of flattened, pointed phyllaries. The outermost disk flowers are enlarged and 2-lipped. **Desert pincushion** (*C. stevioides*) has cobwebby-hairy stem bases, twice-pinnately lobed leaves with short, thick segments, and blunt-tipped, glandular phyllaries. **Mojave pincushion** (*C. macrantha*) has flattened, once-pinnately lobed leaves, nodding flower heads, and numerous leafy bracts subtending the phyllaries. The anthers do not protrude, and the cream-colored flowers open mostly at night.

Chaenactis carphoclinia

Chaenactis fremontii

Chaenactis stevioides

ROSE HEATH

Chaetopappa ericoides (Torr.) G. L. Nesom
Sunflower Family (Asteraceae)

Description: This clump-forming, bushy perennial with erect, branching stems spreads by underground rhizomes. The somewhat linear, leathery, ½"-long leaves have longitudinal grooves and a raised midvein on the upper surface, and they are overlapping and crowded along the entire length of the stem. Flower heads have 12–24 white ray flowers and 12–24 yellowish disk flowers subtended by a hemispheric involucre of green, pointed phyllaries with purplish tips. The pappus is composed of around 25 bristles with tiny barbs.

Bloom Season: April to September

Habitat/Range: Rose heath occupies dry slopes and flats from 3,800 to 9,500' in blackbush scrub, Joshua tree woodland, and pinyon-juniper woodland in the mountains of the eastern Mojave Desert to Wyoming, Nebraska, Texas, and northern Mexico.

Comments: This species is highly variable within its range, especially in the amount of pubescence and the number of flowers per head. The genus name *Chaetopappa* is derived from the Greek words *chatte*, for bristle, and *pappos*, for seed down.

DESERT THISTLE

Cirsium neomexicanum A. Gray
Sunflower Family (Asteraceae)

Description: This cobwebby-hairy biennial usually has 1 erect stem that often grows to over 6' tall, bearing a few ascending branches in the upper portion. The greenish-gray leaves have many long spines along the margins and tips, and they clasp the stem at the base. The lower leaves are 2–7" long and the upper are reduced, sometimes to just spines with no blade near the very top. The rounded, flat-topped flower heads are produced singly at the tops of the main stems and branches, each subtended by a 1"-long and 2"-wide involucre of spiny, spreading to reflexed phyllaries. Numerous dirty-white to pink or pale-lavender disk flowers are crowded into each head.

Bloom Season: April to May

Habitat/Range: Fairly common from 2,500 to 7,000' in the eastern Mojave Desert and northwestern Sonoran Desert to Colorado and New Mexico.

Comments: The southern Paiute harvested young plants, prior to the thorns hardening, and stripped the "bark" to eat the centers of the stems. A cold infusion of the root was used as an eyewash. The caterpillars of the Mylitta crescent (*Phyciodes mylitta*) and painted lady butterflies (*Vanessa cardui*) use thistles as food plants.

127

CARVESEED, KEYSIA
Glyptopleura setulosa A. Gray
Sunflower Family (Asteraceae)

Description: This tufted, 2"-high, milky-sapped annual grows from a strong taproot. The light-green, 1–2"-long leaves are pinnately lobed with hardened, bright-white, toothed edges. The sweet-smelling flower heads have 7–14 ray flowers only, these creamy or yellowish. Each head has an involucre with an outer, scant row of linear phyllaries and an inner row of 7–12 narrow, equal-length phyllaries. The ⅙"-long cypsela has a pappus of white bristles, and it is 5-angled and curved, giving the common name of carveseed.

Bloom Season: April to July

Habitat/Range: Sandy or rocky dry flats and slopes up to 6,000' in the western Mojave to southern Owens Valley, Utah, and Arizona.

Comments: The similar *G. marginata*, which is more prevalent in the northern and eastern Mojave, has smaller, much less exserted, white to cream flowers and a more conspicuous white leaf margin. The common name *keysia* is for pioneer-rancher William Keys and his wife, who settled in the Little San Bernardino Mountains. The Paiute tribe ate the leaves and stems of this plant as greens.

WHITE TIDY-TIPS
Layia glandulosa (Hook.) Hook. & Arn.
Sunflower Family (Asteraceae)

Description: This erect, 4–20"-tall annual has branched, purplish stems with black glands. The thin, roughened basal leaves are toothed or lobed while the upper leaves are entire. Single flower heads are produced at the ends of branches, each with numerous ¼"-long, yellow disk flowers, 10–14 white, 3-lobed ray flowers, and 1 row of ¼–½"-long, glandular-hairy phyllaries. The hairy akenes are topped by a pappus of 10–15 narrow, bright-white, flattened scales. This plant has a pleasant, spicy odor.

Bloom Season: March to June

Habitat/Range: White tidy-tips are found in sandy soil below 8,000' in many vegetation types in the Mojave and Sonoran Deserts and elsewhere in California, as well as throughout the western United States.

Comments: This genus was named for George Tradescant Lay (1799–1845), an early 19th-century naturalist aboard the *Blossom*, a ship that was assigned to follow and check up on the infamous *Bounty*. Lay later became a missionary to China. Tidy-tips (*L. platyglossa*), with yellow, white-tipped rays, occur on the western edge of the Mojave Desert.

MOJAVE DESERTSTAR
Monoptilon bellioides (A. Gray) H. M. Hall
Sunflower Family (Asteraceae)

Description: This 2–6"-tall, cushion-like, stubble-haired annual has entire, somewhat linear, ¼–½"-long leaves in tufts below the flower heads. Each head has 1 row of equal, linear, firm phyllaries, numerous yellow disk flowers, and 12–20 white, ¼–½"-long ray flowers. The pappus has up to 12 straight bristles and shorter, alternating, divided scales.

Bloom Season: February to May, and sometimes in September following summer rain

Habitat/Range: Mojave desertstar is common on sandy and gravelly flats and washes below 3,000' in creosote bush scrub in the Mojave and Sonoran Deserts.

Comments: The similar daisy desertstar (*Monoptilon bellidiformae*) has wider, spoon-shaped leaves and slightly shorter ray flowers. The pappus has a cup of tiny scales and 1 much longer, feathery-tipped bristle. Both species of desertstar are true "belly plants," since you have to get on your belly to really see the details.

129

EMORY ROCK-DAISY
Perityle emoryi Torr.
Sunflower Family (Asteraceae)

Description: This brittle, 6–24"-tall, glandular-hairy annual has 1–4"-long, rounded, toothed or lobed leaves that are opposite near the base and alternate above. The flower heads have numerous tiny, yellow disk flowers and 8–12 white ray flowers. The boat-shaped, ¼"-long phyllaries occur in 1–2 rows, and they are fringed with hairs at their tips.

Bloom Season: February to June

Habitat/Range: Emory rock-daisy is common among boulders, on slopes, and in washes below 3,000' in creosote bush scrub in the central, eastern, and southeastern Mojave Desert to coastal southern California, the Channel Islands, and Baja California and Sonora, Mexico.

Comments: This plant was named in honor of Major W. H. Emory (1811–1887), who completed the Mexican Boundary Survey in 1855, resulting in the moving of the international boundary in southern Arizona and New Mexico to its present location. Other less common species of *Perityle* in the Mojave Desert are perennial, lack ray flowers, and are found in the higher mountains of the eastern Mojave. An interesting study in which numerous desert annuals were grown in chambers and subjected to various levels of air pollutants showed Emory rock-daisy to be quite resistant to ozone damage and moderately resistant to sulfur dioxide.

BUSH ARROWLEAF
Pleurocoronis pluriseta (A. Gray) R. M. King & H. Rob.
Sunflower Family (Asteraceae)

Description: This slender and straggly, highly branched, tangled subshrub can grow up to 18" tall. The unique, glandular-hairy leaves are trident-shaped at the top, narrowing to thin petioles at the base. Each cylindrical, ¼–½" flower head contains only disk flowers and is subtended by 25 recurved phyllaries with glandular hairs and darkened tips.

Bloom Season: October to June

Habitat/Range: Found in rocky canyons and washes below 5,500' in creosote bush scrub and other desert scrub communities in the Mojave and Sonoran Deserts to Utah, Arizona, and northern Mexico.

Comments: The sunflower family has the largest number of species of any plant family and is fairly complex. It is broken into subgroups called tribes. This species is in the Eupatory tribe, as is the genus *Brickellia* in this book. This tribe also includes the genus *Stevia*, which is a South American species used commercially as a sugar substitute.

PORE-LEAF, ODORA
Porophyllum gracile Benth.
Sunflower Family (Asteraceae)

Description: The wiry, erect, 1–2' tall, very slender stems of this foul-smelling, branched subshrub bear hairless, linear leaves covered with numerous translucent, dark-purple oil glands. The narrow, cylindrical flower heads bear white to purplish disk flowers and are subtended by 5 equal-length, bluish-tinged phyllaries with oil glands.

Bloom Season: October to June

Habitat/Range: Found in the southern and eastern Mojave Desert to Texas and Mexico.

Comments: Pore-leaf is called *hierba del venado* (deer grass) by the people of Baja California, Mexico. They make tea for respiratory and intestinal illnesses from the bitter dried leaves. The Havasupai rubbed a decoction of the pounded plant as a liniment. Research has shown that having more glands per leaf results in reduced herbivory, and that the number of glands is not primarily a hereditary trait; it can be increased by adding nitrogen to the soil.

DESERT CHICORY
Rafinesquia neomexicana A. Gray
Sunflower Family (Asteraceae)

Description: This hairless, 6–24"-tall, milky-sapped annual has weak, zigzag stems that often grow up through shrubs for support and protection against herbivores. The 1½–4"-long basal leaves wither by the time the stem develops, and the smaller stem leaves are sessile, toothed, and alternate. The large, showy flower heads occur singly at the ends of branches. They have numerous white, strap-shaped flowers that extend well beyond the pointed, ½–1"-long phyllaries. The pappus consists of white, plumose bristles with tangled hairs.

Bloom Season: March to May

Habitat/Range: Occurs in sandy and gravelly soils in creosote bush scrub and Joshua tree woodland in the Mojave and Sonoran Deserts to Texas and northern Mexico.

Comments: California chicory (*R. californica*) differs from desert chicory with its stout, erect, self-supporting stems, inconspicuous flowers, and brownish pappus. It occasionally occurs on the deserts but is more common elsewhere in California to Utah and Baja California, Mexico. California chicory is among plants known to accumulate nitrates from the soil in sufficient quantities to cause distress or death to cattle if they consume enough of it.

Johnstonella angustifolia

FORGET-ME-NOTS, CAT-EYES

Cryptantha, Greeneocharis, Johnstonella, Eremocarya, and *Oreocarya* species
Borage Family (Boraginaceae)

Genus Description: Forget-me-nots generally have tiny, white, 5-parted flowers with a raised yellow area (the fornice) in the center. They often occur in coiled, spike-like clusters, and like many borages, they are covered with bristly hairs. The ovary is divided into 4 parts called nutlets, each with 1 seed, some of which may abort during development. The forget-me-nots were all formerly placed in the genus *Cryptantha*, but recent molecular studies have led to the recognition of five genera, including *Cryptantha. Johnstonella* species are annuals with 1 large, persistent nutlet and 3 smaller ones that abort. Species in the genus *Greeneocharis* are annuals with an overall dome shape, sepals fused at the base, capsules that open with a "lid," and roots that are red or purple when dried. *Eremocarya* species are similar, but the sepals are separate, and the fruit does not open by a lid. Plants of the genus *Oreocarya* are generally much taller than the other genera, are biennial to perennial, and have well-developed basal leaves. Plants remaining in the genus *Cryptantha* are all annuals with various-size nutlets that are rough or dull to shiny, have varying numbers of whitish bumps, and have wings of variable widths. See the first or second edition of this book for nutlet photos.

Cryptantha barbigera

Cryptantha dumetorum

Cryptantha juniperensis

Cryptantha maritima

Cryptantha mohavensis

Cryptantha nevadensis

Cryptantha pterocarya

Cryptantha recurvata

Cryptantha utahensis

Greeneocharis similis

Johnstonella costata

Oreocarya virginensis

Pectocarya heterocarpa

Pectocarya linearis subsp.
ferocula

Pectocarya penicillata

Pectocarya platycarpa

Pectocarya recurvata

Pectocarya setosa

COMB-SEED
Pectocarya species
Borage Family (Boraginaceae)

Genus Description: Most of these desert annuals have numerous 1–10"-long, decumbent to erect stems with alternate, bristly-haired leaves up to 1¼" long. The funnel-shaped, white, 5-parted flowers are very tiny and inconspicuous. As the flower ages and the fruit matures, the petals fall and the 4 nutlets that make up the fruit enlarge. They eventually spread to release the seeds, while remaining attached at the bases, to form a butterfly-shaped structure that remains on the stem. Species can be distinguished by their nutlets of different shapes with variable hairs, projections, and margins. Most species are widespread in clearings of sandy, gravelly, and sometimes disturbed soils throughout the desert. They are usually among the first bloomers of spring, often beginning in early March. *Pectocarya setosa* is characterized by entire, rounded nutlets, 3 with wide, membranous wings, 1 with narrow wings and some bristles hooked at the tips. The nutlets of *P. penicillata* have bristles along the margins starting in the middle and getting longer near the tips, while nutlet bristles on *P. linearis* are found along the entire margin. The nutlets of *P. recurvata, P. platycarpa,* and *P. heterocarpa* have wide, membranous, jagged margins, but differ in the margin width, curvature, and symmetry of nutlets.

CALIFORNIA MUSTARD

Caulanthus lasiophyllus (Hook. & Arn.) Payson
Mustard Family (Brassicaceae)

Description: The erect stems of this 8–40"-tall, often branched annual have alternate, dark green, pinnately lobed to dentate lower leaves; these are reduced in size up the stem. The long, narrow inflorescences are produced on stem tips, with each white flower bearing the typical mustard family structure of 4 sepals, 4 claw-shaped petals, and 6 stamens, 2 short and 4 long. The elongated fruits are flattened backward against the stem, often with the tips slightly curved outward.

Bloom Season: March to June

Habitat/Range: California mustard is found in many varied habitats below 4,600' throughout the deserts and most of California to Utah, British Columbia, and northwestern Mexico.

Comments: This is the host plant for caterpillars of the spring white butterfly (*Pontia sisymbria*) and the California marble butterfly (*Euchloe hyantis*).

SPECTACLE-POD

Dithyrea californica Harvey
Mustard Family (Brassicaceae)

Description: This 4–12"-tall annual has somewhat thick, 1–6"-long basal and lower leaves that are shallowly pinnately lobed or toothed, while the upper stem leaves are shorter and entire to toothed. The flowers are produced in dense clusters on upper stems. Each white, 4-parted flower is about ½" long, and the somewhat reflexed petals have 3 veins. The distinctive, flattened fruits have 2 round lobes resembling eyeglasses.

Bloom Season: March to May

Habitat/Range: Found in sandy soil and washes below 4,000' in creosote bush scrub in both the Mojave and Sonoran Deserts to Nevada, western Arizona, Baja California, and the coastal areas of Sonora, Mexico.

Comments: The genus name is Greek for "2 shields," referring to the 2 lobes of the fruit. In this species, the seed coat clings to the root after germination and persists throughout the plant's entire life cycle. Since the seed coat reflects seed size, this made it possible for researchers to dig up plants and figure out the size of the seed from which they developed. They discovered that larger seeds have a higher chance of germination than do smaller seeds, and plants that developed from larger seeds have higher survival rates and higher seed production.

DESERT ALYSSUM, BUSH PEPPERGRASS
Lepidium fremontii S. Watson
Mustard Family (Brassicaceae)

Description: This 1–4'-tall, grayish perennial has alternate, 1–4"-long leaves that are either linear and entire or pinnately lobed with linear segments. Great masses of small, 4-parted flowers with white, clawed petals are produced in branched, leafy clusters, making this normally drab plant look white and suddenly conspicuous when in flower. The ¼"-long, ovate, flattened fruits have a notch in the top.

Bloom Season: March to May

Habitat/Range: Desert alyssum is common in sandy soil and rocky areas below 5,000' in creosote bush scrub and Joshua tree woodland in the Mojave and Sonoran Deserts and in the western Great Basin Desert.

Comments: Crushing the foliage will yield a smell similar to broccoli and cabbage, also in the mustard family. Native Americans ate the leaves and seeds. Desert alyssum, Shockley's goldenhead, desert mallow, and shadscale have been shown to be good pioneer species in the northern Mojave Desert. They are capable of invading relatively dry, nutrient-poor, bare, and disturbed areas between established shrubs, where they create new fertile sites, adding organic matter to the soil and attracting soil moisture, enabling other species to become established.

MOJAVE DWARF
Nemacladus californicus (A. Gray) Morin
Bellflower Family (Campanulaceae)

Description: This modest but unique species of *Nemacladus* consists of very tiny, very low-growing tufts that are interconnected by stems that creep along the ground. The ¼–¾" oblanceolate, entire leaves narrow to slender petioles. The 5-parted flowers are white, open, and bell-shaped with spreading lobes, and unlike most *Nemacladus* species, they have nearly radial symmetry. The stamens have curled filaments with a paddle-shaped attachment at the base, and the fruit is a ¼" rounded capsule that opens by a dome-like lid.

Bloom Season: April to May

Habitat/Range: Occurs in the central Mojave Desert and also in the Coast Ranges in Ventura, Santa Barbara, and San Luis Obispo Counties.

Comments: The genus was first described in 1843 by Thomas Nuttall. He assigned the name *Nemacladus*, which in Greek means "thread-branch," to describe the very tiny nature of this most overlooked group. Asa Gray stated that "to the scientific botanist there is no more interesting genus than Nuttall's *Nemacladus*." Gray originally described this particular plant as belonging to the genus *Parishella* in honor of its discovery at Rabbit Springs by the Parish brothers from San Bernardino; however, it is now recognized as belonging to the genus *Nemacladus*. The flowers of this species are larger than any other species in this genus; they reach an outstanding length of around ⅙"!

Nemacladus glanduliferus

Nemacladus morefieldii

Nemacladus orientalis

Nemacladus rubescens

Nemacladus sigmoideus

Nemacladus tenuis var. *tenuis*

THREAD-STEM
Nemacladus species
Bellflower Family (Campanulaceae)

Genus Description: It is very easy to overlook these extremely tiny annuals, but they are unusual and interesting! The basal rosette withers by the time the flowers appear, and the alternate stem leaves, in species which have them, also shrivel early. The stem, which is often branched above the middle, is so thin that it is nearly invisible. The flowers are produced in a sparse, raceme-like cluster, with each flower subtended by a bract. The 5 petals are somewhat triangular with various degrees of fusion, often resulting in the flowers having bilateral symmetry with the 3 upper petals more pigmented and patterned than the 2 lower petals. In some species flowers are inverted, with 2 petals on the top and 3 on the bottom. The filaments are separate near the base but fused around the middle or top of the style, and the anthers bend backward as the 2 style lobes separate. The partially inferior ovary has 3 nectar glands at the apex. Clear, elongate cells that look like rods are attached to some of the filament bases; some are seen in the photos. These have unknown function, but it's been postulated they may be involved in pollinator attraction—they may mimic shiny nectar; they may absorb heat to warm pollinators; or they may aid in moving the filaments around the style. The flowers of most *Nemacladus* species are only 1–2mm in size, making these the ultimate belly flowers! Nancy Marin recently described several new species, including *N. morefieldii*, shown here.

FROST MAT, ONYX FLOWER
Achyronychia cooperi Torrey & A. Gray
Pink Family (Caryophyllaceae)

Description: Frost mat is a flattened, branched, mat-forming annual with opposite, spatulate leaves up to ¾" long. The leaves in each pair are not equal, and they have ovate, fringed, white stipules. Clusters of 20–60, or more, tiny, white flowers are produced in leaf axils. Each flower has 5 petal-like sepals, no true petals, and 2 style branches.

Bloom Season: January to May

Habitat/Range: Frost mat is found in washes and on sandy flats and slopes below 3,000' in creosote bush scrub in both the Mojave and Sonoran Deserts to Baja California and coastal areas of Sonora, Mexico.

Comments: A perennial, Rixford rockwort (*Scopulophila rixfordii*) is a very similar-looking species that occurs on limestone in the northern Mojave Desert. It differs from frost mat in that it has 3 style branches, it is somewhat woody at the base, and it is erect. Some botanists believe that Rixford rockwort and frost mat should be placed in the same genus based on the similarities of the flowers and seeds.

SMALL-TOOTHED DODDER
Cuscuta denticulata Engelm.
Morning Glory Family (Convolvulaceae)

Description: This slender, parasitic, twining, annual vine sends tiny rootlets (haustoria) into host tissues to absorb water and nutrients, after which its own root system dies. The hairless, yellow to orange stems have minute, scale-like leaves. Small, spike-like clusters of tiny, 5-parted, bell-shaped flowers are produced in leaf axils. The rounded, minutely toothed calyx lobes overlap and enclose the corolla tube. The corolla lobes are bent backward, and the corolla tube length is less than its width. Both the calyx and corolla have fine teeth on the margins, and both have an artistic vein pattern that can be seen with a 10X hand lens. The fruit is a cone-shaped capsule.

Bloom Season: May to October

Habitat/Range: Dodder is parasitic on numerous shrub species, including creosote bush (*Larrea tridentata*) and cheesebush (*Ambrosia salsola*). It occurs below 4,000' in creosote bush scrub and Joshua tree woodland in the Mojave Desert and in the Sonoran Desert to Washington, Colorado, and Baja California, Mexico.

Comments: Other species of *Cuscuta* that have been collected from the Mojave Desert include *C. californica*, *C. nevadensis*, *C. occidentalis*, *C. salina*, and *C. subinclusa*. The features that distinguish these species are difficult to discern with a hand lens—much expertise and a dissection microscope are required.

BRANDEGEA
Brandegea bigelovii (S. Watson) Cogn.
Gourd Family (Cucurbitaceae)

Description: The stems of this hairless perennial, which arise from a white, fleshy, 1"-diameter taproot, cling and climb over shrubs by means of unbranched tendrils. The alternate, rounded, palmately lobed leaves have white gland-dots on the upper surfaces. The tiny, cup-shaped flowers are white and very fragrant. Male flowers are produced in small clusters in leaf axils, with a single female flower on a slender stalk below at the same node. The dry, prickly fruit is around ¼" long.

Bloom Season: March to April and sometimes following late summer rain

Habitat/Range: Locally common in washes and canyons below 3,000' in creosote bush scrub in the southern Mojave Desert to Sonora and Baja California, Mexico.

Comments: This genus was named in honor of Townshend Stith Brandegee (1843–1925) and Mary Katharine Brandegee (1844–1920). Townshend came to California after studying botany under Professor William Brewer at Yale. He married Mary Katharine Layne Curran, who was the curator of botany for the California Academy of Sciences. Their honeymoon was spent hiking and botanizing from San Diego to San Francisco.

SMALL-SEED SANDMAT
Euphorbia polycarpa Benth.
Spurge Family (Euphorbiaceae)

Description: Small-seed sandmat is a perennial with diverging, prostrate to ascending stems and milky sap. The round to ovate, opposite, more or less sessile, entire, ¼–½"-long leaves are asymmetrical at the base. The stipules on the bottom sides of the stem are fused, forming a line across the stem at the nodes, while on the top side of the stems, the stipules look like overlapping triangles. Each flower cluster looks like a single flower but is in fact 1 female flower and 15–32 male flowers surrounded by 5 fused bracts. Each bract has a raised, gold to yellowish, oblong gland with a white to reddish appendage. The 3-lobed fruit is on a drooping peduncle.

Bloom Season: All year

Habitat/Range: Widespread on dry slopes, flats, sandy areas, and roadsides below 3,000' in the Mojave Desert, the Sonoran Desert, and other habitats throughout southern California to Nevada and Mexico.

Comments: Native Americans applied the milky juice of small-seed sandmat and other prostrate spurges to rattlesnake bites and scorpion stings, and they used it to treat yeast infections. Extracts of this species have shown anticancer activity, but the specific compounds responsible for cancer cell death have not yet been identified.

Euphorbia albomarginata

Euphorbia setiloba

Euphorbia serpillifolia

Euphorbia micromera

PROSTRATE SPURGES
Euphorbia species
Spurge Family (Euphorbiaceae)

Genus Description: The prostrate spurges are herbaceous, somewhat mat-forming, and mostly annual species of *Euphorbia*. The spreading stems have opposite leaves, often with stipules and sometimes with short petioles. What looks like 1 flower is really an inflorescence of 5 fused bracts (the "showy" parts), which often bear red or yellow glands. The bracts surround a cluster of flowers with very reduced parts—1 female flower that matures into a little, hanging, 3-chambered fruit on a curved stalk, and several male flowers consisting of stamens. You will likely not see the stamens, as they fall off after the pollen is released. The species are distinguished by bract sizes, gland colors, leaf characteristics, and stipule features. They all yield white, milky sap full of latex. There are 11 species of prostrate spurge in the Mojave Desert.

LAYNE MILKVETCH

Astragalus layneae Greene
Pea Family (Fabaceae)

Description: The erect, 1–7"-high stems of this coarsely hairy perennial grow from a deep rhizome. The pinnately compound leaves have 11–23 ovate to round leaflets. The pea-type flowers are in a raceme-like cluster on long pedicels arising from leaf axils. The sepals are covered with black hairs, but there may be some white hairs interspersed. The petals are white, although the banner petal and tips of the wings may be tinged with lilac to purple. The strongly curved, leathery fruits are covered with white hairs, and they have 2 seeds per chamber.

Bloom Season: March to June

Habitat/Range: Occurs in sandy washes and on dry slopes up to 5,000' throughout the Mojave Desert to the White and Inyo Mountains, southern Nevada, and northwestern Arizona.

Comments: This species was named for Mary Katharine Layne Curran (1844–1920), who later married Townshend Stith Brandegee (1843–1925), a botanist who made collections in California, Nevada, and Baja. Dr. M. K. Brandegee worked for the California Academy of Science, where she was the first female curator of botany.

HELIOTROPE

Heliotropium curassavicum L. var. *oculatum* (A. Heller) I. M. Johnst. Ex Tidestr.
Heliotrope Family (Heliotropiaceae)

Description: This fleshy, bluish, 4–24"-tall perennial spreads from underground rootstocks to form mat-like clumps. The inversely lanceolate, 1–3"-long leaves are wedge-shaped at the base. Numerous tiny, sessile flowers are produced in 2–4 coiled spikes at the ends of branches. Each white to purple, 5-parted, bell-shaped flower has a yellow center. The fruit consists of 4 smooth nutlets.

Bloom Season: March to October

Habitat/Range: Occurs in moist, sandy, alkaline springs and streams and moist roadside ditches below 7,000' in many plant communities throughout California to Utah and Arizona.

Comments: This species produces alkaloid compounds in sufficient quantities to cause occasional cattle poisoning, and human liver toxicity is a recurring problem in Afghanistan, where seeds of a particular *Heliotropium* species regularly contaminate grain supplies. A related species, *H. convolvulaceum* var. *californicum* occurs in the Mojave Desert around 29 Palms and in Utah and Arizona. It is a nonfleshy annual with large, showy flowers that occur singly on short stalks in leaf axils.

AVEN NELSON'S PHACELIA

Phacelia anelsonii J. F. Macbr.
Waterleaf Family (Hydrophyllaceae)

Description: This erect, 10–20"-tall annual has short, stiff hairs with dark glands. The 1–3"-long lower leaves have deep, rounded lobes along the margins, while the lobes of upper leaves tend to be more shallow with teeth. The ¼"-long, widely bell-shaped flowers are white to pale blue or lavender, with the stamens not protruding from the corolla. The fruit is a 2–4-seeded capsule with tiny, glandular hairs.

Bloom Season: March to May

Habitat/Range: This species is found in gravels and sand along sheltered cliff and rock sites from 4,000 to 5,000' in creosote bush scrub and desert woodlands from the eastern Mojave Desert mountains to southwestern Utah and southeastern Nevada.

Comments: This species was named for Aven Nelson (1859–1952), a botanist who specialized in Rocky Mountain flora. He taught at the University of Wyoming and wrote several books and papers on the floras of Wyoming and Montana. He also served as president of both the University of Wyoming and the Botanical Society of America.

IVES PHACELIA

Phacelia ivesiana Torr.
Waterleaf Family (Hydrophyllaceae)

Description: This 2–10"-tall, glandular-hairy annual has stems that tend to branch at the base and spread to form a widened crown. The ½–1½"-long lower leaves are pinnately divided to the midrib into entire or toothed, oblong segments; the upper leaves are smaller. The narrow, funnel-shaped flowers are up to ⅛" long and are white with a yellowish tube.

Bloom Season: March to June

Habitat/Range: Ives phacelia is found in dry, sandy soil, desert pavement, and dunes below 3,000' in creosote bush scrub in scattered locations from Palmdale, California, through the Mojave Desert, to Colorado and Wyoming.

Comments: Ives phacelia was at one time considered for listing by the California Native Plant Society but was determined to be too common. This species was named for Joseph Christmas Ives (1828–1868), the first white explorer of the Grand Canyon.

ALKALI PHACELIA
Phacelia neglecta M. E. Jones
Waterleaf Family (Hydrophyllaceae)

Description: This small annual bears up to 2"-long, nicely rounded leaves with wavy margins. The petioles are equal or shorter in length than the leaf blades. The creamy-white, ¼"-long, bell-shaped flowers are produced in a glandular, curved inflorescence typical of many *Phacelia* species.

Bloom Season: March to May

Habitat/Range: Found in alkali and clay soils in creosote bush scrub on flats, mild slopes, and desert pavement up to 3,000' elevation throughout the Mojave to Arizona, southern Nevada, and Baja California, Mexico.

Comments: The similar *P. rotundifolia* can be most easily distinguished from *P. neglecta* in the field by its scalloped to toothy, rather than wavy, leaf margins. Also, the petioles of *P. rotundifolia* are longer than the leaf blade.

ROUND-LEAVED PHACELIA
Phacelia rotundifolia S. Watson
Waterleaf Family (Hydrophyllaceae)

Description: This low, glandular annual is covered with short, stiff hairs. The ½–1½"-long, round, toothed leaves are on stalks longer than the blades. Narrow, bell-shaped, ¼"-long flowers can vary in color from white to lavender or pink, and they have pale-yellow tubes. The capsules are less than ¼" long with 50–100 tiny, pitted seeds.

Bloom Season: April to June

Habitat/Range: Most often found wedged in crevices and on rocky cliff faces below 6,000' in creosote bush scrub, Joshua tree woodland, and pinyon-juniper woodland in the Mojave and Sonoran Deserts.

Comments: Edward Palmer (1829–1911) was the first to collect this species in southern Utah. Palmer was a self-taught British botanist who emigrated to the United States in 1850. He collected extensively, and around 200 taxa are named for him. He was also interested in archaeology and participated in surveys of Indian mounds in the eastern United States.

WHITE FIESTA FLOWER

Pholistoma membranaceum (Benth.) Constance
Waterleaf Family (Hydrophyllaceae)

Description: This somewhat fleshy yet brittle annual can grow up to 40" tall, it branches freely, and it can form tangles. Narrow-winged petioles support the deeply pinnately lobed leaves, the lower opposite, and the upper alternate and reduced. The inflorescences are 2–10-flowered cymes produced in leaf axils on pedicels up to ¾" long. The spreading, oval calyx lobes have bristly hairs along the margins. The white, rotate corolla is less than ½" wide with a greenish-yellow color visible down the throat, and each corolla lobe has a purple stripe. The anthers are often light blue.

Bloom Season: February to May

Habitat/Range: White fiesta flower is found in desert washes up to 4,600' in the Mojave and Sonoran Deserts and in coastal areas and other plant communities in southern California and the San Joaquin Valley to Baja California, Mexico.

Comments: The genus name is derived from the Greek words for "scale" (*pholis*) and "mouth" (*stoma*). This plant was originally described by George Bentham (1800–1884), who authored the *Handbook of the British Flora*, *Flora Hongkongensis*, and *Flora Australiensis*. He was a longtime president of the Linnaean Society.

MOJAVE PENNYROYAL

Monardella exilis (A. Gray) E. Greene
Mint Family (Lamiaceae)

Description: This erect, 2–12"-tall annual has purplish stems that branch at the base or below the middle. The opposite, lanceolate leaves have a pleasant smell. A rounded, 1"-diameter flower cluster is produced at the top of the main stem and branches. Each cluster has numerous broad, pointed, purple-veined bracts below. Each small, white flower has an erect, 2-lobed upper lip, a 3-lobed lower lip, and 4 stamens.

Bloom Season: April to June

Habitat/Range: Occurs in dry, sandy areas from 2,000 to 6,000' in creosote bush scrub, Joshua tree woodland, and pinyon-juniper woodland in the western Mojave Desert, Kern Plateau, and southern Sierra.

Comments: Due to its limited distribution, this species has been proposed as an addition to the California Native Plant Society's List 4. *Monardella linoides* subsp. *linoides* occurs in the mountains of the southwestern Mojave Desert, and *M. boydii*, from the Ord and Rodman Mountains, was recently discovered and described. Both are perennials. The Shoshone and Paiute used this plant to treat stomachache. This genus and the genus *Monarda* were named in honor of Nicholas Monardes (1493–1588), a Spanish botanist and physician.

SANDPAPER PLANT

Petalonyx thurberi A. Gray subsp. *thurberi*
Loasa Family (Loasaceae)

ROCK NETTLE, STING-BUSH

Eucnide urens (A. Gray) C. Parry
Loasa Family (Loasaceae)

Description: Numerous clumped, 1–3'-tall stems grow from the woody base of this perennial. Be careful, as the alternate, oval, toothed, 1–2"-long leaves have long, sharp, stinging hairs that can deliver a painful blister! The cream-colored, 5-parted, 1–2"-long flowers are produced on bracted stalks in leaf axils. They have numerous stamens, 5 stigma lobes, and an inferior ovary with tiny seeds.

Bloom Season: April to June

Habitat/Range: Rock nettle is found in rocky areas and washes below 4,000' in creosote bush scrub. It ranges from Red Rock Canyon State Park to Utah, Arizona, and Baja California, Mexico. It is very common in the Death Valley region.

Comments: The rash caused by this plant is not an allergic reaction but due to irritation by toxins released from the sharp, tubular leaf hairs when they are bumped. Interestingly, the toxins do not seem to affect aphids that feed on the plant juices; they perhaps are small enough to dodge the hairs. Dead syrphid flies, predators attracted to aphids, have been observed on this plant. Killing a species that could eat its herbivores may seem to be counterproductive for the plant, but the stinging hairs must confer an overall advantage to the plant in warding off other types of herbivores.

Description: This branched, bleached-gray, 1–3½'-tall shrub has short, stiff, down-turned hairs, which give it a sandpapery texture. The sessile, triangular to heart-shaped leaves are larger near the base of the plant and reduced upward. The 5-parted, white to cream-colored flowers, which are less than ¼" long, occur in narrow, dense, ½–1¾" clusters at the ends of branches. Oddly, the protruding stamens appear to be placed outside of the petals, which are fused along the upper part of their narrow, clawed bases.

Bloom Season: May to June and September to November

Habitat/Range: Sandpaper plant is fairly common in open, sandy or gravelly places below 4,000' in creosote bush scrub in both the Mojave and Colorado Deserts to northern Mexico.

Comments: The photosynthetic stems of sandpaper plant remain active during the hottest part of summer, allowing for fall flowering. Death Valley sandpaper plant (*P. thurberi* A. Gray subsp. *gilmanii*) is similar but with shorter stamens and soft, spreading hairs, which give the young leaves and stems a felt-like texture. It occurs on sand dunes and in washes below 3,500' in creosote bush scrub. It is known from only around 20 occurrences in Death Valley National Park, and is listed in the California Native Plant Society's Inventory of Rare and Endangered Plants of California.

151

DEATH CAMAS, DESERT ZYGADENE
Toxicoscordion brevibracteatum (M. E. Jones) R. R. Gates
False-Hellebore Family (Melanthiaceae)

Description: This perennial has an underground bulb from which numerous rosette leaves and 12–20"-tall flowering stems arise. The narrow, 4–10"-long leaves have rough margins and are folded lengthwise. The cream-colored, ¼"-long flowers with 6 equal segments are produced in an open, branched, 4–14" flower cluster. The fruit is an oblong, ½–¾"-long capsule with numerous seeds.

Bloom Season: April to May

Habitat/Range: Found in sandy areas from 2,000 to 5,000' in creosote bush scrub and Joshua tree woodland in the western and southern Mojave Desert and in the Colorado Desert to San Luis Obispo County, California.

Comments: Many species of *Toxicoscordion* have highly toxic alkaloid compounds, zygacine and zygadenine, that affect humans and livestock, especially sheep. The alkaloids act on the nervous system, producing the initial symptoms of difficulty speaking and walking, nausea, vomiting, and altered heart rhythm. It is deadly in high doses.

CARPET-WEED
Mollugo cerviana (L.) Ser.
Carpet-Weed Family (Molluginaceae)

Description: This tiny, slender-stemmed, 1–6"-tall summer annual is often overlooked. It has 5–10 linear leaves in a whorl at each node. The minute, inconspicuous flowers are produced in whorls on thread-like stalks in leaf axils. Each flower has 5 sepals, which are white on the inside, and 3 stigmas. The fruit is a tiny, round capsule with brown, net-veined seeds.

Bloom Season: September to October in the Mojave Desert, following summer rainfall

Habitat/Range: Uncommon in sandy areas below 5,000' in creosote bush scrub and Joshua tree woodland in the Mojave Desert and in scattered locations in the western states and Mexico.

Comments: There is some speculation that carpet-weed is an introduction from the Old World. However, it lacks a weedy habit, it almost always grows in undisturbed places, and it is responsive to summer, and not winter, rainfall. *Mollugo verticillata*, a related species not found in the desert, has the leaf anatomy, cell structure, and products of photosynthesis that appear to be intermediate between regular C3 plants and those that perform heat-efficient C4 photosynthesis. It is the first plant ever reported with a blend of C3 and C4 characteristics.

DESERT POT-HERB, DESERT PUSSY-PAWS
Cistanthe ambigua (S. Watson) Carolin ex Hershk.
Miner's Lettuce Family (Montiaceae)

Description: Several spreading to erect stems up to 7" tall arise from the root of this succulent annual, each bearing juicy, cylindrical leaves up to nearly 2" long. The dense inflorescences are nestled within the leaves, each flower with 2–5 membranous-margined, green sepals and 3–5 separate, white petals, greenish at the base, and up to nearly ¼" long. There are 5–10 stamens with yellow anthers, and the style has 3 stigmas. The tiny, 3-valved capsules have 6–15 shiny, black seeds.

Bloom Season: November to February

Habitat/Range: Occurs in sandy washes and slopes, often on alkaline soils, in desert scrub communities below 3,000' in the eastern Mojave Desert and the Sonoran Desert to southwestern Arizona and northwestern Mexico.

Comments: Native Americans and early settlers used the juicy leaves as greens. They are said to have a cool, salty flavor. John Lemmon (1832–1908) was the first to collect this plant on the plains of El Rio along the Colorado River. Lemmon was a pioneer California botanist, a schoolteacher, and a conifer specialist.

YERBA SANTA

Eriodictyon trichocalyx A. Heller var. *trichocalyx*
Nama Family (Namaceae)

Description: This erect, evergreen, 1–6'-tall shrub has spreading, gummy branches. The alternate, lanceolate, 2–5"-long leaves are dark green and sticky on the upper surface, and grayish-green with fine hairs and a netted vein pattern on the lower surface. They have entire to toothed, somewhat inrolled margins, and they are on ¼–½"-long stalks. Open, curved clusters of white, ¼–½"-long, funnel-shaped, 5-parted flowers with 2 styles are produced on the ends of branches. The fruit is a tiny capsule with 4–8 dark-brown seeds.

Bloom Season: May to August

Habitat/Range: Yerba santa occurs on dry, rocky hillsides below 8,000' in Joshua tree woodland and pinyon-juniper woodland along desert slopes of the San Gabriel and San Bernardino Mountains and in other habitats in southern California to Baja California, Mexico.

Comments: *Yerba santa* means "holy herb" in Spanish. This plant is high in flavonoids, and a tea made from the leaves is a very effective decongestant and allergy reliever. *Eriodictyon angustifolium* is a very similar species with narrower, linear leaves. It is found in the eastern Mojave Desert.

SPINY MENODORA

Menodora spinescens A. Gray var. *spinescens*
Olive Family (Oleaceae)

Description: The angled branches of this rounded, 1–3'-tall shrub become very spiny with age. The linear, entire, somewhat fleshy, ¼–½"-long leaves are mostly alternate and sometimes clustered at the nodes. The white, ½" flowers are produced singly or in clusters on short stalks in leaf axils; the corolla tube is less than ⅕" long. The ¼"-long capsules have round, pitted, dark-brown seeds.

Bloom Season: April to May

Habitat/Range: This variety of spiny menodora occurs on dry slopes and flats between 3,000 and 6,500' in shadscale scrub, blackbush scrub, and Joshua tree woodland in the northern and eastern Mojave Desert to the Great Basin Desert of western Nevada.

Comments: The genus name was derived from Greek words meaning "force" and "spear," probably in reference to the strong, spiny branches. *Menodora spinescens* var. *mohavensis*, with longer corolla tubes (>¼"), is known only from the Ord and Rodman Mountains, the Waterman Hills north of Barstow, and Joshua Tree National Park. It is on the California Native Plant Society's watch list.

BROWN-EYED PRIMROSE

Chylismia claviformis (Torr. & Frém.) A. Heller
subsp. *claviformis*
Evening Primrose Family (Onagraceae)

Description: This annual has a well-developed rosette of purple-spotted, pinnate leaves with large lateral leaflets. Flower clusters are produced at the tips of drooping, 4–24" stalks. The 4-parted flowers have white or yellowish petals with dark spots near the inner base, giving the plant its common name. The straight, stalked fruit is over ⅛" wide and has 2 rows of unwinged seeds per chamber.

Bloom Season: March to May

Habitat/Range: This subspecies is common in sandy soils and washes below 4,000' in creosote bush scrub and Joshua tree woodland in the Mojave Desert. Numerous other subspecies are found in many other habitats throughout the western United States.

Comments: There are colossal population outbreaks of hungry white-lined sphinx moth (*Hyles lineata*) larvae that migrate through the desert, stripping foliage of this and other evening primrose family members bare. This plant has one of the highest photosynthetic rates ever recorded in the field. In that experiment, leaf temperatures were consistently a few degrees below the air temperature due to a high transpiration rate, while leaves of other surrounding species were at air temperature or above.

BOOTH'S PRIMROSE

Eremothera boothii (Douglas) W. L. Wagner & Hoch subsp. *condensata* (Munz) W. L. Wagner and Hoch
Evening Primrose Family (Onagraceae)

Description: This stout, erect, often branched, 2–12"-tall annual with whitish, shining, and peeling stems bears lanceolate, 1–4"-long, generally entire leaves that decrease in size up the stem. A well-developed basal rosette of leaves is still present early in the flowering season. Clusters of white, 4-parted flowers are produced on pendant stem tips, subtended by conspicuous leafy bracts. The sessile, woody fruits curve outward but not downward. They are enlarged at the base and taper toward the tip, with 1 row of seeds in each of the 4 chambers.

Bloom Season: February to May

Habitat/Range: This subspecies of Booth's primrose is found on sandy soils in washes and desert scrub communities below 4,000' in both the Mojave and Sonoran Deserts to southern Utah, western Arizona, and northwestern Mexico.

Comments: Subsp. *desertorum* also occurs throughout the Mojave Desert. It tends to have somewhat shorter leaves, it does not have conspicuous inflorescence bracts, and the fruits arch strongly downward and are not woody. Subsp. *boothii*, with spreading hairs and smaller flowers, is a summer and fall bloomer that grows in sandy flats and washes from creosote scrub to pinyon-juniper woodlands.

155

LONG-CAPSULED SUN-CUP
Eremothera chamaenerioides (A. Gray) W. L. Wagner & Hoch
Evening Primrose Family (Onagraceae)

Description: This erect, slender, glandular-hairy, 3–20"-high annual differs from many related species by its lack of a basal rosette. The narrowly elliptic leaves are up to around 3" long with scattered tiny teeth along the margins. The dusk-opening flowers, which have ⅛"-long white petals that may fade to pink, are borne on a nodding inflorescence, and their anthers protrude farther than the stigma. The cylindric, straight fruits arise from an inferior ovary. They are narrow and the same width throughout, with 1 row of seeds per chamber.

Bloom Season: March to June

Habitat/Range: Found in sandy soils in desert scrub communities up to 4,200' in both the Mojave and Sonoran Deserts to Utah, Texas, and northwestern Mexico.

Comments: *Eremothera refracta* is very similar but can be distinguished by its larger flowers (up to a little over ¼" long). Its stigma protrudes farther than the anthers.

DEVIL'S LANTERN, BASKET EVENING PRIMROSE
Oenothera deltoides Torr. & Frém. subsp. *deltoides*
Evening Primrose Family (Onagraceae)

Description: This annual to short-lived perennial has a loose basal rosette that sends up an erect main stem, which develops several decumbent lateral branches. All stems are pale-colored, spongy-textured, and peeling. The alternate, dull, coarse, greenish-gray, diamond-shaped to oblanceolate leaves are 1–6" long and reduced in size along the stems. Lighter-colored veins often show up prominently on larger leaf undersurfaces. The showy, solitary flowers are produced from nodding buds in axils of reduced upper leaves, each flower with 4 narrow sepals that bend downward when the flowers open, 8 yellow stamens, a yellow style with a cruciform, 4-parted stigma, and 4 white, 1–1½"-long petals that fade pink as the flower ages. The inferior ovary develops into a narrow, twisted, 1–2"-long, cylindric capsule with numerous seeds. Stems can persist with dried fruits, yielding the birdcage-like structure shown above.

Bloom Season: March to May

Habitat/Range: Basket evening primrose is found in sandy areas and dunes below 3,600' in both the Mojave and Sonoran Deserts to southern Nevada, western Arizona, and northwestern Mexico.

Comments: Similar taxa include *Oenothera avita* var. *californica*, which spreads by shoots from lateral roots, forming mats. It is densely hairy, giving it a grayer look, and the leaves are narrower, often with wavy margins. *Oenothera caespitosa*, also hirsute-hairy, is similar to both *O. deltoides* and *O. avita* var. *californica*, but it has a warty fruit surface, and the leaves tend to be variously pinnately lobed.

157

WILD HONEYSUCKLE, LINDA TARDE

Oenothera suffrutescens (Ser.) W. L. Wagner & Hoch
Evening Primrose Family (Onagraceae)

Description: This perennial sends up clumps of erect to ascending, 8–20"-tall stems from a belowground, branched, woody caudex. The alternate, lanceolate, soft-hairy, grayish-green leaves have irregular teeth and are wavy on the margins. The flowers are produced in dense, 2–7" spikes on stem tips, each flower with 4 reflexed sepals, 8 stamens with long anthers, and 4 clawed, white petals that turn dark red as they age and shrivel. The style, with its 4-parted stigma, is longer than the stamens and is somewhat pendulous. The sessile fruits have flattened hairs, are strongly 4-angled, and abruptly narrow to an 8-ribbed structure at the base.

Bloom Season: April to June

Habitat/Range: Found on dry, mostly limestone slopes and flats in Joshua tree woodland and pinyon-juniper woodland below 5,200' in the eastern Mojave Desert to western Canada, the central United States, and Mexico. It also inhabits cismontane southern California.

Comments: This species is vespertine (flowers open at dusk) and is pollinated by noctuid moths. It has long been known as *Guara coccinea*, but it has recently been included within the genus *Oenothera* based on molecular similarities and morphological similarities in flower structure.

PRICKLY POPPY
Argemone corymbosa E. Greene
Poppy Family (Papaveraceae)

Description: This bristly, erect, 16–32"-tall annual has orange, milky juice. The alternate, 3–6"-long, pinnately toothed or lobed leaves have stiff hairs on the veins and margins, especially on the lower surface. White flowers with 4 or 6 separate petals and 100–120 yellow stamens are produced singly on the ends of stems, followed by 1–1¼"-long, ovate capsules with numerous tiny, dark-brown seeds.

Bloom Season: April to May

Habitat/Range: Common along roadsides and in dry, sandy areas and valley bottoms below 3,500' in creosote bush scrub throughout the Mojave Desert.

Comments: Roasted prickly poppy seeds were eaten by the Kawaiisu tribe to induce vomiting and as a laxative, and they used mashed seeds as a treatment for wounds and head lice. The similar chicalote (*A. munita*), which occurs above 4,000', has yellow sap, 150–250 stamens, and stiff hairs along veins on both the upper and lower leaf surfaces. Stamen counting can be daunting; however, just count a quarter of all the stamens and multiply by four, or break a leaf (if you dare) to look at sap color.

PYGMY POPPY
Canbya candida A. Gray
Poppy Family (Papaveraceae)

Description: This 1"-tall, tufted, hairless annual has linear to oblong, fleshy basal leaves with entire margins. Very short, leafless stems each bear a single flower with 6 separate, white, ovate petals and 6–9 stamens. The 3 sepals fall off before the flower opens. The fruit is a tiny, ovate capsule with minute, shiny, brown seeds.

Bloom Season: April to May

Habitat/Range: Occurs on sandy soil from 2,000 to 4,000' in creosote bush scrub, saltbush scrub, Joshua tree woodland, and pinyon-juniper woodland in the western Mojave Desert from Hesperia and Victorville, east to the Lancaster area, and north to Kramer, Calico, Owens Lake, and Walker Pass.

Comments: Development and the invasion of non-native species, as well as trampling by livestock, are threats to this rare species. However, it is not in immediate danger of extinction and is not currently listed as threatened or endangered. This species was named for W. M. Canby (1831–1904), a banker and plant collector from Delaware.

CREAM CUPS
Platystemon californicus Benth.
Poppy Family (Papaveraceae)

Description: Beautiful shaggy, spreading hairs decorate the leaves, stems, and flower buds of this 1–12"-tall annual. The narrowly oblong to lanceolate, entire, up-to-3"-long leaves are basal and alternate on lower stems. Flowers are produced singly from nodding buds on up-to-10"-long peduncles in leaf axils and at the stem tips. Each flower has 3 hairy sepals, which fall off at flowering time, 6 separate, ¾"-long, spreading, cream-colored petals with yellow tips or bases, and a profusion of cream-colored stamens with flat filaments.

Bloom Season: March to May

Habitat/Range: Found in open, sandy areas and grasslands and on loose soils below 3,300', mostly in the western Mojave, but also in scattered locations in the eastern Mojave. It is more common throughout cismontane California, California's Channel Islands, and the San Joaquin Valley to Oregon, Utah, Arizona, and Baja California, Mexico.

Comments: Cream cups are highly variable throughout their range, especially in terms of pubescence and flower color patterns. The genus has in the past been divided into over 50 species, but it is believed that the variation results more from environmental conditions, rather than genetic differences. The genus name is from the Greek word *platys*, which means "broad or flat," and *stemon*, for "stamen"; this name describes the broad, flattened filaments of the outer stamens.

DESERT PLANTAIN
Plantago ovata Forssk. var. *fastigiata* (Morris) S. C. Meyers & A. Liston
Plantain Family (Plantaginaceae)

Description: This erect, 2–10"-tall annual is covered with silky, flattened hairs. The narrow, linear, 1–7"-long leaves occur in a clump at the base of the plant. Numerous papery, 4-parted flowers and bracts are produced in dense, woolly, cylindrical, ½–1½"-long spikes at the tops of the leafless stems. The small, ovate capsules open by lids to release shiny, yellowish-red seeds.

Bloom Season: March to April in the Mojave Desert

Habitat/Range: Found on gravelly or sandy flats and slopes below 4,000' in creosote bush scrub and Joshua tree woodland in the Mojave Desert and throughout the western states to Baja California, Mexico.

Comments: There is speculation that desert plantain is an introduced weed from the Mediterranean region. If so, the introduction likely occurred very long ago, as it is widespread and does not behave like a weed. Furthermore, it is very closely related to another widespread and more coastal species, *P. erecta*, possibly indicating that there has been ample time since the suspected introduction for these to diverge into separate species.

161

MANYBRANCHED IPOMOPSIS, FORKED GILIA

Ipomopsis polycladon (Torr.) V. E. Grant
Phlox Family (Polemoniaceae)

Description: Glandular, reddish to purplish, 1–4"-long stems spread from the base of this annual. The dark-green, white-hairy, pinnate leaves, which can be up to ¾" long, are only present in clusters below the packed inflorescences. The tubular, white, ¼"-long corolla flares into a limb with 5 sharp lobes, each with some yellow near the throat. The anthers and stigma protrude just slightly from the tube.

Bloom Season: March to July

Habitat/Range: Occurs on sand, rock, or gravel soils and slopes from 2,500 to 7,000' in creosote bush scrub, Joshua tree woodland, and pinyon-juniper woodland in the Mojave Desert to Oregon, Colorado, and Texas.

Comments: Sand is entrapped on this plant's surfaces; having this sand armor is called psammophory. Researchers removed surface sand from a species of *Abronia*, and they supplemented sand levels in a species of *Navarretia*. The more sand a plant was coated with, the less it got eaten, which shows that this feature aids in the plant's physical defense. Was sand merely camouflaging the plants so they didn't get eaten? They coated some with green sand to match stem color and others with brown sand to match the background soil, but it made no difference in herbivory. Those with the most sand got eaten less, no matter what color the sand.

HUMBLE GILIA, DESERT-SNOW
Linanthus demissus (A. Gray) Greene
Phlox Family (Polemoniaceae)

Description: This somewhat glandular annual grows only to 4" high and branches from the base. The leaves are opposite with 3–5 lobes at the tips. The flowers are sessile in terminal clusters, subtended by numerous leaves. Each flower has a calyx nearly ⅛" long, the 5 narrow lobes separated by membranous margins. The ¼"-long, bell-shaped, white corolla has a very short tube, and each oblong lobe is marked with 2 purple or maroon streaks below the base. The 5 yellow anthers and 3-parted stigma protrude slightly from the tube.

Bloom Season: March to May

Habitat/Range: Found on dry flats, sandy soils, desert pavement, and often on limestone in creosote bush scrub and Joshua tree woodland below 4,000' in the Mojave Desert, the northeastern Sonoran Desert, and the foothills of the eastern Sierra Nevada Range in Inyo County to Utah and Arizona.

Comments: The rules of botanical nomenclature require the use of the first validly published name, but those rules are not always followed! In 1868, Torrey first described this plant and named it *Gilia dactylophyllum*; this appeared in the Ives report on the Colorado River Exploration. However, in 1870, Asa Gray published the name and description as *Gilia demissa*. Greene later transferred it into the genus *Linanthus* in 1892. In 1917, Rydberg called it *Linanthus dactylophyllum*, which should be its rightful name now if the rules were consistently applied.

EVENING SNOW
Linanthus dichotomus Benth. subsp. *dichotomus*
Phlox Family (Polemoniaceae)

Description: The shiny, purple to reddish-brown, wiry stems of this hairless, 2–8"-tall annual bear 1–2 pairs of opposite leaves with 3–7 thin, palmate lobes. The white, funnel-shaped corolla is the width of a quarter when fully open, and the hairless sepals have spreading, green tips. Since it is closed during the daytime, unless it is cloudy, you are unlikely to notice this plant until the evening when it opens up and carpets the ground with white brilliance and fills the air with a delightful fragrance.

Bloom Season: April to June

Habitat/Range: Occurs in the Mojave Desert in sandy or gravelly sites below 5,000', growing between shrubs in creosote bush scrub and Joshua tree woodland. It is more widespread in other areas of California and throughout the western United States.

Comments: *Linanthus dichotomus* subsp. *meridianus*, which occurs in northern California where subsp. *dichotomus* is also present, has its flowers open during the day. Researchers found that it produces some of the same volatile compounds as does subsp. *dichotomus*, but in different quantities; the blend in subsp. *dichotomus* is more attractive to nocturnal moths, while that of subsp. *meridianus* attracts a more varied suite of insect visitors. In the Mojave Desert, the similar *Linanthus jonesii* can be distinguished from *L. dichotomus* by its smaller flowers and glandular-hairy calyx. The flowers of both are closed during the day.

PYGMY PINK-SPOT, SPOTTED GILIA, LITTLE SAN BERNARDINO MOUNTAINS LINANTHUS

Linanthus maculatus (Parish) Milliken
Phlox Family (Polemoniaceae)

Description: This hairy little annual "belly plant" is not much more than 1" tall with oblong, ¼"-long leaves. The dense, sessile inflorescence bears tiny flowers with 5 slightly recurved, ⅛"-long, white petals, each with 1–2 tiny, red spots at the bases and sometimes with a notched tip. The pollen is yellow, and the 3-parted stigma is slightly exserted.

Bloom Season: April to May

Habitat/Range: Rare in sandy washes and flats in creosote scrub and Joshua tree woodland from Lucerne Valley to Morongo and Joshua Tree National Park, areas surrounding the park's west end, and the Sonoran Desert from the Palm Springs area to south of Anza-Borrego.

Comments: This species is threatened by development and off-highway vehicles that frequent sandy habitats in which these plants are found. Researchers from UC Riverside found evidence that the introduced Mediterranean grass, *Schismus barbatus*, which is expanding due to nitrogen deposition, outcompetes *L. maculatus* and excludes it from areas of its potential range, possibly by preempting resources, stabilizing loose soil and preventing *L. maculatus* seed scarification, or altering the microhabitat in terms of water availability.

SCHOTT GILIA, LITTLE SUNBONNETS
Loeseliastrum schottii (Torrey) S. Timbrook
Phlox Family (Polemoniaceae)

Description: This tufted, 1–4"-tall annual has ½–1½"-long, linear leaves with comb-toothed margins and bristle-tipped teeth. The white to yellow, pink, or pale-lavender, ¼–½"-long corolla is weakly bilateral, with a 3-lobed upper lip and 2-lobed lower lip, but it sometimes looks nearly radial. The stamens are shorter than the upper lip, and they have yellow pollen. The pointed sepals are up to half as long as the corolla tube.

Bloom Season: March to June

Habitat/Range: Schott gilia is found in gravelly and sandy soil in washes and valleys below 5,000' in creosote bush scrub and Joshua tree woodland in the Mojave Desert to the San Joaquin Valley and Mexico.

Comments: This species was named in honor of Arthur Schott (1814–1875), a naturalist, artist, and special scientific collector on the Mexican Boundary Survey of 1848–1855. Numerous plant taxa are named for him, as are two North American reptiles: Schott's whipsnake (*Masticophis schotti*) and Schott's tree lizard (*Urosaurus ornatus schotti*).

MOJAVE SPINEFLOWER
Chorizanthe spinosa S. Watson
Buckwheat Family (Polygonaceae)

Description: The 2–10"-long stems of this loosely branched annual can form a low clump or stand erect. The oblong, petioled, 1"-long basal leaves have hairy undersurfaces and form a rosette, while the upper portions of the plant have plentiful green, hairy, awl-shaped bracts in whorls of 3, each with a long, brown, tapering, spiny tip. Flowers are produced in small, 4–5-toothed, axillary involucres with 1 tooth much longer than the others. The protruding tepals are white with 3 broad outer lobes and 3 narrower, smaller inner lobes. There are 9 stamens per flower.

Bloom Season: April to July

Habitat/Range: Occasionally found on sandy or gravelly soil from 1,950 to 4,350' in creosote bush scrub or Joshua tree woodland. Its distribution is restricted to the western Mojave Desert, with one record for the Caliente Range in eastern San Luis Obispo County.

Comments: The genus name is derived from the Greek word *chorizo*, meaning "divided," and *anthos* for "flower." Mojave spineflower is on the California Native Plant Society's List 4.2 as a species of limited range that needs more study.

FLAT-TOPPED BUCKWHEAT, SKELETON WEED

Eriogonum deflexum Torrey var. *deflexum*
Buckwheat Family (Polygonaceae)

Description: This 4–28"-tall annual has 1 or a few slender, erect, hairless flowering stems from a basal rosette. The ½–1"-long, heart-shaped to kidney-shaped leaf blades have dense, white wool on the undersurfaces, and they are on ½–2"-long leaf stalks. The spreading flower cluster has 3 triangular bracts at the branching points, and the broad, flat-topped crown can be up to 2' across on larger plants. The tiny, white to pink flowers are produced within ⅒"-long, more or less sessile, downward-hanging involucres. As the plant ages, the stems turn dark-reddish-brown or black and persist for several seasons, giving the plant the common name of skeleton weed.

Bloom Season: May to October

Habitat/Range: Flat-topped buckwheat is widespread in sandy and gravelly soil below 6,000' in both the Mojave and Sonoran Deserts to Baja California, Mexico.

Comments: *Eriogonum deflexum* var. *baratum*, with inflated stems and involucres on short peduncles, is found from 3,000 to 9,500' on north slopes of the Transverse Ranges and in scattered desert mountain ranges to southern Nevada. The desert metalmark butterfly (*Apodemia mejicanus deserti*) larvae use skeleton weed as a food plant.

MOJAVE DESERT CALIFORNIA BUCKWHEAT

Eriogonum fasciculatum Benth. var. *polifolium* (Benth.) Torry & A. Gray
Buckwheat Family (Polygonaceae)

Description: The branched stems of this 1–3'-tall shrub have alternate clusters of ¼–¾"-long, sessile, oblong to linear leaves with dense, short hairs and slightly inrolled leaf margins. The round, compact, head-like flower clusters are produced on leafless, 1–4" stalks with leafy bracts below. The fuzzy, whitish, 6-parted flowers become pink with age, and as they dry, they turn a rich, burnt-orange color. Dried flower clumps often persist until the next flowering season.

Bloom Season: April to November

Habitat/Range: This variety is very common on dry hillsides and in canyons and washes below 7,000' in sagebrush scrub, Joshua tree woodland, and pinyon-juniper woodland in the Mojave Desert to Inyo County and in the Sonoran Desert. Other varieties occur throughout California to northwestern Mexico.

Comments: California buckwheat is a food plant for the Mormon metalmark butterfly (*Apodemia mormo mormo*), which flies from April to June and August to September in the northern and eastern Mojave Desert. Native Americans gathered and stored seeds of various *Eriogonum* species in the fall; tea made from the flowers was used as an eyewash; and a drink made from the leaves cured headache and stomachache. Buckwheat teas were used for gargling and douching, as astringents, and as remedies for kidney problems and excessive menstrual bleeding.

PALMER BUCKWHEAT

Eriogonum palmerianum Rev.
Buckwheat Family (Polygonaceae)

Description: This 2–12"-tall annual has a basal rosette of stalked leaves with round, ¼–1¼" blades and hairy undersurfaces. The slender stems arise from the base and branch to form a spreading crown. Pressed against the flowering stems are tiny, sessile, bell-shaped involucres with 5 teeth at the tips. The hairless, 6-parted flowers vary in color from light yellow to white to light pink. The outer 3 petal-like segments have spreading, fan-shaped tips, while the inner 3 are narrow and erect.

Bloom Season: April to October

Habitat/Range: Palmer buckwheat is found in sandy or gravelly soils from 2,000 to 8,000' in both the Mojave and Sonoran Deserts to California's Mono County, Colorado, and New Mexico.

Comments: The birdnest buckwheat (*E. nidularium*) is very similar to Palmer buckwheat, but the flowers are a brighter yellow and the flowering stem tips tend to curve inward instead of spreading, forming a birdnest effect. Buckwheat grown as a crop, *Fagopyrum sagittatum*, is in this same family.

PUNCTURED BRACT
Mucronea perfoliata (A. Gray) A. Heller
Buckwheat Family (Polygonaceae)

Description: The slender, 4–12"-long, glandular-hairy, green and reddish stems of this annual have forked, horizontal branches. The inversely lanceolate, ½–2½"-long leaves occur in a basal cluster, and they have hairs along the margins. The upper nodes each have 3 bracts that are fused into a ½–1"-wide, angled, funnel-shaped involucre with short, fleshy to spiny tips in the corners. The tiny, white flowers occur in small clusters within the involucres.

Bloom Season: April to July

Habitat/Range: Punctured bract is common in sandy or gravelly soil from 2,500 to 6,000' in creosote bush scrub, Joshua tree woodland, and pinyon-juniper woodland in the Mojave Desert north to Lassen County.

Comments: The larvae of the small blue butterfly (*Philotes speciosa*) feed only on the short, fleshy bract tips of punctured bract. The apple-green, white-haired larvae curl up around the stem inside of the bracts when they are not eating. It is unclear whether perfoliate leaves or bracts (those that form a disk or cup around the stem) confer an advantage for plants. Perhaps the cup-like structure may collect water during a drought, or it might impede herbivorous insects as they move up the stem, limiting damage to growing tips or reproductive organs.

APACHE PLUME
Fallugia paradoxa (D. Don) Torr.
Rose Family (Rosaceae)

Description: This erect to sprawling, 1–5'-tall shrub with grayish bark has rust-colored, flaky patches and short, white hairs. The alternate, ½"-long leaves have 3–7 pinnate lobes with rolled-under margins. For much of the year, Apache plume looks like a disheveled mass of branches with a few leaves, until it sends up long stalks with showy, white, 5-parted flowers. As the cluster of akenes from each flower matures, the styles enlarge and turn pinkish, feathery, and very ornate.

Bloom Season: May to June

Habitat/Range: Apache plume is found on dry hillsides from 4,000 to 5,500' in Joshua tree woodland and pinyon-juniper woodland in the mountains of the eastern Mojave Desert and throughout the western states to Texas.

Comments: This genus was named for Abbot Virgilio Fallugi (1627–1707), an 18th-century Italian botanist and monk who declined a position as botany professor at the University of Padua. This species is widely used as a drought-tolerant ornamental in gardens in the southwestern United States.

DESERT ALMOND
Prunus fasciculata (Torrey) A. Gray var. *fasciculata*
Rose Family (Rosaceae)

Description: This rounded, deciduous, angular-branched, spiny, 3–6'-tall shrub has narrow, alternate, entire, ¼–½"-long leaves that are bundled into very small, bud-like branches. Inconspicuous, white, sessile flowers occur singly or in groups of 2–3 along the branches. The immature fruit resembles a tiny, fuzzy, green peach, but when mature, the 1-seeded, ½"-long fruit is brownish and fibrous.

Bloom Season: March to May

Habitat/Range: Desert almond is found in dry canyons and washes from 2,500 to 6,000' in creosote bush scrub, Joshua tree woodland, and pinyon-juniper woodland along the north bases of the Transverse Ranges and in mountains throughout the Mojave and Sonoran Deserts.

Comments: The web-like tents of the tent caterpillar moth (*Malacosoma* species) are often found in profusion on desert almond in the spring. The larger, least active caterpillars often occupy the center of the web, while smaller ones move about along the tent margins. A related tent moth species causes much damage to peaches and plums (which are also members of the genus *Prunus*) in the eastern United States.

BITTERBRUSH, ANTELOPE BUSH

Purshia tridentata var. *glandulosa* (Curran) M. E. Jones
Rose Family (Rosaceae)

Description: This highly branched, evergreen shrub has somewhat sticky, alternate, ¼–½"-long leaves with 3–5 pinnate lobes, inrolled margins, and sunken glands on the upper surface. Cream-colored, 5-parted, ¼" flowers are often produced in profusion, making the plant very fragrant. As the akene develops, the feathery style enlarges to nearly 1" long.

Bloom Season: April to June

Habitat/Range: Bitterbrush is found on slopes from 2,500 to 8,000' in Joshua tree woodland and pinyon-juniper woodland. It grows on the north-facing slopes of the Transverse Ranges and in various other mountain ranges throughout the Mojave Desert. It is also found throughout Nevada, Utah, and Arizona to northern Baja California, Mexico.

Comments: The Owens Valley Paiute used bitterbrush for firewood, fiber, violet dye, and many medicinal treatments. The Behr's hairstreak butterfly (*Satyrium behrii behrii*) uses bitterbrush as a food plant. This genus is named for Frederick Traugott Pursh (1774–1820), botanic garden curator and author of the first flora book of North America, *Flora Americae Septentrionalis*, which included many collections from the Lewis and Clark Expedition. He had a competitive, turbulent relationship with Thomas Nuttall and other botanists of the early 1800s, so it seems fitting that bitterbrush should be named for him.

YERBA MANSA

Anemopsis californica (Nutt.) Hook. & Arn.
Lizard's-Tail Family (Saururaceae)

Description: This 6–20"-tall perennial spreads by creeping, woody rhizomes. The oblong to elliptic, 4–6"-long basal leaves are on long stalks, while the stem leaves are sessile, ovate, and sparse. The terminal, stalked flower cluster has 5–8, 1"-long white bracts that may be mistaken for petals. Individual greenish flowers appear in a cone-shaped spike above the bracts. The dried, rusty-brown flower clusters persist for a long time after flowering season.

Bloom Season: March to September

Habitat/Range: Found in moist, alkaline soil around seeps, springs, and playas in the Mojave Desert to Texas and Mexico.

Comments: *Yerba mansa* means "gentle herb" in Spanish. Native Americans boiled the bark and drank the liquid as a cure for ulcers and chest infections; it was also used as a wash for wounds. Because of the drying of habitat in parts of its range, some are worried that yerba mansa populations will decline before adequate research is conducted to determine whether it has real medicinal value.

JIMSON WEED, THORN-APPLE, SACRED DATURA
Datura wrightii Regel
Nightshade Family (Solanaceae)

Description: This conspicuous, 2–5'-tall perennial has up to 8"-long, dark-green, ovate leaves with smooth or slightly lobed edges. The 6–8"-long, white, trumpet-shaped flowers open in the morning and evening. Each flower has 5 wing-like ribs toward the base of the calyx. The round, drooping fruits are at least 1" long, are covered with prickles, and contain flat, tan seeds.

Bloom Season: April to October

Habitat/Range: Jimson weed is commonly found in sandy soils, roadsides, and disturbed places below 7,000' throughout the Mojave Desert and southwestern United States to New Mexico and Texas.

Comments: This plant contains several toxic alkaloid compounds. Symptoms of ingestion include extreme thirst, visual disturbances, nausea, fever and delirium, incoherency, and even respiratory arrest and death. The amounts of toxic alkaloids vary, so taking any amount of the plant material can be very dangerous. However, these same compounds, when concentration is strictly controlled, are very useful in modern pharmaceuticals. Important constituents include scopolamine, a motion-sickness medication, and atropine, which counteracts muscle spasms. Native Americans used this plant in several rituals.

ANDERSON'S BOX-THORN, WOLFBERRY
Lycium andersonii A. Gray
Nightshade Family (Solanaceae)

Description: This rounded, highly branched, spiny shrub can be up to 6' tall. The alternate, ¼–¾"-long leaves are somewhat succulent and cylindrical to spatulate or pear-shaped, and they are often in small bundles. Flowers are produced singly or in twos in leaf axils on ⅛–⅓"-long pedicels. Each flower has a tiny, cup-shaped calyx and a white to lavender, tubular to narrowly funnel-shaped corolla with 5 flaring, ⅒" lobes. The yellow stamens protrude slightly from the corolla tube. The bright-red, fleshy fruit is around ¼" long.

Bloom Season: March to May

Habitat/Range: Common on gravel and in washes below 6,200' in creosote bush scrub, pinyon-juniper woodland, sagebrush, scrub, and other plant communities in the Mojave and Sonoran Deserts to Utah, New Mexico, and northwestern Mexico.

Comments: The fruit is edible and tastes somewhat like a tomato. The similar *Lycium torreyi* has longer, less succulent leaves, flowers with more lavender coloration and pointed lobes, and hairs on the margins of the corolla lobes.

COOPER'S BOX THORN, PEACH THORN

Lycium cooperi A. Gray
Nightshade Family (Solanaceae)

Description: This thorny, 3–5'-tall, winter-deciduous shrub has sturdy, rigid stems and pinkish-brown bark, which ages to a brownish-black color and then peels. The alternate, inversely lanceolate, ½–1¼"-long leaves often occur in tight clusters. The flowers are produced singly or in groups of 2–3 in leaf axils. The lobes of the bowl-shaped calyx are at least ⅛" long, and the narrowly funnel-shaped, ½"-long corollas are white to greenish. The green, egg-shaped ¼"–⅜"-long fruits are notched at the apex and have a horizontal constriction above the middle.

Bloom Season: March to May

Habitat/Range: Cooper's box thorn is found on dry slopes and in washes below 5,000' in creosote bush scrub, Joshua tree woodland, blackbush scrub, and pinyon-juniper woodland in the Mojave and Colorado Deserts.

Comments: This species was named for Dr. J. G. Cooper (1830–1902), a geologist with the US Geological Survey in California, who collected plants in the Mojave Desert from Cajon Pass to Camp Cady in 1861. The Cooper Ornithological Society was named in his honor.

COYOTE TOBACCO
Nicotiana obtusifolia Martens & Galeotti
Nightshade Family (Solanaceae)

Description: This sticky, glandular, perennial herb develops clumps of erect, 8–36" stems. The dark-green, triangular to ovate lower leaves are up to 6" long, while upper leaves are smaller and clasp the stem. Flowers occur in a loose cluster on the upper stems. Each dingy-white, ½–1"-long, funnel-shaped flower has a narrow throat and petal lobes that spread abruptly. The fruit is a dry, ¼–½"-long, 2-chambered capsule with numerous seeds.

Bloom Season: March to June

Habitat/Range: Coyote tobacco is found on ledges and in crevices in rocky canyons below 4,000' in creosote bush scrub and Joshua tree woodland. It occurs in the Mojave and Sonoran Deserts to Texas and Mexico. It is especially common on basalt and desert varnish.

Comments: Coyote tobacco was dried and smoked for rituals and pleasure by various groups of Native Americans, although Indian tobacco (*N. quadrivalvis*) was preferred. The Paiute mixed it with mistletoe and stuffed it into the inflated stems of desert trumpet (*Eriogonum inflatum*), using them as pipes. This genus was named for Jean Nicot (1530–1604), who introduced tobacco to France in the mid-1500s. He was the French ambassador to Portugal and the author of one of the first French dictionaries.

CROWNED MUILLA
Muilla coronata Greene
Brodiaea Family (Themidaceae)

Description: The 1–2"-tall stem of this perennial arises from a swollen stem base 1–3" below the ground. There is 1 narrow, somewhat cylindrical leaf arising from the base of the stem; it is 2–2½ times as long as the stem. Up to 4 flowers are produced in an umbel subtended by 2–4 membranous bracts. Each flower is on a 1"-long pedicel and has 6 white, spreading segments with dark-green linear bands on the outside. The crown-like structure in the middle of the flower is made up of 6 yellow anthers attached to 6 very widened, white, erect, petal-like filaments, which are expanded and overlapping on the sides. The fruit is a globe-shaped, 3-angled capsule with black seeds.

Bloom Season: March to April

Habitat/Range: Found in creosote bush scrub, Joshua tree woodland, pinyon-juniper woodland, and shad-scale scrub communities from 2,300 to 6,500' in the Mojave Desert and into the Kern Plateau and Owens Valley to western Nevada.

Comments: *Muilla* is *Allium* (the genus of onion) spelled backwards. Although the flowers superficially resemble *Allium*, *Muilla* does not have the characteristic onion odor, it differs in the number and arrangement of inflorescence bracts, and it arises from a corm rather than a bulb. These are also the characteristics of the entire Brodiaea family that separate it from the onion family.

YELLOW FLOWERS

This section includes flowers that are light yellow to deep-golden yellow. Cream-colored flowers grade into yellow, so be sure to check the "White to Cream Flowers" chapter if you cannot find the flower you are looking for here. Yellow flower colors are produced by water-soluble pigments called flavonols (derived from the Latin word for "yellow") and fat-soluble carotenes, also found in many yellow fruits and vegetables.

DESERT PARSLEY
Lomatium mohavense (J. Coulter & Rose) J. Coulter & Rose
Carrot Family (Apiaceae)

Description: This lacey, thick-rooted, 4–12"-tall perennial has 3–4 times pinnately divided leaves on 1–5" leaf stalks. The tiny, yellow or dark-maroon flowers are produced in a compound umbel on a 3–8" flower stalk. The round, flattened, ¼–½" fruits have wings that are at least as wide as the fruit body.

Bloom Season: April to May

Habitat/Range: Common on dry slopes and flats from 2,000 to 5,000' in creosote bush scrub, Joshua tree woodland, and pinyon-juniper woodland along the northern base of the Transverse Ranges and the western Mojave Desert to Barstow and Inyo County in California, and south along the western border of the Colorado Desert to Baja California, Mexico. It also occurs in coastal ranges of southern California.

Comments: Although this plant bears the name desert parsley, it is not considered edible. Many plants in this family are poisonous, often due to a wide variety of coumarin compounds, which the plants produce to defend against herbivory. Several limonene compounds have been isolated from this species, which have potential to have anti-inflammatory, antioxidant, antiviral, or anticancer properties. *Lomatium dissectum*, native to Canada and the western United States, is already in use as an alternative antifungal and antibacterial agent by some naturopathic practitioners; however, there appears to be a serious rash and other potential side effects associated with it. It is advisable to avoid using any such remedy until there has been controlled research, clinical trials, and FDA approval.

MOJAVE MILKWEED
Asclepias nyctaginifolia A. Gray
Dogbane Family (Apocynaceae)

Description: The ascending stems of this milky-sapped perennial bear opposite, dark-green, ovate, pointed, 1½–2¾"-long leaves with somewhat wavy margins. Sessile umbels are produced at and near branch ends. Each flower has 5 light-yellowish-green, reflexed corolla lobes. In the center of the flower are the fused anthers and stigma surrounded by 5 tall, narrow hoods in which copious nectar is stored. The fruit is a slender, 2–2½"-long follicle.

Bloom Season: May to August

Habitat/Range: Occurs in dry areas from 4,000 to 5,000' in creosote bush scrub and pinyon-juniper woodland in the mountains of the eastern Mojave Desert to Nevada and New Mexico.

Comments: Mojave milkweed is rare in California but more common elsewhere. It occurs in the footprint of the Ivanpah solar field, where a population genetic study suggested that the destruction of just one individual would lead to a potentially significant loss of genetic diversity for the population. Queen butterflies (*Danaus gilippus*) lay plenty of eggs on it, but monarch butterfly eggs were not found.

RUSH MILKWEED, AJAMETE
Asclepias subulata Decne.
Dogbane Family (Apocynaceae)

Description: This greenish-white, 2–5'-tall perennial has rigid, rush-like stems, which give it a shrubby character. The opposite, sessile, thread-like leaves usually fall early, so plants appear mostly leafless. The cream-colored, ¼–½"-long flowers are produced in rounded umbels at and near the branch tips. They have reflexed petals and hoods with horns. The slender, smooth, 2–4"-long fruits contain smooth, tufted, ¼" seeds.

Bloom Season: April to December

Habitat/Range: Found along washes and in hot, sandy areas below 2,000' in creosote bush scrub in the eastern Mojave Desert and from the Sonoran Desert to western Sonora and Baja California, Mexico.

Comments: The milky juice of rush milkweed contains good-quality latex rubber, although it is not used commercially. Rush milkweed may be confused with white-stemmed milkweed (*A. albicans*), to be looked for in the mountains at the southern edge of the Mojave. It is distinguished by having hoods exceeded by anther heads, and it usually has 3 leaves per node.

UTAH VINE MILKWEED

Funastrum utahense (Engelm.) Liede & Meve
Dogbane Family (Apocynaceae)

Description: The hairless, very slender stems of this perennial often twist near the ground as they arise from a branched crown below. The opposite, sessile, thread-like leaves often bend downward as the plant ages. The tiny, yellow flowers, which age to a burnt orange, are in umbels in leaf axils. Each flower has 5 narrow, triangular, pointy calyx lobes and 5 incurved corolla lobes that meet above the fused anthers; this makes each flower look like a 5-lobed, closed bud. The fruit is a follicle up to nearly 2½" long.

Bloom Season: April to September

Habitat/Range: Occurs in dry, sandy places below 3,000' in creosote bush scrub in the southern and eastern Mojave Desert to Arizona and Utah.

Comments: This plant lacks the hoods and horns that help position pollinating insects in other milkweeds. The flowers seem to remain closed so that an insect cannot enter at all! However, the inrolled corolla lobes do have tiny, slit-like openings at the top, into which an insect can insert its proboscis.

SHOCKLEY'S GOLDENHEAD

Acamptopappus shockleyi A. Gray
Sunflower Family (Asteraceae)

Description: The seasonal twigs of this rounded, branching, ½"–2'-tall subshrub are covered in small, rough hairs. The alternate, sessile, ⅓"-to nearly 1"-long, lanceolate leaves are sometimes bundled due to development of axillary buds, and they taper to a narrow base. The flower heads are produced singly at ends of branch tips, each with 14–80 yellow disk flowers and 4–14 yellow ray flowers subtended by a hemispheric, nearly ½"-high involucre with several rows of rounded, greenish, papery phyllaries with clear margins.

Bloom Season: April to June

Habitat/Range: Found on rocky slopes and washes below 6,000', often in creosote bush scrub, in the eastern Mojave Desert to the White and Inyo Mountains and southern Nevada.

Comments: Rayless goldenhead (*A. sphaerocephalus*) has smaller flower heads with disk flowers only. It is found on flats and in washes up to 4,500' in creosote bush scrub and Joshua tree woodland in the central, northern, and eastern Mojave Desert and the western edge of the Sonoran Desert.

COOPER'S DYSSODIA, COOPER'S GLANDWEED

Adenophyllum cooperi (A. Gray) Strother
Sunflower Family (Asteraceae)

Description: The stout, ridged stems of this 1–2'-tall perennial grow from a woody base. The toothed, alternate, ovate leaves are less than 1" long. Each flower head has 7–13 ray flowers, numerous disk flowers, and 3 rows of ½" phyllaries, the outer ones comparatively shorter. The pappus consists of 15–20 scales, each dissected into 5–9 bristles. The phyllaries, foliage, and stems have conspicuous, translucent oil glands that yield a pungent, turpentine-like odor.

Bloom Season: April to June and again in September to November in years when summer showers occur

Habitat/Range: Found on open slopes and sandy washes from 2,000 to 5,000' in creosote bush scrub and Joshua tree woodland from Victorville, California, to Arizona, Nevada, and the northeastern Sonoran Desert. It is fairly common in the eastern Mojave Desert and on the north-facing slopes and bases of the San Bernardino Mountains.

Comments: The genus name means "gland leaf." A similar species, *A. porophylloides*, occurs on dry, rocky hillsides in the Sonoran Desert but can occasionally be found in the southern Mojave Desert. It has pinnately divided leaves, opposite lower leaves, and shorter phyllaries than Cooper's dyssodia.

CHAFFBUSH

Amphipappus fremontii Torr. & A. Gray var. *fremontii*
Sunflower Family (Asteraceae)

Description: The widely spreading branches of this hairless shrub are gray below and whitish on upper portions. They often have a striped appearance and/or a yellowish-green cast. The ovate, entire leaves are usually around ½" long with 1 main vein. Each gummy head has 3–7 narrow disk flowers and 1–2 yellow, 2–3-toothed ray flowers, subtended by 7–12 overlapping, appressed, pale-green phyllaries that are nearly as tall as the disk flowers. The pappus is composed of 25 twisted, flattened scales that are less than ⅛" long.

Bloom Season: April to May

Habitat/Range: Found in open, often alkaline areas below 5,200' in Death Valley National Park and the northern and eastern Mojave Desert to Inyo County, southern Nevada, and northwestern Arizona.

Comments: The very similar *A. fremontii* var. *spinosus* is covered with dense, short, roughened hairs. It is found in the eastern Mojave Desert to Utah and Arizona.

SCALE-BUD
Anisocoma acaulis Torrey & A. Gray
Sunflower Family (Asteraceae)

Description: This milky-sapped annual generates 1 to several leafless, 2–8"-tall flower stalks from a basal rosette of pinnately toothed or divided leaves. The 1" cylindrical flower heads are produced singly, each with numerous pale-yellow, strap-shaped flowers. The flattened, serial phyllaries have red tips and papery margins. The inner phyllaries are long and narrow, grading to short and round outermost layers. The pappus is composed of 10–12 bright-white, feathery bristles in 2 unequal rows.

Bloom Season: April to June

Habitat/Range: Scale-bud is found in sandy soil in creosote bush scrub, Joshua tree woodland, and pinyon-juniper woodland from 2,000 to 7,800' in the Mojave Desert to southwestern Kern County, California. Its range extends to northwestern Arizona, Nevada north of Reno, and into the Sonoran Desert to Baja California, Mexico.

Comments: This plant is included in the chicory tribe of the sunflower family, the same tribe that includes lettuce. The genus name means "unequal clumps of hair," referring to the 2 unequal rows of pappus bristles.

PARISH'S GOLDENEYE
Bahiopsis parishii (Greene) E. E. Schill. & Panero
Sunflower Family (Asteraceae)

Description: Numerous branching stems arise from the base of this rounded, rough-hairy subshrub. The dark-green, triangular leaves can be up to nearly 1½" long on petioles up to ⅓" long, they have 3 main veins from the base, and they are opposite, at least on lower stems. The hemispheric flower heads are solitary or in small clusters on 1–5"-long peduncles, each head with numerous golden disk flowers and 8–15 narrow, bright-yellow, ½–⅔"-long ray flowers subtended by broadly lanceolate, often hairy phyllaries with abruptly narrowed tips. The pappus is of 2 awns, and the receptacle bears scales that partially enclose the fruits.

Bloom Season: February to June and September to October

Habitat/Range: Found in canyons, washes, and on slopes below 5,000' in creosote bush scrub in both the Mojave and Sonoran Deserts to Nevada, Arizona, and northwestern Mexico.

Comments: It is curious that the type specimen was collected in 1881 by the Parish brothers at San Luis Rey, but there have been no other collections or observations of this species from this original coastal location. In addition, several specimens with the same collection number, and now housed in various herbaria, were actually collected at different locations and on different dates. Botanists are often meticulous about details, but someone slipped up here!

185

DESERT MARIGOLD
Baileya multiradiata A. Gray
Sunflower Family (Asteraceae)

Description: This 8–20"-tall, short-lived perennial has white-woolly stems that branch from a taproot. The 1–4"-long, spatulate to oblong, pinnately lobed leaves occur on the lower half of the stem and in a basal rosette. The 4–12"-long, stout, leafless flower stalks bear ½–1½" heads with numerous yellow, hairy, gland-dotted disk flowers and 50–60 bright-yellow ray flowers that are arranged in several rows. The strap-shaped corollas of the ray flowers dry and bend backward as the flowers age. The fruit is a cylindrical akene with no pappus.

Bloom Season: April to July, and again in October after summer rain

Habitat/Range: Desert marigold is common in sandy and rocky flats, washes, and hillsides from 2,000 to 5,000' in creosote bush scrub and Joshua tree woodland in the Mojave and Sonoran Deserts to eastern Texas and central Mexico.

Comments: Woolly desert marigold (*B. pleniradiata*) is distinguished from desert marigold by having leafy flower stalks; the basal leaves wither by the time the flowers open. There are 20–60 ray flowers, and the akenes have prominent, angled ribs. A series of sesquiterpene chemicals isolated from both desert marigold and woolly desert marigold were found to markedly inhibit the growth of mouse leukemia cells in vitro; further testing may prove it to be useful against human cancers as well.

LAX-FLOWER, COLORADO DESERT MARIGOLD
Baileya pauciradiata A. Gray
Sunflower Family (Asteraceae)

Description: This 4–20"-tall, branched annual is covered with soft, woolly hair. The 1½–5½"-long stem leaves are entire and linear to lanceolate, while the 1–4"-long basal leaves have 2–5 pairs of short, pinnate lobes. The basal leaves wither before the flowers open. The ¼–½" flower heads are produced in loose clusters with distinct, woolly phyllaries below. Each head has numerous disk flowers and 4–8 light-yellow ray flowers, which become papery and bend backward as they age. No pappus is present on the pale akenes.

Bloom Season: February to June, and also in October following summer rain

Habitat/Range: Lax-flower occurs on very loose, sandy soil and dunes below 3,500' in creosote bush scrub in the eastern Mojave Desert. It is more common in the Sonoran Desert to northwestern Mexico.

Comments: The genus name honors Jacob Whitman Bailey (1811–1857), a pioneer of microscopic technique and professor of geology and chemistry at West Point. His son, William Whitman Bailey, was a professor of botany at Brown University.

SWEETBUSH

Bebbia juncea (Benth.) Greene var. *aspera* Greene
Sunflower Family (Asteraceae)

Description: This 2–5'-tall, rounded, broom-like shrub has slender, brittle stems, which are covered with short hairs with swollen bases, making it rough to the touch. It often appears leafless, since the linear leaves fall early when drought-stressed. The entire plant has a strong odor. The ¼–½" hemispheric flower heads are produced on ½–2½" stalks. They have numerous yellow disk flowers and lanceolate phyllaries in several rows. The receptacle has chaffy bracts, and the pappus consists of 15–20 bristles.

Bloom Season: April through July

Habitat/Range: Occurs on gravelly slopes and in rocky washes below 4,000' in creosote bush scrub throughout the Mojave Desert and cismontane southern California to Baja California, Mexico, and throughout the Sonoran Desert to New Mexico and Sonora, Mexico.

Comments: The genus name is in honor of Michael Schuck Bebb (1833–1895), who was a resident of San Bernardino and an authority on willows of North America. The late desert naturalist Edmund C. Jaeger noted that sweetbush flowers are relished by desert tortoises. In addition to numerous pollinators, there is also a plethora of insect taxa that feed on the sap and foliage of this species, representing 22 insect families and 34 species. A study showed that many of these are generalist feeders and are found to also feed on other shrubs with similar plant architecture in the sunflower family.

YELLOW TACK-STEM

Calycoseris parryi A. Gray
Sunflower Family (Asteraceae)

Description: This 2–6"-tall, branched annual has milky sap throughout. The pinnately divided, 1–5"-long leaves occur at the base of the plant and along the stem. The stalked, 1–1½" flower heads have yellow, strap-like flowers and numerous narrow phyllaries with membranous edges and dark-reddish, tack-shaped glands. The tapered, beaked akenes are topped with a pappus of white, slender bristles.

Bloom Season: March to May

Habitat/Range: Found on slopes and in washes below 6,000' in creosote bush scrub, Joshua tree woodland, and pinyon-juniper woodland in the Mojave Desert to the Owens Valley, western Nevada, and the Sonoran Desert, to Arizona, to Guerrero Negro in Baja California, Mexico, and to the far northwestern corner of Sonora, Mexico.

Comments: This plant is often confused with desert dandelion (*Malacothrix glabrata*), which does not have tack-shaped glands or beaked akenes. White tack-stem (*Calycoseris wrightii*) is a white-flowered species with tack-shaped glands that is found in the eastern Mojave Desert and in the Sonoran Desert. It is featured in the "White to Cream Flowers" chapter of this book.

RED ROCK TARPLANT
Deinandra arida (D. D. Keck) B. G. Baldwin
Sunflower Family (Asteraceae)

Description: This 1–3'-tall, branched annual has a bristly feel due to its sparse, short, stiff hairs. The lower leaves are inversely lanceolate and hairless with toothed margins, while upper leaves are entire with bristly hairs. Flat-topped clusters of flower heads are produced at the tops of stems. Each ¼" head has 18–25 yellow disk flowers and 5–10 pale-yellow ray flowers. The bristly, glandular phyllaries halfway enclose the akenes of the ray flowers.

Bloom Season: May and November

Habitat/Range: Red Rock tarplant occurs on clay and volcanic soils in washes from 1,000 to 3,000'. It is known only from the western Mojave Desert in the vicinity of Red Rock Canyon State Park.

Comments: Off-highway vehicles posed a threat to Red Rock tarplant, but roads have now been closed to protect substantial portions of the population. A similar species with entire lower leaves, Mojave tarplant (*D. mohavensis*), was presumed to be extinct until rediscovered in Short Canyon and in the foothills of the San Jacinto Mountains in the early 1990s. It had not been seen since the type specimen was collected in 1933 from what is now the Mojave Forks Dam. It is hairy and sticky, with 5 ray flowers, 8 disk flowers, and 5–9 disk pappus scales. It is listed as state endangered.

ACTON ENCELIA
Encelia actoni Elmer
Sunflower Family (Asteraceae)

Description: Acton encelia is a rounded, 1½–4'-tall shrub that produces slender branches from the base. The bark of older stems is cracked while the younger stems are yellow-green and covered with velvety hairs. The entire, ovate to triangular, 1–2"-long leaves have short, soft hairs, giving them a silvery, whitish appearance. Flower heads have numerous disk flowers and 14–25 ray flowers, each with ½–1"-long, shallowly toothed, strap-shaped corollas. The ovate phyllaries are in 2–3 rows. The akenes have no pappus and are surrounded by receptacle chaff.

Bloom Season: March to July

Habitat/Range: Acton encelia can be found on rocky slopes, open areas, and roadsides below 5,000' in creosote bush scrub. It is widespread in the western and southern Mojave Desert to the western Transverse Ranges, White and Inyo Mountains, San Joaquin Valley, and Baja California, Mexico.

Comments: This genus was named in honor of Christoph Entzelt (1517–1583), a Lutheran clergyman who wrote about medicinal uses of plants. The type specimen was collected in Acton in the western Mojave Desert. *Encelia virginensis* is similar to *E. actoni*, but it occurs primarily in the eastern Mojave. The flower heads have 11–21 deeply toothed ray flowers, and the greener leaves have some longer hairs in addition to short, soft hairs. A compound isolated from *Encelia* kills variegated cutworm moth (*Peridroma saucia*) larvae, which feed on over 120 different plant species, including important crops such as corn, cotton, and soybeans.

BRITTLEBUSH, INCIENSO
Encelia farinosa A. Gray ex Torr. var. *farinosa*
Sunflower Family (Asteraceae)

Description: The white stems of this aromatic, rounded, 1–5'-tall shrub ooze golden resin when broken. The alternate, ovate, 1–4"-long leaves have short, dense, white-silvery hairs and mostly entire margins. The 1"-wide flower heads are produced in branched clusters on long, leafless stalks that rise above the leaves, forming a rounded, yellow arch over the silvery dome of foliage. Each flower head has numerous disk flowers and 11–21 ray flowers with ½"-long, strap-shaped corollas. The ¼"-long, flattened akenes have silky hairs on the margins, but no pappus is present.

Bloom Season: March to May in the Mojave Desert

Habitat/Range: Brittlebush grows on rocky slopes and fans below 3,000' in creosote bush scrub in the Death Valley region and eastern and southern Mojave Desert and in the Sonoran Desert to Baja California and Sonora, Mexico. It is not well adapted to the cooler temperatures of the western and northern Mojave Desert, although the California Department of Transportation has hydroseeded it along some highways there for erosion control.

Comments: Fossilized pack-rat midden data show brittlebush present in the southern Mojave 9,500 years ago. This species is readily drought-deciduous, with larger leaves dropping first. Small retained leaves become thick and hairy, reflecting sunlight and cooling the plant by reducing evaporation. Spanish missionaries used the gold resin from woody stems as incense, and the Cahuilla heated the resin and rubbed it on the chest to reduce pain. A boiled decoction of flowers, stems, and leaves was placed on a tooth to relieve toothache. This species is often cultivated as an ornamental for drought-tolerant landscapes. Variety *phenicodonta*, of the southeastern Mojave Desert, has red to brownish disk flowers.

RAYLESS ENCELIA, GREEN BRITTLEBUSH

Encelia frutescens (A. Gray) A. Gray
Sunflower Family (Asteraceae)

Description: The whitish stems of this rounded, 3–5'-tall shrub are rough to the touch. The dark-green, ovate, 1"-long leaves have blister-like swellings at the base of the coarse leaf hairs. Single ½–1" flower heads with numerous yellow disk flowers and no ray flowers are produced on leafless stalks. The akenes are black and flattened, and they have silky hairs along their margins.

Bloom Season: February to May in the Mojave Desert; in the lower Sonoran Desert, these plants bloom in response to summer rain

Habitat/Range: Rayless encelia is often found in washes and on rocky flats and slopes in creosote bush scrub in the Mojave, Sonoran, and southern Great Basin Deserts to western Colorado and New Mexico, and to Baja California and northwestern Sonora, Mexico.

Comments: This plant can maintain low levels of photosynthesis with very low water availability, but if the water reserves are too low, the leaves drop. It is also capable of photosynthesis at quite high temperatures (to 104 degrees F), but it evaporates a lot of water in the process. In the hottest, driest parts of its range in the lower Sonoran Desert, these characteristics restrict the plant to desert wash habitats, where soil moisture may be more reliable.

PANAMINT DAISY

Enceliopsis covillei (Nelson) S. F. Blake
Sunflower Family (Asteraceae)

Description: This stately perennial can grow to heights of over 40", branching from the woody base. The silvery, 3-veined, diamond-shaped leaves with winged petioles are tufted at the bases of branches. The 3½–5"-diameter flower heads with numerous yellow disk and ray flowers are produced on 12–20"-long stalks. Each head is subtended by a ¾"-tall involucre of lanceolate phyllaries. The akenes are nearly ½" long with a pappus of 2 short scales.

Bloom Season: March to June

Habitat/Range: Panamint daisy is found only on rocky slopes and in canyons from 1,300 to 4,000' along a 20-mile stretch of the western side of the Panamint Mountains, entirely within the limits of Death Valley National Park.

Comments: Although not legally protected as an endangered or threatened species, the Panamint daisy has a very limited distribution and has in the past been threatened by mining, grazing, and horticultural collecting. It has been adopted as the official logo for the California Native Plant Society.

NAKED-STEMMED DAISY

Enceliopsis nudicaulis (A. Gray) Nelson var. *nudicaulis*
Sunflower Family (Asteraceae)

Description: This 4–16"-tall perennial has mostly leafless stems from a woody base. The dull, gray-green, ovate leaves are around 1–2½" long with tufts of woolly hairs in the leaf axils. The flower heads are produced on 6–18"-long, gray-fuzzy stalks. Each 1½–3½"-diameter head has numerous disk flowers and 21 ray flowers, subtended by 3 rows of narrowly lanceolate, gray-fuzzy phyllaries. The akenes are slightly over ¼" long, and they are covered with silky hairs.

Bloom Season: April to May

Habitat/Range: Naked-stemmed daisy occupies rocky slopes and canyons from 3,000 to 6,000' in the mountains of the eastern and northern Mojave Desert to the White and Inyo Ranges, Utah, Idaho, and northern Arizona. It often occurs on volcanic or carbonate soils.

Comments: This plant is rare in California but somewhat widespread elsewhere, and it is not in danger of extinction at this time. More information is needed on the Ash Meadows daisy (*E. nudicaulis* var. *corrugata*), which has corrugated leaf margins. It is state-listed as critically endangered in Nevada and is known only from the vicinity of Ash Meadows.

COOPER'S GOLDENBUSH

Ericameria cooperi (A. Gray) H. M. Hall var. *cooperi*
Sunflower Family (Asteraceae)

Description: This 1–2'-tall, gummy-textured shrub has long, slender, alternate leaves that are approximately ½" long, but with age, the axillary buds become active, and dense clumps of ¼" leaves develop. Clusters of stalked, ¼" flower heads are produced abundantly over the top portion of the plant. Each head has 4–7 disk flowers and 0–2 ray flowers. Between 9 and 15 short-haired phyllaries occur in 3–4 rows; the outer phyllaries are ovate and the inner phyllaries are oblong. The pappus consists of soft, white bristles, and the nearly cylindrical akenes have silky hairs.

Bloom Season: March to June

Habitat/Range: Cooper's goldenbush is common on dry flats and mesas from 2,000 to 6,000', mostly in Joshua tree woodland; it is usually absent in the lowest, hottest, driest areas of the desert. It occurs from Antelope Valley and the Little San Bernardino Mountains to Mono County in California and Nevada.

Comments: These plants have shallow, spreading root systems that compete for limited water in surface soil layers, while rabbitbrush (*E. nauseosa* var. *mohavensis*) has taproots to access deeper, more reliable water sources. This species was named for J. G. Cooper (1830–1902), a US Geological Survey geologist.

CLIFF GOLDENBUSH
Ericameria cuneata (A. Gray) McClatchie var. *spathulata* (A. Gray) H. M. Hall
Sunflower Family (Asteraceae)

Description: This 4–20"-tall, spreading, gland-dotted shrub has crowded, green-glossy, spoon-shaped leaves that are up to 1" long with entire margins. They stay on the plant all year but change to a duller grayish-green in the very cold months. Flower heads consist of 7–15 disk flowers and 0–3 ray flowers. The linear to oblong phyllaries are in 4–6 rows, forming a ¼"-high involucre. The akenes have dense, flattened hairs with a sparse, brownish pappus.

Bloom Season: September to November

Habitat/Range: Cliff goldenbush grows in granitic rock cracks and crags between 2,600 and 6,000' in Joshua tree woodland and pinyon-juniper woodland. It can be found across the Mojave Desert and parts of southern California to the eastern Sierra Nevada, Arizona, and northwestern Mexico.

Comments: It is curious that this plant is almost never found in regular soil. It could be restricted to rocks because it is unable to compete with other shrubs, or it may be escaping herbivores. A study of rock cliffs in Joshua Tree National Park found that this shrub occurs in lower densities on cliffs that are heavily used by rock climbers.

INTERIOR GOLDENBUSH, LINEAR-LEAVED GOLDENBUSH, STENOTOPSIS

Ericameria linearifolia (DC.) Urb. and J. Wussow
Sunflower Family (Asteraceae)

Description: The resinous, erect twigs of this highly branched, 1–5'-tall shrub bear crowded, bundled, alternate leaves that are linear, cylindrical, and ½–2" long. The ¼–¾"-wide flower heads are produced at the ends of nearly leafless flower stalks. Each head has numerous disk flowers and 13–18 ray flowers. The lanceolate phyllaries with stalked glands, a green center, and fringed margins occur in 2–3 rows. The flattened, silky-haired akene has 6–8 veins and a white pappus.

Bloom Season: March to May

Habitat/Range: Interior goldenbush is common on dry hillsides below 6,500' in creosote bush scrub, Joshua tree woodland, and pinyon-juniper woodland. It occurs throughout the Mojave Desert to central Arizona, the southern Coast Ranges, and Baja California, Mexico.

Comments: If there are California junipers nearby, a light tapping of the interior goldenbush might scare up perched juniper hairstreak butterflies (*Mitoura siva juniperaria*). The larvae feed on the juniper, and the adults suck nectar from the interior goldenbush. The similar turpentine-brush (*E. laricifolius*) has much narrower leaves, fewer than 11 ray flowers, and flower heads smaller than ¼" wide. It occurs from 3,000 to 6,000' in the mountains of the eastern Mojave Desert.

RUBBER RABBITBRUSH

Ericameria nauseosa (Pursh) G. L. Nesom & G. I. Baird var. *mohavensis* (Pall.) G. L. Nesom & G. I. Baird
Sunflower Family (Asteraceae)

Description: This 2–8'-tall, highly variable shrub has numerous parallel, erect yet flexible branches. The stems are coated with a fine layer of dense wool, giving the plant a light-bluish or grayish cast. Leaves, when present, are alternate, narrowly linear, and ½–1" long. Many small heads of 5 yellow disk flowers are produced in crowded, rounded, or elongated clusters. Below each head are erect, hairless, angled phyllaries that are in distinct, vertically aligned rows. The pappus is composed of numerous thin bristles.

Bloom Season: September to October

Habitat/Range: Common on roadsides and disturbed areas below 7,800' in creosote bush scrub, Joshua tree woodland, and pinyon-juniper woodland throughout the Mojave Desert to cismontane central California and eastern Nevada.

Comments: This plant was investigated as a potential source of rubber during World War II, but the yield would have been too small for the effort required. Native Americans made a tea from the leaves or roots for stomachaches and colds, and root extract was used to make chewing gum. You may notice the chubby, purplish-black, clear-winged cactus fly (*Volucella mexicana*), a frequent visitor. Its larvae feed on decaying cacti, especially prickly pear and cholla.

BLACK-BANDED RABBITBRUSH
Ericameria paniculata (A. Gray) Rydb.
Sunflower Family (Asteraceae)

Description: The erect, loosely branched stems of this hairless, resinous, 2–5'-tall shrub often have irregular, distinct, black, gummy bands. The alternate, light-green, ½–1½"-long leaves are cylindrical, each narrowing abruptly to a pointed tip. Heads with 5–8 yellow disk flowers are grouped into large, branched, dense clusters. The ¼"-long phyllaries are in 4–5 rows, and the pappus consists of numerous brownish-white, soft, thin bristles.

Bloom Season: June to December

Habitat/Range: Black-banded rabbitbrush inhabits dry washes with subsurface water from 1,300 to 5,200' in creosote bush scrub throughout the Mojave Desert and along the western and northern borders of the Colorado Desert.

Comments: The black, gummy stem bands found on many branches are possibly from a smut fungus infection or insect attack. Essential oil from this species is marketed online, with the aroma being described as "sweet and warm, with notes of cumin and licorice."

BARSTOW WOOLLY SUNFLOWER
Eriophyllum mohavense (I. M. Johnston) Jepson
Sunflower Family (Asteraceae)

Description: This ½–1"-tall, tufted annual is covered with long, woolly hairs. The spoon-shaped leaves may have 3 pointed teeth near the wider tip. The stalked flower heads have 3–4 disk flowers and 3–4 linear, concave phyllaries. The pappus consists of 12–14 oblong scales.

Bloom Season: April to May

Habitat/Range: Rare in open loamy, gravelly, or clay soil from 1,500 to 3,000' in creosote bush scrub and saltbush scrub from the northeastern edge of Edwards Air Force Base to Kramer Hills, Boron, the Harper Dry Lake area, Opal Mountain, and Cuddeback Lake. It has also recently been observed from Ridgecrest and from Grant, a tiny town just south of Owens Lake.

Comments: This species is threatened in nearly its entire range by vehicles, grazing, military activities, and energy development, but it does not have legal protection. Researchers placed seeds of this species and the more common Wallace's woolly daisy (*E. wallacei*) in experimental plots beneath the shade of solar panels at various locations in the Mojave. Even in a year with plentiful rainfall, the seeds of this rare species did not do as well as expected; however, the solar panels had little effect on the seed germination of Wallace's woolly daisy.

PRINGLE'S WOOLLY DAISY
Eriophyllum pringlei A. Gray
Sunflower Family (Asteraceae)

Description: This ½–3"-tall, tufted annual is branched from the base. The spoon-shaped, woolly leaves usually have 3 rounded lobes near the tip, and the margins curl under. The unstalked, ⅛–¼" flower heads are produced in small clusters in the leaf axils and at the branch tips. Each head has 10–25 tiny disk flowers with 6–8 phyllaries below; there are no ray flowers. The tiny akenes have some long, flattened hairs, and the pappus scales have a shredded appearance.

Bloom Season: April to June

Habitat/Range: Pringle's woolly daisy is found in open, sandy areas from 1,000 to 7,000' in creosote bush scrub, Joshua tree woodland, and sagebrush scrub in both the Mojave and Sonoran Deserts.

Comments: This species was named for Cyrus Guernsey Pringle (1838–1911), a Quaker who was imprisoned for being a conscientious objector during the Civil War. After being released he returned home and developed improvements to several varieties of crop plants. Asa Gray of Harvard sent him on numerous plant collection trips to the western states and Mexico, where he collected about 500,000 specimens, many new to science.

WALLACE'S WOOLLY DAISY
Eriophyllum wallacei (A. Gray) A. Gray
Sunflower Family (Asteraceae)

Description: Wallace's woolly daisy is a tufted, woolly, 1–3"-tall annual with spoon-shaped, entire, ¼–¾"-long leaves. The flower heads are produced singly on ½–1"-long stalks. Each head consists of numerous yellow disk flowers, 5–10 yellow ray flowers (often 8), and 5–10 pointed, overlapping, ¼" phyllaries. The tiny, club-shaped akenes are usually nearly hairless, and the pappus is less than ¹⁄₁₆" long.

Bloom Season: As early as December in the southern part of its range, to July

Habitat/Range: Common in sandy soil below 6,000' in creosote bush scrub, Joshua tree woodland, and pinyon-juniper woodland in the Mojave and Sonoran Deserts to Mono County and mountains of southern California to northern Baja California, Mexico.

Comments: This plant may be confused with its larger relative, *E. ambiguum* var. *paleaceum*, which has longer flower stalks and tends to occur on steep, rocky slopes. Also see comment for the similar false woolly daisy (*Syntrichopappus fremontii*) later in this chapter. This species is named for William A. Wallace (1815–1893), who moved to California from New England in 1850 and made extensive plant collections in the Los Angeles area in the mid-1800s. He also worked as a gold miner, schoolteacher, and newspaper editor.

DESERT SUNFLOWER
Geraea canescens Torr. & A. Gray
Sunflower Family (Asteraceae)

Description: This up-to-2'-high annual or biennial branches from the base, producing alternate, ½–4"-long, slightly roughened, elliptic leaves with entire or toothed margins. The lower leaves have winged petioles, while the upper leaves are sessile. The 1–3"-wide flower heads are produced in loose, branched clusters, each head with numerous disk flowers and 10–21 golden-yellow ray flowers. The narrow, white-fringed phyllaries are in 2–3 rows, forming a ¼–½"-high involucre. The flattened, wedge-shaped, ¼"-long disk flower akenes are black with long, white hairs on the margins.

Bloom Season: February to May, and also in October and November following summer rain

Habitat/Range: Occurs in sandy flats below 3,000' in creosote bush scrub in the central and eastern Mojave Desert to the Sonoran Desert; it also occurs in Sonora and Baja California, Mexico.

Comments: The root word of the genus name means "old," probably in reference to the long, white hairs of the disk flower akenes. Desert sunflower has been known to hybridize occasionally with *Encelia farinosa*, which is not surprising when considering that *Geraea*, *Encelia*, and *Enceliopsis* are very closely related. In years with plentiful rainfall, this plant forms showy yellow carpets on the floor of Death Valley.

STICKY SNAKEWEED, MATCHWEED
Gutierrezia microcephala (DC.) A. Gray
Sunflower Family (Asteraceae)

Description: This 8–24"-tall, highly branched perennial has a gummy, fibrous texture and upward-curving, furrowed stems that are yellow to greenish above and brown and somewhat woody near the base. The linear, entire, dark-gray-green leaves have gland-dots. Numerous skinny, cylindrical flower heads are produced in clusters of 5–6 on upper branches. Each head has 4–6 phyllaries, 1–2 disk flowers, and 1–2 ray flowers with ⅛"-long, strap-shaped corollas.

Bloom Season: July to October

Habitat/Range: Common on roadsides and in disturbed and open, sandy areas below 7,500' in saltbush scrub, creosote bush scrub, and Joshua tree woodland throughout the Mojave and Sonoran Deserts to Colorado and central Mexico.

Comments: This genus was named for Pedro Gutiérrez Bueno, a chemist from Madrid. His chemistry textbook promoted the then-popular narrative that rusting and burning were due to phlogiston, a mysterious substance released from fire. When Gutiérrez incorporated LaVoisier's new ideas about oxidation into his second edition, the angry old-schoolers closed his laboratories! Native Americans used the leaves for a tea for colds and a poultice for sprained muscles. However, livestock avoid the leaves, which contain soapy and toxic saponins, which means it spreads rapidly in overgrazed areas. A common related species, *Gutierrezia sarothrae*, differs from sticky snakeweed in that it is a smaller plant with larger, globular to ovate heads with up to 8 ray flowers.

NEVADA GOLDENEYE

Heliomeris multiflora Nutt. var. *nevadensis* (A. Nelson) W. F. Yates
Sunflower Family (Asteraceae)

Description: This perennial has several erect, 1–3'-tall stems arising from a branched, woody root. The simple, narrow, entire, up-to-2"-long leaves are opposite on lower parts of the stem, and the margins tend to roll under. Flower heads are single or in loose panicles on 2–6"-long peduncles with numerous golden-yellow disk flowers and 8–15 oblong, yellow ray flowers subtended by a hemispheric involucre of narrow, lanceolate phyllaries with flattened, rigid, straight hairs. The receptacle is chaffy, and the hairless fruits lack a pappus.

Bloom Season: May to September

Habitat/Range: Found on rocky and gravelly canyons in pinyon-juniper woodland and sagebrush scrub from 4,000 to 7,500' in the mountains of the northern and eastern Mojave Desert to Utah, Nevada, New Mexico, and northern Mexico.

Comments: In 1899, Wyoming botany professor Aven Nelson (1859–1952) hired high school student Leslie Goodding (1880–1967) to help on a Yellowstone expedition. This sparked Goodding's interest in plants, and he went on to study botany under Nelson. He eventually collected Nevada goldeneye as a botanist with the Soil Conservation Service. Nelson officially described it. Years later, Nelson became a widower and married his student, Ruth Ashton Nelson, who authored *Handbook of Rocky Mountains Plants*. This is the same book that this book's coauthor, Tim Thomas, used in 1972 to key a plant for the very first time, sparking his interest in botany!

COOPER'S RUBBERWEED
Hymenoxys cooperi (A. Gray) Cockerell
Sunflower Family (Asteraceae)

Description: This erect biennial to short-lived perennial has hairy, somewhat branched, up-to-3'-tall, reddish to purplish stems. The linear to pinnately divided, 1½–3½"-long leaves are gradually reduced in size up the stem. Flower heads have numerous yellow disk flowers surrounded by 9–14 somewhat reflexed, ½–1"-long ray flowers, subtended by a ½"-high, cup-shaped involucre of 12–14 lanceolate, keeled, pointed phyllaries surrounding more rounded inner phyllaries. The pappus is composed of 5 oblong to ovate scales.

Bloom Season: May to September

Habitat/Range: Found in rocky, open places in pinyon-juniper woodland from 3,300 to 11,500' in the Little San Bernardino Mountains in Joshua Tree National Park and in the mountains of the eastern Mojave Desert to Arizona, Nevada, Utah, and Oregon.

Comments: This plant was collected in 1861 in the Providence Mountains by James G. Cooper (1830–1902), a California Geological Survey zoologist who collected plants as well. His Cooper's rubberweed collection happened to be a "top snatch," meaning it was missing the lower part of the plant. Although this makes it hard to describe or identify, Asa Gray (1810–1888), Harvard botany professor and the most influential botanist of that era, provided the description, in spite of it being a substandard collection.

ALKALI GOLDENBUSH
Isocoma acradenia (E. Greene) E. Greene var. *acradenia*
Sunflower Family (Asteraceae)

Description: The brittle, ascending, shiny, hairless, and densely branched stems of this 1–2½'-tall, rounded shrub bear resinous, gland-dotted, oblong, ½–2"-long leaves with entire or few-toothed margins. The flower heads are clustered tightly in groups of 4–5, each with 6–12 yellow disk flowers, no ray flowers, and 22–28 firm phyllaries in 3–4 rows. The cylindrical corolla tube expands abruptly near the throat, which is a diagnostic characteristic of this genus. The blunt phyllary tips appear swollen and wart-like due to conspicuous resin pockets.

Bloom Season: August to November

Habitat/Range: Found in alkaline soils below 3,000' in scattered locations throughout the Mojave Desert to the Grand Canyon, southern Utah, and the eastern Sonoran Desert to northern Sonora, Mexico; also found in cismontane California from central California to Baja California, Mexico.

Comments: The Cahuilla drank tea and inhaled vapor from boiled roots to cure colds. It was also used as a poultice and an insect repellent on horses. Some look-alike species have poisons that can cause liver damage. Var. *bracteosa* in the northwestern Mojave has toothed leaves, 10–17 flowers, and 25–36 phyllaries per head. Var. *eremophila* in the Mojave and Sonoran Deserts has 15–25 flowers per head, fewer than 28 phylla-ries with widely rounded tips, and 4–6 soft-pointed teeth per leaf side.

GOLDFIELDS
Lasthenia gracilis (DC.) Greene
Sunflower Family (Asteraceae)

Description: This silky-haired annual is 4–16" tall. The slender stems are either simple or branched from the base, with opposite, linear, hairy leaves that are ¼–2½" long. The hemispheric flower heads, which often nod in bud, have numerous disk flowers, 6–13 ray flowers, and 4–13 separate, hairy phyllaries.

Bloom Season: February to June

Habitat/Range: Goldfields inhabit open, sandy areas below 3,000' in creosote bush scrub in the western, southern, and central Mojave Desert to Oregon and Baja California, Mexico.

Comments: Goldfields often show up in profusion after winter rain, turning entire landscapes yellow. Although the very similar *L. californica* grows adjacent to *L. gracilis* in some cismontane areas in California, these species are actually occupy-ing different, adjacent soil types. The *L. gracilis-californica* complex is being used as a model to study rapid speciation to adapt to different edaphic conditions. Lasthenia, for whom this genus was named, was supposedly a female student of Plato.

203

BIGELOW'S TICKSEED, BIGELOW'S COREOPSIS
Leptosyne bigelovii (A. Gray) A. Gray
Sunflower Family (Asteraceae)

Description: This 4–12"-tall, hairless, slender-stemmed annual has 1–3"-long, basal, pinnate leaves with linear lobes. The leafless stems bear individual heads with 20–50 disk flowers and 5–10 ray flowers. The 4–7 outer phyllaries are ¼–½" long and linear, while the 4–8 inner phyllaries are longer and oval to oblong. Each flattened, oblong disk fruit has marginal hairs and a pappus of 2 tiny, bright-white scales; ray akenes lack both hairs and pappus. Dry bracts are fused to the base of the disk flower fruits; when they fall, these dry bracts still cling to the fruit, so the dried receptacle is bare.

Bloom Season: March to May

Habitat/Range: Bigelow's coreopsis is common on dry, gravelly slopes under 6,000' in creosote bush scrub, Joshua tree woodland, and pinyon-juniper woodland. It occurs in the central, eastern, and northern Mojave Desert to northern California, and in southern California to the Santa Monica Mountains.

Comments: The former genus name, *Coreopsis*, means "resembling a tick" in Greek, referring to the akene shape. The similar *L. californica* has similar disk and ray fruits (cypselae), but they are hairless with irregularly thickened corky wings, and the dry bracts on the receptacle remain there after the cypselae are gone.

LEAFSTEM TICKSEED
Leptosyne calliopsidea (DC.) A. Gray
Sunflower Family (Asteraceae)

Description: The erect, stout stems of this hairless, 4–20"-tall annual bear basal and alternate once, or twice, pinnately divided leaves; leaves are simple near the top. Flower heads have 8–10 obovate, widely spreading, bright-yellow ray flowers, numerous golden-yellow disk flowers to which receptacle chaff adheres, and an involucre of outer, spreading phyllaries that are shorter than the inner ones. The oblong fruits are shiny on one side and silky on the other, their margins are covered with long, silky hairs, and they have a pappus of 2 yellowish awns.

Bloom Season: February to June

Habitat/Range: This species occurs in open, sandy and grassy habitats in the western Mojave Desert and the Transverse Ranges, southern Coast Ranges, and San Joaquin Valley to the San Francisco Bay region.

Comments: Species author DC. refers to Swiss botanist Augustin Pyramus de Candolle (1778–1841), who began his career working at an herbarium. He developed a system of plant classification that recognized that plants in similar environments may develop similar characteristics over time, even though they may not be related— the idea of convergent evolution. He also was one of the first to describe circadian rhythms in plants, with regard to their leaf movements.

SNAKE'S HEAD
Malacothrix coulteri Harv. & A. Gray
Sunflower Family (Asteraceae)

Description: The erect, leafy, sparsely branched stems of this annual are light-greenish with a smooth, powdery coating. The alternate, bluish, 1½–4"-long, lanceolate leaves are somewhat fleshy-looking with wavy margins. The rounded flower heads have numerous rows of membranous-margined phyllaries, each with a dark midrib; the involucre somewhat resembles the keeled scales of a snake, hence the common name. The heads contain numerous light-yellow ray flowers but no disk flowers.

Bloom Season: March to May

Habitat/Range: Found in sandy basins below 3,500' in creosote scrub and other plant communities from the San Joaquin Valley to Utah, Arizona, and Argentina. It is believed to be extirpated from the Channel Islands.

Comments: This chicory tribe plant has milky sap. It was named for Thomas Coulter (1793–1843), an Irish botanist who traveled from Monterey south along the El Camino Real, visiting California missions en route to San Diego, collecting plants and documenting Native American vocabularies along the way. He traveled from there to the confluence of the Colorado and Gila Rivers, collecting the first plant records from the Colorado Desert.

DESERT DANDELION
Malacothrix glabrata A. Gray
Sunflower Family (Asteraceae)

Description: This mostly hairless, 2–16"-tall annual has a basal rosette of linear-lobed or toothed leaves that withers by the time the flowers open; sparse leaves are found up the stem. The stalked flower heads have numerous ½–1"-long, lemon-yellow, strap-like ray flowers, sometimes with an orange-tinged spot near the center of the cluster. The hairless, overlapping phyllaries are up to ¾" long. The small akenes have veins and a pappus of teeth and bristles.

Bloom Season: March to June

Habitat/Range: This species is one of the most common spring annuals on roadsides, vacant lots, sandy flats, and washes below 6,000' in creosote bush scrub, Joshua tree woodland, and saltbush scrub. It seems to be very tolerant of disturbance. It occurs in both the Mojave and Sonoran Deserts and in adjacent cismontane valleys from San Diego County to Santa Barbara County and Idaho.

Comments: Related species in the Mojave Desert include *M. californica*, which has hairs on the basal leaves and no stem leaves, and *M. sonchoides*, with fleshy basal leaves with toothed lobes. This plant is not in the same genus as the edible and medicinal weedy dandelion (*Taraxacum officinale*) and should never be used as a substitute for it. The Navajo used *M. sonchoides* to induce vomiting.

LOBE-LEAF GROUNDSEL

Packera multilobata (Torr. & A. Gray) W. A. Weber
& A. Löve
Sunflower Family (Asteraceae)

Description: Several somewhat erect, up-to-14"-high stems arise from the short taproot of this hairless perennial. The lower leaves, which are up to 3" long, including the petiole, are pinnately divided with a rounded, large, terminal lobe and smaller lateral lobes. The upper leaves are smaller and sessile. The flower heads are in flat-topped clusters, each with a bell-shaped involucre of 13 or 21 green, yellow-tipped, hairless phyllaries enclosing 40–50 disk flowers and 8 yellow ray flowers from ¼" to nearly ½" long.

Bloom Season: May to July

Habitat/Range: Common on dry slopes from 3,600 to 11,000' in the mountains of the eastern Mojave Desert to the eastern Sierras and Great Basin Desert to Wyoming, Colorado, and New Mexico.

Comments: The type specimen of this plant was collected by John C. Frémont (1813–1890) during his second expedition (1843–1844), which was designed to map the second part of the Oregon Trail. From Oregon his party turned south, eventually traveling through the San Joaquin Valley, over Tehachapi Pass, and finally through the Mojave Desert to the vicinity of Las Vegas and eastward.

CHINCH-WEED

Pectis papposa Harvey & A. Gray var. *papposa*
Sunflower Family (Asteraceae)

Description: This gland-dotted, ½–8"-tall, mound-forming or spreading annual has a pungent, spicy odor. The opposite, narrow, sessile leaves are ½–1½" long with bristly hairs on the margins, especially along the winged bases. Numerous ¼–½" flower heads are produced in dense, branched clusters, each with 6–14 disk flowers, 8 ray flowers, and a row of 8 green phyllaries, each with a gland near the tip and glands along the margins. The small, cylindrical disk fruits have a pappus of bristles, while the pappus on the ray fruit forms a low crown of small scales.

Bloom Season: September to November, following summer rains

Habitat/Range: Occurs on dry flats and rocky slopes below 5,000' in creosote bush scrub and Joshua tree woodland in all of the deserts of North America. It is rare in the western Mojave, but has been observed as far west as Victorville.

Comments: Worldwide, there are about 90 species of *Pectis*. Many, including this species, have the C4 photosynthesis, which makes them well-adapted to hot climates. The major essential oil of chinch-weed is a cumin oil similar in composition and odor to the common cooking spice cumin. Chinch-weed has been suggested as a commercial source, since the plant grows rapidly and thrives in hot weather. Pectis oil has also been shown to be antifungal and antibacterial.

PYGMY-CEDAR
Peucephyllum schottii A. Gray
Sunflower Family (Asteraceae)

Description: This evergreen shrub or small tree superficially resembles a conifer, with its dense, shiny green, needle-like leaves that are less than 1" long. Solitary, cylindrical flower heads are produced on ⅓–1" stalks, each with 12–21 pale-yellow, ½"-long disk flowers. Each head has 1 row of 9–18 thick, pointed, ¼–½"-long phyllaries that are gland-dotted near the tips. The tiny, blackish akenes have a pappus of fine bristles.

Bloom Season: May to December

Habitat/Range: Pygmy-cedar can be found on rocky outcrops, canyons, upper alluvial fans, and sometimes roadcuts below 3,000' in creosote bush scrub. It occurs in both the Mojave and Sonoran Deserts to north-western Mexico.

Comments: Studies in Death Valley have shown that pygmy-cedar is not able to handle drought stress as well as its neighbors, creosote bush (*Larrea tridentata*) and desert holly (*Atriplex hymenelytra*). Fossilized pack-rat midden data show that this plant probably occupied its present range beginning about 10,000 years ago. Individuals of pygmy-cedar can live at least 100 years, as shown by repeat photography. This species was named for Arthur Schott (1814–1875), a naturalist of the Mexican Boundary Survey.

TURTLEBACK, VELVET ROSETTE
Psathyrotes ramosissima (Torrey) A. Gray
Sunflower Family (Asteraceae)

Description: This dense, gray, dome-shaped, 2–6"-tall annual has a strong resinous or turpentine odor. The young stems are covered with soft white hair, but the older stems are smooth and hairless. The thick, velvety, ¼–¾"-long leaf blades have irregular, rounded teeth, prominent veins, and long leaf stalks. The flower heads are produced on short stalks in leaf axils, each with 16–32 small, yellow to purplish disk flowers subtended by 2 rows of ¼" phyllaries, the outer row reflexed. The tiny akenes have numerous brownish pappus bristles in 3–4 rows.

Bloom Season: March to June

Habitat/Range: Occurs on sandy flats and in washes below 3,000' in creosote bush scrub in the Mojave Desert to Owens Valley, Nevada, and Utah, although it seems to be absent in much of the western Mojave. It also occurs in the Sonoran Desert to central Arizona, and to Baja California and northwestern Sonora, Mexico.

Comments: Native Americans used this as a tea for intestinal and urinary tract disorders, as a dressing for snakebite, as an eyewash, and as a cure for toothache. *Psathyrotes pilifera* occurs in the northern Mojave Desert in Nevada and into the Grand Canyon. It is differentiated by the entire leaf margin and longer, multicellular leaf hairs. *P. annua* has 10 to 20 flowers per head, and the phyllaries in the outer row are erect. It is found in alkali soils up to 6,000' in the Mojave and on the desert slopes of the San Bernardino Mountains and southern Sierra Nevada Range.

PAPER DAISY
Psilostrophe cooperi (A. Gray) E. Greene
Sunflower Family (Asteraceae)

Description: This 8–24"-tall, nearly spherical perennial has numerous branched, white-woolly stems arising from a woody base. The alternate, linear, 1–2"-long leaves have a fuzzy coating that wears off as the leaves age. The showy flower heads are produced on 1–3" stalks. Each head has up to 25 protruding disk flowers and 4–8 wide, ovate, ¼–¾"-long ray flowers with 3 teeth at the tips. These fold back and become very papery with age, clinging to the plant until the akenes are shed. The tiny, hairless akenes bear a pappus of short scales.

Bloom Season: April to June, and in late fall following summer rain

Habitat/Range: Occurs on alluvial slopes and rocky flats from 2,000 to 5,000' in creosote bush scrub and Joshua tree woodland in the eastern Mojave Desert to southern Nevada, southwestern Utah, and the northern Sonoran Desert to New Mexico and northern Mexico.

Comments: Paper daisy will quickly drop its leaves with the onset of drought. This species is named in honor of Dr. James Graham Cooper (1830–1902), who worked as a geologist for the Geological Survey of California. He collected Mojave Desert plants in the early 1860s, and several species have been named after him.

ABERT'S SANVITALIA
Sanvitalia abertii A. Gray
Sunflower Family (Asteraceae)

Description: This erect to spreading, 2–12"-tall summer annual is covered with stiff, appressed hairs. The leaves are mostly opposite and narrowly lanceolate with a pointed tip. The flower heads are on peduncles up to 1¼" long and are subtended by 3–11 pointed, hairless phyllaries with prominent veins. For each phyllary there is 1 ovate, 2-lobed ray flower that starts out yellow but dries white. The tiny disk flowers are yellow and dry to a cream color. The pappus is composed of 3 tiny awns, and the disk flower fruits (cypselae) are warty with 4 angles.

Bloom Season: August to October

Habitat/Range: Found in scrublands and pinyon-juniper woodlands from 4,700 to 5,800' in the eastern Mojave Desert in California to Texas and south to Baja California, Sonora, Chihuahua, and Coahuila, Mexico.

Comments: Lt. James William Abert (1820–1897), an explorer, soldier, and artist, was hired to document John Frémont's third expedition with his drawings. It was on this trip that he collected the type specimen of Abert's sanvitalia, between Bent's Fort and Santa Fe, New Mexico.

CALIFORNIA BUTTERWEED

Senecio flaccidus Less. var. *monoensis* (E. Greene)
B. L. Turner & T. M. Barkley
Sunflower Family (Asteraceae)

Description: This 1–3'-tall, hairless, green perennial has furrowed, arching stems from a strong taproot. The alternate, 1–4"-long leaves are linear and entire or pinnately divided into linear segments. Flower heads are produced in a loose cluster on the upper stems, each with numerous disk flowers and 8, ½–1"-long ray flowers. The involucre consists of an inner row of 13 or 21 even, lanceolate phyllaries and an outer row of very short, spreading phyllaries. The soft-hairy, cylindrical akenes are less than ¼" long with a pappus of thin bristles.

Bloom Season: March to May, and in the fall following summer rain

Habitat/Range: This variety of California butterweed occurs in washes in creosote bush scrub, Joshua tree woodland, and pinyon-juniper woodland in the Mojave Desert and in the northern Sonoran Desert to Mono County, Utah, Arizona, Texas, and northwestern Mexico.

Comments: Black, shiny, solitary bees are often seen in the evening resting in the foliage of California butterweed on the north slopes of the San Gabriel Mountains. Many species of *Senecio* have been used as alternative treatments as diuretics, to promote sweating, and as a laxative. The active compound is a pyrrolizidine alkaloid that can cause loss of appetite, vomiting, diarrhea, liver toxicity, and even liver cancer.

MOJAVE BUTTERWEED

Senecio mohavensis A. Gray
Sunflower Family (Asteraceae)

Description: This branched, hairless, 8–16"-tall annual has green, 1–3½"-long, lobed or toothed leaves distributed alternately along the entire length of the purplish stems; the upper leaves have clasping bases. Loose clusters of ½" flower heads are produced atop the stems, each with numerous disk flowers and sometimes a few inconspicuous ray flowers. There is 1 main row of 8 or 13 linear, ¼"-long phyllaries with very pointed tips, and there may also be some very short, outer phyllaries. The tiny, cylindrical akenes have soft, short, white hairs.

Bloom Season: March to May

Habitat/Range: Occupies shady areas under shrubs and among boulders on rocky slopes below 3,000' in the eastern and southern Mojave Desert and in the Sonoran Desert to northwestern Mexico.

Comments: This species is indistinguishable from *S. flava* from the Middle East. Both species are self-fertilizing, and the mucilaginous seeds remain viable for 15 years. It has been suggested that Mojave butterweed might have been introduced from that region fairly recently by bird-dispersed seeds. If so, it is curious that our species has an endemic tephritid fly that feeds on the flowers, since recently introduced plants are usually not hosts to endemic insects.

FALSE WOOLLY DAISY
Syntrichopappus fremontii A. Gray
Sunflower Family (Asteraceae)

Description: This 1–4"-tall, branched annual is covered with short hairs. The linear to spoon-shaped, ¼–¾"-long leaves may have 3 teeth near the tip. Flower heads have several yellow disk flowers, 5 ray flowers, and 5 hardened, boat-shaped phyllaries with dry, thin margins that partly enclose the ray akenes. The strap-shaped corollas of the ray flowers are strongly 3-lobed or toothed. The small, hairy akene has a pappus of 30–40 bright-white bristles that are united at the base.

Bloom Season: March to June

Habitat/Range: This plant grows in sandy or gravelly soil between 2,500 and 7,500' in creosote bush scrub and Joshua tree woodland throughout the Mojave Desert to the Owens Valley, southern Nevada, southwestern Utah, and northwestern Arizona.

Comments: False woolly daisy is commonly confused with Wallace's woolly daisy (*Eriophyllum wallacei*). However, Wallace's woolly daisy usually has 5–10 ray flowers, which are not strongly lobed, and the pappus, if present, consists of 6–10 oblong scales less than ¹⁄₂₅" long. The phyllaries are not as well defined, and the plants are usually lower in stature. It is usually found in low, sandy areas, while false woolly daisy is often above the desert floor.

COTTON-THORN
Tetradymia axillaris Nelson var. *longispina* (M. E. Jones) Strother
Sunflower Family (Asteraceae)

Description: The white-woolly stems of this spiny, 2–5'-tall shrub have straight, ½–2"-long spines, and clusters of short, green, linear, up-to-½"-long leaves in the spine axils; they are hairy when very young but quickly become hairless with maturity. Clusters of 1–3 flower heads are produced on hairy stalks, each head with 5–7 pale-yellow, ¼–³⁄₈"-long disk flowers and 5 narrowly ovate, hairy, ¼"-long phyllaries. The densely hairy akene is less than ¼" long, and it has a pappus of approximately 25 slender scales.

Bloom Season: May to August

Habitat/Range: Occurs on dry slopes and flats from 3,500 to 7,000' along the desert slopes of the Transverse Ranges to Joshua Tree National Park and north along the eastern slopes of the Sierra Nevada to Nevada and southwestern Utah. It is also found in Death Valley National Park and the northern Mojave National Preserve.

Comments: *Tetradymia stenolepis* has silvery, hairy leaves and straight spines. *T. spinosa* has hairless leaves and curved spines, while *T. canescens* is a silvery, spineless shrub of the Transverse Ranges, desert mountains, and Great Basin Desert.

ANGELITA DAISY

Tetraneuris acaulis (Pursh) Greene var. *arizonica* (Greene) K. F. Parker
Sunflower Family (Asteraceae)

Description: The erect, leafless, 4–12"-tall stems of this tufted perennial arise from a branched caudex. The gray-silky-hairy, gland-dotted, narrowly oblanceolate basal leaves are up to 2" long. Solitary flower heads on 2–6"-long peduncles have 9–15 bright-yellow, ½–⅔"-long, somewhat reflexed ray flowers, numerous small, golden-yellow disk flowers, and a ¼–½"-high involucre of lanceolate to ovate phyllaries with long, white hairs. The fruits have long, silky hairs, and the pappus is composed of 5–7 short, membranous, abruptly awned scales.

Bloom Season: April to September

Habitat/Range: In grassy areas, meadows, and forest edges, largely on limestone soils, from 4,000 to 8,000' in the mountains of the eastern Mojave Desert to Idaho, Colorado, and Arizona.

Comments: The genus name *Tetraneuris* refers to the 4 veins present in the ray florets; they are, however, 3-lobed. There are 13 species of *Tetraneuris* and 4 varieties of *T. acaulis*; the variety *arizonica* is the only Mojave Desert representative.

THYMOPHYLLA

Thymophylla pentachaeta (DC.) Small var. *belenidium* (DC.) Strother
Sunflower Family (Asteraceae)

Description: This 6–12"-tall, gland-dotted perennial has very slender stems that are somewhat woody at the base. The opposite, ½–1¼"-long leaves are pinnately divided into 3–5 stiff, spine-tipped, linear lobes. The ¼" flower heads are produced singly on 1–2" stalks. Each head has numerous disk flowers, 13 ray flowers, 2 rows of ¼"-long inner phyllaries, and an outer row of a few short, triangular phyllaries. The tiny akene has a pappus of 10 scales, each divided into 3 awns.

Bloom Season: April to June, and may also bloom September to October when there has been adequate rain

Habitat/Range: Found on dry, gravelly benches and slopes, often on limestone soils, from 1,500 to 5,600' in creosote bush scrub and Joshua tree woodland in the eastern Mojave Desert, the western Sonoran Desert, and the Chihuahuan Desert of Texas and Mexico.

Comments: This plant is sometimes confused with chinch-weed (*Pectis papposa*), which only blooms in the fall, has simple leaves, and never develops woody tissue. The irritating odor may be due to sesquiterpene lactones, which are found in several genera of the marigold tribe (Tageteae) of the sunflower family, including *Pectis*, *Dyssodia*, *Nicolletia*, *Porophyllum*, and *Adenophyllum*, all of which are featured in this book. A small percentage of people develop contact dermatitis when exposed to these chemicals.

YELLOW-HEADS
Trichoptilium incisum A. Gray
Sunflower Family (Asteraceae)

Description: This 2–10"-tall annual has fuzzy stems that may branch near the base. The ½–1¼"-long, inversely lanceolate, toothed leaves are concentrated at the base of the plant and along the lower stems. They taper to short, winged petioles, and they are densely white-hairy; resin dots are visible under the hairs. The rounded flower heads with numerous yellow disk flowers and 2 rows of lancolate, glandular-hairy, ¼"-long phyllaries occur singly on 1–4"-long, glandular-hairy stalks. Ray flowers are absent. The tiny akenes have a pappus of 5 divided scales.

Bloom Season: February to May, and sometimes October to November following summer rain

Habitat/Range: Yellow-heads are found on rocky slopes or desert pavement below 2,200' in creosote bush scrub in the Mojave Desert (except the western Mojave) to southern Nevada and northwestern Arizona. It hugs the eastern slopes of the Peninsular Ranges south and makes it into Baja California, Mexico. However, it is absent in a swath from the Salton Sea south through the Imperial Valley to the Gran Desierto, as this is largely unsuitable sandy habitat. Its distribution picks up farther east in the Sonoran Desert to central Arizona and the Pinacate volcanic field in Sonora, Mexico.

Comments: The flowers of this species look like yellow versions of pincushions (*Chaenactis* species), to which they are likely closely related. The genus name is derived from the Greek words for "hair-like" (*tricho*) and "feather" (*ptilon*), referring to the pappus scales.

TRIXIS, AMERICAN THREEFOLD
Trixis californica Kellogg var. *californica*
Sunflower Family (Asteraceae)

Description: This erect, leafy, 1–3'-tall shrub has white, brittle stems. The lanceolate, alternate, bright-green leaves are 1–4" long with entire to minutely toothed margins. The ½–1"-tall flower heads are produced in somewhat flat, branched, leafy-bracted clusters. Each head bears numerous disk flowers with 2-lipped, yellow corollas and 8–10 green, pointed phyllaries. The narrow akenes have a pappus of white to beige bristles.

Bloom Season: February to April

Habitat/Range: Trixis occurs on rocky slopes, canyons, and washes below 3,000' in creosote bush scrub in the southern Mojave Desert, as in the Sheep Hole Mountains. It is more common in the Sonoran Desert to western Texas and northern Mexico.

Comments: Native Americans in the Sonoran Desert smoked the leaves of this plant like tobacco, and a tea was made from the roots to aid in childbirth. The genus name *Trixis* is from the Greek *trixos*, for "three folds," describing the 3-cleft corolla. This plant belongs to a unique group of sunflowers (Tribe Mutisieae) that has 2-lipped disk flowers.

ANNUAL BRISTLEWEED

Xanthisma gracile (Nutt.) D. R. Morgan & R. L. Hartm.
Sunflower Family (Asteraceae)

Description: The erect, bristly, branched stem of this annual can grow to 10" high. The alternate, oblanceolate, pinnately lobed leaves have bristly hairs on the surface and margins. Heads of yellow disk and ray flowers are subtended by 4–6 rows of green, hairy, bristle-tipped phyllaries. The brownish-red akenes have a pappus of bristles that are slightly wider at the base.

Bloom Season: April to September

Habitat/Range: Occurs in sandy, rocky, or clay soils below 5,000' in the eastern Mojave Desert to Colorado, Texas, and northern Mexico.

Comments: Annual bristleweed has extra chromosomes that do not have functional genes. Only 15 percent of eukaryotic species have these so-called B chromosomes, which are not inherited in a normal Mendelian fashion, and for which little is known. In this species, plants with B chromosomes have dark-purple akenes, and studies are under way to determine if this has any influence on plant survival or reproduction.

DEVIL'S LETTUCE, CHECKER FIDDLENECK

Amsinckia tessellata A. Gray var. *tessellata*
Borage Family (Boraginaceae)

Description: This erect, bristly, 8–24"-tall annual has alternate, entire, lanceolate leaves. The stiff leaf hairs have bulbous bases that can be seen with a hand lens. The 5-parted, ⅓"–⅔"-long, yellow to orange flowers occur in a 2–5"-long, coiled spike at the top of the stem. Each corolla is less than ¼" wide, and the flower tubes are cylindrical. Some of the calyx lobes are fused, so there appears to be 3–4 lobes instead of 5; the lobes have white hairs on the margins.

Bloom Season: March to May

Habitat/Range: Common throughout both the Mojave and Sonoran Deserts to eastern Washington and Baja California, Mexico. Although it is present in nondesert areas of southern California, it is very uncommon there.

Comments: A study involving removal of the introduced annual grasses, *Bromus* and *Schismus*, resulted in better growth of this species, showing that these introduced grasses are strong competitors. This plant can grow in large swaths that seem to be monocultures. When walking through dried patches, one quickly learns that this plant's stiff hairs are really good at infesting socks and the insides of pant legs, causing extreme discomfort! Common fiddleneck (*A. intermedia*) differs from devil's lettuce by having 5 distinct calyx lobes rather than 3–4.

215

SAHARA MUSTARD
Brassica tournefortii Gouan
Mustard Family (Brassicaceae)

Description: The high-branched, stiff-hairy, 4–40"-tall stems of this annual have a basal rosette of dark-green, pinnately lobed leaves up to 12" long. The leaves get smaller up the stem till only tiny bracts are present within the racemose inflorescence. The 4-parted, pale-yellow, ⅓"-long flowers are on pedicels that are longer than the sepals. The elongated fruits have a narrow beak on the end, and they have 2 rows of seeds in each chamber.

Bloom Season: January to June

Habitat/Range: This species has invaded disturbed soils in the Mojave and Sonoran Deserts and throughout southern California and the San Joaquin Valley, to southern Nevada, Texas, and Baja California, Mexico. It is now found in sandy soils in undisturbed sites, and it sometimes occupies rockier soils when there are seasons with adequate rain.

Comments: The extremely invasive nature of Sahara mustard is due to uprooted plants spreading their seeds while tumbling in the wind, as well as animal dispersal. It rapidly moves into recently burned sites, where it provides biomass that increases fire frequency and depletes soil of nutrients. So far, efforts at control are inadequate; it thrives after prescribed burning, and it covers too much area for hand-pulling to be practical. Biological control would likely have negative impacts on crop species of *Brassica*, including broccoli, cauliflower, Brussels sprouts, and cabbage.

YELLOW PEPPER-GRASS
Lepidium flavum Torrey var. *flavum*
Mustard Family (Brassicaceae)

Description: This 2–16"-tall, hairless, yellow-green annual often grows flat on the ground with stem tips upturned. The pinnately lobed, 1–2"-long, spoon-shaped leaves are in a basal rosette, with smaller, toothed leaves toward the stem tip. The tiny flowers have 4 separate, bright-yellow petals, 4 greenish-yellow sepals, and 6 stamens. The flattened, ovate fruit has 2 wing-like projections near the notch at the top.

Bloom Season: March to May

Habitat/Range: Yellow pepper-grass occurs in alkaline flats, playas, puddles, and washes below 4,500' in creosote bush scrub and Joshua tree woodland in the western, central, and northern Mojave Desert. It is especially abundant in Death Valley, Lucerne Valley, and around Lancaster. It is uncommon in the Sonoran Desert. Its range extends to Nevada and Baja California, Mexico.

Comments: This plant has a spicy flavor and odor similar to many members of the mustard family, especially watercress. It is a source of carvacrol, a phenolic compound also found in the extracted oils of oregano, thyme, wild bergamot, and other species. Carvacrol is known to have strong anti-oxidant, anticancer, and antimicrobial activities. However, there have been no human trials, so there are no clinical uses yet.

BEADPOD, BLADDERPOD
Physaria tenella (A. Nelson) O'Kane & Al-Shehbaz
Mustard Family (Brassicaceae)

Description: This annual has several ascending, branched, 4–24"-long stems with 1–2½"-long, entire or coarsely toothed or lobed basal leaves, and shorter, linear to inversely lanceolate stem leaves. The showy, bright-yellow flowers are produced in 3–8"-long clusters on the upper stems. Each flower has 4 sepals and 4 rounded, ¼–½"-long petals that taper to a claw-like base. The plump, spherical, ⅛" fruits are on ½"-long, S-shaped stalks, and the reddish-brown, flattened seeds have a narrow wing on the margin. The entire plant, including the fruit, is densely covered with stellate hairs.

Bloom Season: March to May

Habitat/Range: Beadpod grows in sandy areas below 3,500' in the eastern Mojave Desert and northeastern Sonoran Desert. Its range extends to southwestern Utah, southern Nevada, New Mexico, and to northern Sonora and Baja California, Mexico.

Comments: The seeds of *Physaria* species contain abundant hydroxy fatty acids, like those found in castor oil, which are used in plastics, biofuels, pharmaceuticals, cosmetics, and more. Since castor bean is no longer grown in the United States due to its toxic ricin content, castor oil is imported, but *P. fendleri*, with a range extending into the Mojave Desert in northwestern Arizona, is rapidly being developed as a replacement.

PRINCE'S PLUME
Stanleya pinnata (Pursh) Britton var. *pinnata*
Mustard Family (Brassicaceae)

Description: Prince's plume is a 16–60"-tall perennial with a thick, branched, woody base. The hairless, 2–6"-long lower leaves have deep pinnate lobes, while the upper leaves are shorter and mostly entire. Showy, yellow flowers are produced in 4–12"-long clusters on upper stems. Each ½–¾"-long flower has 4 sepals, 4 petals, and 6 stamens. The petals taper into claws with dense, long, wavy hairs on the inside surfaces.

Bloom Season: April to September

Habitat/Range: Prince's plume is found in washes and on slopes from 1,000 to 7,500' in creosote bush scrub, Joshua tree woodland, and pinyon-juniper woodland throughout the Mojave Desert and many western states.

Comments: Prince's plume accumulates soil selenium to levels that are toxic to livestock and humans. The Paiute and Shoshone consumed young stems and leaves, but the plants had to be repeatedly boiled, rinsed, and squeezed, and the first cooking water was discarded. The plants were then dried and boiled again later when needed, effectively reducing the toxins to a safe level. Livestock seem to avoid consuming this plant. The similar Panamint plume (*S. elata*) has entire leaves and is not a selenium accumulator.

LONGBEAK STREPTANTHELLA
Streptanthella longirostris (S. Watson) Rydb.
Mustard Family (Brassicaceae)

Description: This slender, branched annual has entire leaves, the lower up to 2" long, and the upper, smaller and sessile. The flowers, produced on short pedicels, have 4 green, erect sepals with purple tips, 2 of them enlarged at the base. The 4 petals are up to ¼" long, yellowish to white with purplish veins, clawed or spoon-shaped, and often with wavy margins. There are 6 stamens, with 2 shorter than the other 4. The reflexed fruits are linear, flattened siliques that open near the tip, and they have a narrow, ⅛–¼"-long beak.

Bloom Season: March to June

Habitat/Range: Often abundant around shrub bases and in sandy washes and flats below 6,000' in creosote bush scrub, Joshua tree woodland, and pinyon-juniper woodland in the Mojave, Sonoran, and Great Basin Deserts to Washington, Colorado, New Mexico, and Baja California, Mexico. It is also found in the southern San Joaquin Valley and southern Coast Ranges.

Comments: This is a monotypic genus, meaning it has only one species. It was once placed in the genus *Streptanthus*, but it lacks the wavy petal margins typical of that genus, and *Streptanthus* species lack the fruit beak.

COTTON-TOP

Echinocactus polycephalus Engelm. & J. M. Bigelow var. *polycephalus*
Cactus Family (Cactaceae)

Description: Each plant consists of a clump of 10–30 rounded to cylindrical, 10–21-ribbed, 1–2'-tall stems, which are 8–14" in diameter. They have 3–4 central, 2–3"-long spines that are fuzzy when young, but as they mature they become red or gray and flattened, with crosswise markings. There are also 6–8 similar but shorter radial spines. The 1–2"-long yellow flowers are produced at the top of the stems, surrounded by woolly fibers. The ¾–1½"-long, densely woolly fruits, which contain angled seeds, persist on the plant for a year, or longer.

Bloom Season: March to August

Habitat/Range: Occupies rocky slopes and ridges from 2,000 to 5,000' in creosote bush scrub and saltbush scrub communities from the central and northern Mojave Desert and Sonoran Desert to northwestern Sonora, Mexico.

Comments: Native Americans ate the seeds, applied baked and ground-up plants to burns, and used the thick spines as needles and boring tools. Grand Canyon cottontop (*Echinocactus polycephalus* var. *xeranthemoides*) is found from just southwest of Lake Mead, where it hybridizes with *E. polycephalus* var. *polycephalus*, and across northern Arizona to the Flagstaff area. It has shorter stems and fewer stems per clump.

CALIFORNIA BARREL CACTUS, VISNAGA

Ferocactus cylindraceus (Engelm.) Orc.
Cactus Family (Cactaceae)

Description: The massive, unbranched, columnar, 2–9'-tall stem of the barrel cactus has 18–27 longitudinal ribs that are almost obscured by dense spines of varying colors. Some have crosswise rings or markings; these are 3–8" long and curved. The showy, 1–2½"-long yellow flowers are produced in a circle at the top of the barrel. The green, 1¼"-long fruits have pitted seeds.

Bloom Season: April to May

Habitat/Range: Occurs on fractured, rocky soils and upper alluvial and gravelly slopes, canyon walls, and wash margins in creosote bush scrub. Its range is the eastern and southern Mojave Desert and the Sonoran Desert to coastal Sonora and Baja California, Mexico.

Comments: This plant is highly adapted to drought and heat but can't tolerate cold. It occurs on south-facing slopes in the northern parts of its range, with its body tilting south. After rain, special "rain roots" increase water uptake while it is available, but these roots die after the soil water reaches a critical low level. The plant has crassulacean acid metabolism (CAM photosynthesis), opening its stomates at night to minimize water loss. The succulent stems store water and stem ribs allow the stem to expand with water availability; up to 80 percent of stem water can be lost and it will still remain alive.

DESERT PINCUSHION, FRINGE-FLOWERED CACTUS

Escobaria chlorantha (Engelm.) Buxb.
Cactus Family (Cactaceae)

Description: The cylindrical stems of the fringe-flowered cactus occur singly or sometimes in small clumps. Each stem has inconspicuous ribs and is 3–6" tall and up to 3½" wide. Each areole has fewer than 8 straight, white central spines with dark tips and 12–20 slender, straight, white radial spines that nearly conceal the stem surface. The straw-colored to yellow-orangish flowers are produced in a circular pattern at the tops of stems. The outer flower segments have fringed margins, and the erect to ascending stigma lobes are white to green.

Bloom Season: April to May

Habitat/Range: This variety of foxtail cactus is found on limestone soil from 3,000 to 7,500' in the mountains of the eastern Mojave Desert in California, Nevada, southwestern Utah, and northwestern Arizona.

Comments: This cactus is easily recognized when in bloom, as it is the only one of this stature with this unusual flower color. This genus was named for Rómulo and Numa Escobar, authors and teachers who promoted agricultural development in Mexico in the late 19th century.

CLUB CHOLLA, MAT CHOLLA, HORSE CRIPPLER, DEAD CACTUS
Grusonia parishii (Orcutt) Pinkava
Cactus Family (Cactaceae)

Description: The main stems of the densely spiny club cholla creep flat on the ground, forming mats that are 4–6" high and up to 6' across. The erect, club-shaped, terminal pads are narrow at the base and thicker at the apex. Each areole has 1 broad, 1½" central spine flanked by a ring of rounded spines that are nearly the same length. Shorter, slender spines and glochids surround these. Yellow flowers with 1"-long petals and green filaments are produced atop the terminal pads, followed by club-shaped, yellowish-green, 1½–3"-long fruits with yellow glochids.

Bloom Season: May to June

Habitat/Range: Club cholla is found in very dry, sandy, flat areas from 3,000 to 5,000' in creosote bush scrub and Joshua tree woodland. It occurs in the southern and eastern Mojave Desert, from the Little San Bernardino Mountains to Clark Mountain, western Nevada, and southern Arizona.

Comments: This plant is often overlooked, not only because it grows low to the ground, but also because it looks dead most of the time. When conditions are favorable, the new growth will have reddish spines, but older growth looks dehydrated and lifeless. Keep a wary eye out for this species. It's called "horse crippler" for a reason! Repeat photography has shown that patches of this plant can live for more than 80 years.

PANCAKE-PEAR
Opuntia chlorotica Engelm. & J. M. Bigelow
Cactus Family (Cactaceae)

Description: The pancake-pear is unique among the flat-jointed cacti in that it grows up to 7½' tall, and it is quite obvious with its light-yellowish-green, circular, 5–8" pads. Each areole has numerous yellowish, ¼"-long glochids and 3–6 straw-colored spines that are approximately 1–2" long and pointed downward. Large, yellow blossoms are produced on the edges of pads, followed by 1½–2" rounded, spineless, rose-colored fruits, which linger on the plant long after their production.

Bloom Season: May or June

Habitat/Range: The pancake-pear occurs in rocky areas and canyons in creosote bush scrub, Joshua tree woodland, and pinyon-juniper woodland from the Mojave National Preserve in the eastern Mojave Desert to southern Nevada, northwestern Arizona, and New Mexico to northern Sonora, Mexico. It is also found from Rattlesnake Canyon on the east-facing, desert slope of the San Bernardino Mountains, south through the Peninsular Ranges of southern California to Baja California, Mexico.

Comments: A study showed that the pads facing north–south in early spring and winter had more than twice as much light available for photosynthesis than pads oriented in other directions. Other Mojave Desert cacti with flattened pads include the brown-spined prickly-pear (*O. phaecantha*) and Engelmann prickly-pear (*O. engelmannii*). Both are usually shorter and more spreading than pancake-pear, both have short spines (glochids) on the fruits, and both have pads that are more ovate than those of pancake-pear.

OLD MAN CACTUS, MOJAVE PRICKLY-PEAR

Opuntia polyacantha var. *erinacea* (Engelm. & J. M. Bigelow) B. D. Parfitt
Cactus Family (Cactaceae)

Description: The clumped stems of this cactus are generally less than 1½' tall and 3" wide, with flattened, 2–7"-long, elliptical pads. The numerous spines are white to grayish and bent downward, suggesting a bearded appearance and giving the plant one of its common names of "old man cactus." Yellow flowers with white filaments and green stigmas are produced on the upper edges of pads. The dry, short-spiny, 1–1½"-long fruits contain ¼", cream-colored seeds.

Bloom Season: May to June

Habitat/Range: Found in dry, gravelly, and rocky areas from 1,500 to 8,000' in creosote bush scrub, Joshua tree woodland, and pinyon-juniper woodland on the north slopes of the San Bernardino Mountains and in mountains of the eastern and northern Mojave Desert to Washington, New Mexico, and northwestern Sonora, Mexico. It also occurs in the Peninsular Mountains of southern California to northern Baja California, Mexico.

Comments: This plant is found at relatively high elevations, suggesting that it may be somewhat hardy in cold temperatures. The varietal name, *erinacea*, is from the Latin word for "hedgehog."

BLADDERPOD

Cleomella arborea (Nutt. ex Torr. & A. Gray) Roalson & J. C. Hall var. *arborea*
Spiderflower Family (Cleomaceae)

Description: This malodorous, 2–5'-tall shrub bears alternate, green leaves with 3 elliptic, ½–2"-long leaflets. The ½–¾"-long flowers are produced in clusters at the tops of branches, each with 4 partially fused green sepals, 4 bright-yellow petals, and protruding stamens. The 1–2"-long fruit is a smooth, leathery, inflated capsule on a stalk-like receptacle.

Bloom Season: Flowers can be found on bladderpod almost any time of year, even when there has been little rain.

Habitat/Range: Found on roadsides, washes, and flat areas below 4,000' in the western Mojave and Colorado Deserts to Baja California, Mexico.

Comments: Look for the orange and black harlequin bugs (*Murgantia histrionica*), which is one of the few insects able to tolerate bladderpod's secondary compounds. In addition, the yellow to orange eggs of Becker's white butterfly (*Pieris beckeri*) are often seen on the fruits and foliage.

223

MOJAVE STINKWEED

Cleomella obtusifolia Torrey & Frémont
Spiderflower Family (Cleomaceae)

Description: The branched stems of this hairy annual spread to form rounded, 3–6"-tall mats. The compound leaves have 3 obovate, ¼–½"-long leaflets. The dark-yellow, 4-parted, ¼"-long flowers are produced singly on ¼–½" stalks on younger plants and in dense clusters at the ends of branches of older plants. The sepals have hairs on the margins. The odd fruit looks like 2 cones stuck together on a long stalk.

Bloom Season: April to October

Habitat/Range: Mojave stinkweed occurs in sandy and alkaline areas, roadsides, and the edges of playas below 4,000' in creosote bush scrub and Joshua tree woodland throughout the Mojave Desert. It also is found in the Colorado Desert and Inyo County, California.

Comments: Members of this family often contain secondary compounds to prevent herbivory called glucosinolates, which are converted to mustard oils when plant parts are crushed. Most members of this family should be considered toxic, especially after a study showing destructive effects of a related species on the kidneys of sheep and goats. However, the caper (*Capparis spinosa*) is the pungent-tasting, pickled flower bud of another related genus from the Mediterranean region, possibly the only edible member of this family.

DESERT LIVE-FOREVER

Dudleya saxosa subsp. *aloides* (Rose) Moran
Stonecrop Family (Crassulaceae)

Description: This perennial produces a basal rosette of 10–25 succulent, lanceolate, 1½–6"-long leaves that remain on the plant all year, even though they may dehydrate and shrivel in summer. The pinkish-red flower stalk is up to 20" tall, bearing a branched cluster of flowers, each with 5 pink, pointy sepals and 5 yellow to greenish-yellow, ⅓–½"-long petals that are fused at the bases. The terminal branches of the flower cluster are wavy.

Bloom Season: May to June

Habitat/Range: Occurs in crevices on rocky, dry, sheltered slopes at elevations from 3,500 to 7,000' in creosote bush scrub, Joshua tree woodland, and pinyon-juniper woodland in the mountains of the central, eastern, and southern Mojave Desert and also in the San Jacinto and Laguna Mountains to Baja California, Mexico.

Comments: The rarer Panamint dudleya (*D. saxosa* subsp. *saxosa*) is generally smaller with narrower stems, shorter inflorescences, and non-wavy terminal branches. The flowers are yellow, tinged with red. It is endemic to granite and limestone slopes of the Panamint Mountains, but it is not threatened at this time. This genus was named in honor of William Russell Dudley (1849–1911), the first botany professor at Stanford University.

COYOTE MELON
Cucurbita palmata S. Watson
Gourd Family (Cucurbitaceae)

Description: This sprawling, coarse, roughened, perennial vine bears alternate, dark-bluish-green, palmately 5-lobed leaves up to 6" long and wide with grayish-white patches around larger veins. Opposite each leaf is a well-developed, branched tendril. Separate male and female flowers are produced in leaf axils on the same plant, the females on shorter peduncles and the males on longer ones. The large, deep-yellow, 5-lobed, bell-shaped corolla is around 2½–3" long and has triangular lobes. The very bitter, spherical, 3–3½"-diameter fruit is dull green or yellow with vague white markings and stripes; these dry out quickly, leaving their tan to white, hardened shells with bleached seeds littering the desert.

Bloom Season: April to September

Habitat/Range: Occasionally found in dry, sandy soils below 4,000' in the Mojave and Sonoran Deserts, the southern San Joaquin Valley, and throughout much of southwestern California to Arizona and northern Mexico.

Comments: Solitary squash bees (genera *Peponapis* and *Xenoglossa*), which depend on *Cucurbita* pollen for nutrition, show up in the flowers on the day they bloom. This species and its closest relatives, *C. digitata*, *C. cordata*, and *C. cylindrata*, are drought-adapted, with large, tough storage taproots and a perennial life cycle, and they all are capable of vegetative reproduction. Unlike their cultivated relatives, the seeds of these four also have punicic acid, an unusual polyunsaturated fatty acid with antidiabetic, antiobesity, and anticancer properties. It is also found in pomegranate seeds and in the Chinese cucumber (*Trichosanthes kirilowii*), which has been used for centuries in traditional Chinese medicine.

DUNE SPURGE

Euphorbia ocellata Durand & Hilg. subsp. *arenicola*
(Parish) Oudejans
Spurge Family (Euphorbiaceae)

Description: This hairless annual has prostrate
to ascending stems with opposite, lanceolate,
somewhat sessile leaves with thread-like stipules.
Each node has 1 inflorescence with 5 cup-like,
yellow, somewhat petal-like glands surrounding
40–60 male flowers (each consisting of a stamen),
which in turn surround 1 female flower on a stalk.
In fruit, the female part has 3 pronounced lobes
and a noticeable 3-forked style.

Bloom Season: May to September

Habitat/Range: Occupies sandy soils, especially
dunes, below 2,600' at scattered locations in the
Mojave Desert, including the Mojave National Preserve and Death Valley National Park, to western
and southern Nevada and southwestern Utah. It
has also been collected from the Coachella Valley
in the Sonoran Desert and from the San Joaquin
Valley.

Comments: All of the prostrate spurges were, for
a while (in previous editions of this book), placed
in a separate genus, *Chamaecyse*, because of
their prostrate growth form and C4 heat-efficient
photosynthesis. However, they have once again
been merged into the genus *Euphorbia*.

MOJAVE SPURGE

Euphorbia schizoloba Engelm.
Spurge Family (Euphorbiaceae)

Description: This erect, hairless, 4–16"-tall perennial has sessile, ovate, ¼–¾"-long leaves with
pointed tips. What looks like 1 flower is actually
a cluster of 1 female and several male flowers.
Below each flower cluster are 5 small bracts,
which are fused into a bell-shaped involucre.
These have crescent-shaped, yellow glands with
scalloped edges.

Bloom Season: March to May

Habitat/Range: Mojave spurge is found on slopes,
canyons, and rocky places above 3,000' in creosote
bush scrub, Joshua tree woodland, and pinyon-
juniper woodland in the mountains of the eastern
Mojave Desert to southern Nevada and central
Arizona.

Comments: Juba II, king of Mauretania and son-in-
law of Antony and Cleopatra, named this genus for
his Greek doctor, Euphorbus. Juba was supposedly
delighted by the play on words this represented,
since Euphorbus meant "well-fed": The plant being
named (*Euphorbia resinifera*) was fat and succulent, and his doctor was corpulent!

STIFF-HAIRED LOTUS
Acmispon strigosus (Nutt.) Brouillet
Pea Family (Fabaceae)

Description: This prostrate, branching, slender-stemmed, somewhat fleshy annual has stiff, flattened hairs. The pinnately divided, ½–1"-long leaves have 4–9 obovate, alternate leaflets on a flattened rachis. The stalked flower clusters bear 1–3 yellow "pea" flowers that are less than ½" long. The ½–1½"-long fruit is compressed and curved near the tip, and it has sparse, flattened hairs.

Bloom Season: March to June

Habitat/Range: Stiff-haired lotus is common on sandy flats, alluvial slopes, roadsides, and disturbed areas below 7,500' from central California to Baja California, Mexico. Its range includes both the Mojave and Sonoran Deserts to Arizona and Sonora, Mexico.

Comments: Under normal conditions, this plant forms root nodules with bacteria that fix nitrogen, changing it into a usable form for plant uptake. Researchers found that when high levels of nitrogen are deposited in soil from air pollutants, this species' root nodules may fail to develop. This could eventually lead to plant mortality and other negative ecosystem effects.

DESERT ROCK-PEA
Acmispon rigidus (Benth.) Brouillet
Pea Family (Fabaceae)

Description: The erect, firm, branched stems of this 1–4'-tall, somewhat straggly looking perennial are woody at the base. The stem internodes are far longer than the sparse, pinnately divided leaves with 3–5 narrow leaflets, so the plant may seem to be nearly leafless. The yellow, ½–¾"-long "pea" flowers are produced on 1–2½" stalks in umbel-like clusters of 1–3; these may become orange-tinged with age. The straight, hairless, 1½", narrow fruits are erect or spreading.

Bloom Season: March to May, even in the driest years

Habitat/Range: Desert rock-pea is found on dry slopes and in washes below 6,000' in creosote bush scrub, Joshua tree woodland, and pinyon-juniper woodland. It occurs in the southern, eastern, and northern Mojave Desert to Inyo County, California, and in the Sonoran Desert throughout Arizona to Sonora and Baja California, Mexico.

Comments: The roots of desert rock-pea form nodules that house nitrogen-fixing bacteria. The genus name is from the Greek *acme* for "apex," likely referring to the pointed tip of the fruit.

PIG-NUT, HOG POTATO
Hoffmannseggia glauca (Ortega) Eifert
Pea Family (Fabaceae)

Description: This erect annual can grow to 12" tall from deep, tuberous roots. The 2–4¾"-long leaves are bipinnately compound with up to 13 secondary leaflets that tend to fold along the secondary rachis. This orients the leaflets somewhat vertically, giving the pinnae a V-shape. The 2–9"-long, glandular-hairy inflorescence bears showy, bilaterally symmetrical flowers with 5 bright-yellow, spreading, clawed petals with orange to brownish, glandular hairs along the lower margins. There are 10 reddish stamens that protrude forward together, and the pollen is yellow. The fruit is a curved legume up to 1½" long.

Bloom Season: April to June

Habitat/Range: Found occasionally in seasonally wet alkali flats and disturbed habitats below 3,000' in the Pahrump Valley, the Mojave National Preserve, and in Joshua Tree National Park and vicinity in the Mojave Desert. It also occurs in the Sonoran and Chihuahuan Deserts and has a large range across the southwestern United States from southern and central California to Colorado and central Texas. Disjunct populations are also found in southwestern South America.

Comments: The small, potato-like tubers can be eaten if roasted first. This genus is named for Johann Centurius von Hoffmannsegg (1766–1849) a German botanist, ornithologist, and entomologist. He collected plants extensively in Europe and wrote a flora of Portugal. He also established the Zoological Museum in Berlin. A genus of orchid, *Hoffmannseggella*, was also named for him.

HONEY MESQUITE
Neltuma odorata (Torrey & Frém.) C. E. Hughes & G. P. Lewis
Pea Family (Fabaceae)

Description: This deciduous shrub or small tree with arched branches can grow to over 20' tall, and the taproot can reach 100' deep. It has alternate, bright-green, pinnately divided leaves with 1 or 2 pairs of opposite primary leaflets, each with 18–36 linear secondary leaflets that are up to 1" long. There are one or two 1½" spines at each node. The small, cream-colored flowers are produced in dense, slender, 2–4"-long spikes, followed by 3–8"-long pods that are somewhat constricted between the seeds.

Bloom Season: April to June

Habitat/Range: Honey mesquite is common in washes, alkali seeps, dunes, and flats below 5,000' in the Mojave and Sonoran Deserts to the upper San Joaquin Valley, Texas, Louisiana, and Mexico.

Comments: Native Americans relied on honey mesquite for shade and firewood. Fresh green pods were roasted over hot stones or eaten raw as snacks. Hardened mounds of mashed pods were stored, and caches of whole, dried pods have been found in caves. Screwbean or tornillo (*Strombocarpa pubescens*) can be distinguished by its coiled pods.

CATCLAW, WAIT-A-MINUTE BUSH
Senegalia greggii (A. Gray) Britton & Rose
Pea Family (Fabaceae)

Description: This plant can grow as a shrub or as a tree up to 20' tall. The stems bear curved spines resembling cat claws, giving it its common name and entangling the unwary. The twice-pinnate leaves have 2–3 pairs of primary leaflets and 10 pairs of ¼"-long secondary leaflets. Dense, cylindrical, 1½"-long spikes of tiny, light-yellow flowers are produced with the leaves on short branchlets, followed by narrow, flattened, ¼–¾"-long pods that are constricted between the seeds.

Bloom Season: April to June

Habitat/Range: Catclaw is common in canyons and washes, as well as on rocky slopes and flats, below 6,000' in creosote bush scrub, Joshua tree woodland, and pinyon-juniper woodland. It occurs in the eastern and southern Mojave Desert and the Sonoran Desert to Texas, and to Sonora and Baja California, Mexico.

Comments: The genus *Senegalia* was recently separated from *Acacia* on the basis of molecular data. Unlike many members of this family, this species does not seem to form nodules for nitrogen-fixing bacteria. This species is named in honor of Josiah Gregg (1806–1850), an unpopular frontier trader, author, gold seeker, and part-time naturalist who sent botanical specimens to George Engelmann, an eminent botanist from St. Louis, Missouri. Gregg died young after being stranded in a redwood forest during a wet winter.

DESERT SENNA, SPINY SENNA
Senna armata (S. Watson) H. Irwin & Barneby
Pea Family (Fabaceae)

Description: This 2–5'-tall, rounded shrub has yellow-green, hairless, furrowed stems. The pinnately divided leaves, with 2–4 pairs of opposite, ¼" leaflets, appear only after rain, so the plant is often leafless. The leaf axis elongates into a weak, green spine after the leaflets fall. The bright-yellow, 5-parted, ⅓–½"-long flowers are produced in 2–6" clusters at the branch ends and in groups of 1–2 in leaf axils. The spongy, lanceolate, 1–1¾" fruits split apart to release the few seeds they contain.

Bloom Season: April and May

Habitat/Range: Desert senna is locally common in sandy and gravelly washes and in open areas below 3,000' in creosote bush scrub in both the Mojave and Sonoran Deserts.

Comments: This is a host plant for larvae of the cloudless sulfur (*Phoebis sennae*), a bright-yellow butterfly with brownish, circular spots on the underwings. Tea made from Middle Eastern *Senna* species has been used as a laxative for centuries. Since it is difficult to control the amounts of the active ingredient while concocting a tea, pharmaceutical companies have made it available over the counter with standardized amounts of these ingredients. It is not known whether *S. armata* is cathartic, but do *not* try it—*Senna* overdose has resulted in liver toxicity and coma.

WHISPERING BELLS
Emmenanthe penduliflora Benth.
Waterleaf Family (Hydrophyllaceae)

Description: The erect, branched, 4–20"-tall stems of this sticky-hairy, malodorous annual have short-petioled basal leaves and sessile cauline leaves, all deeply pinnately lobed with a linear to oblong outline. The branching inflorescence has pale-yellow, bell-shaped, ¼–¾"-long flowers that droop in bud. There are 5 stamens and a 2-lobed style, neither of which protrude from the flower. The fruit is a dry, ¼"-long capsule with 6–15 brownish, flat seeds with a honeycomb surface texture.

Bloom Season: April to July

Habitat/Range: Occurs on sandy soils and decomposed granite below 7,000'. It is widespread throughout the Mojave Desert and much of California to Arizona, Nevada, and southwestern Utah.

Comments: Whispering bell seeds taken from chaparral plants have been shown to germinate most readily when exposed to charred remains of chamise (*Adenostema fasciculatum*); however, chamise is not present in the desert. When the researchers tested whispering bell seeds taken from desert plants, scarification—or the physical scratching of the seed coat—was the most important factor in determining germination rate; scarification in the desert populations is likely accomplished by the seeds scraping against the coarse sand particles of desert soils.

WHITE-STEMMED STICK-LEAF
Mentzelia albicaulis Hook.
Loasa Family (Loasaceae)

Description: This highly variable, 2–16"-tall, white-stemmed annual has barbed hairs and a basal rosette of leaves with narrow, pinnate, pointed lobes. The upper leaves are usually smaller and entire to lobed. The bright-yellow flowers are less than ½" long, and they have 5 separate, ovate petals with pointed tips. The narrow, tapered, ½–1"-long fruit is straight, with 2–3 rows of seeds in the upper half. The seed surfaces are sculptured with pointed bumps and sharp angles.

Bloom Season: March to June

Habitat/Range: Common in a variety of habitats below 7,000' in both the Mojave and Sonoran Deserts and throughout western North America to Colorado, British Columbia, and Baja California, Mexico.

Comments: Native Americans used the seeds to make a paste similar to peanut butter. Many small-flowered, annual *Mentzelia* species occur in the Mojave Desert, and they are difficult to identify. *M. obscura* differs from *M. albicaulis* in that the seed surfaces have rounded bumps and rounded angles, and *M. affinis* has seeds with grooved angles that are in 1 row in the upper half of the fruit.

SOLITARY BLAZING STAR
Mentzelia eremophila (Jeps.) H. J. Thomps. & J. E. Roberts
Loasa Family (Loasaceae)

Description: This handsome annual has erect, stout, branched stems up to 17" tall. The deeply pinnately lobed leaves are up to 6" long at the base and are reduced in length up the stem. The showy flowers, which open in the morning, have 5 pointy, green sepals, 5 separate, yellow, ½–1"-long petals with mucronate tips, and numerous stamens. The fruit is a narrow, curved, cone-shaped, fibrous, ¾–1½"-long capsule that often splits longitudinally into 3 pieces.

Bloom Season: March to May

Habitat/Range: Occurs on canyon slopes and in washes below 4,000' in the western and north-western Mojave Desert, especially in Red Rock Canyon State Park.

Comments: Dwarf mentzelia (*Mentzelia pumila*) is an interesting relative, also with pinnately lobed leaves. The hooked, Velcro-like hairs covering this plant are so protective that insects, particularly flies, are commonly observed to be entangled and pierced, their dead corpses strewn about the plant. It occupies sandy soils on slopes, flats, and in washes up to 8,000' from Montana to northern Mexico, with a small part of its range reaching into the Mojave Desert from St. George, Utah, to northeastern Arizona. It flowers from February to October.

SAND BLAZING STAR

Mentzelia involucrata S. Watson
Loasa Family (Loasaceae)

Description: This erect, sandpaper-textured, branched annual grows to 18" tall. The basal rosette leaves are toothed or lobed, while the stem leaves are lanceolate and alternate. The ½–2½"-long, funnel-shaped flowers have numerous stamens, 3 stigma lobes, and red-veined, cream-colored to yellowish petals that narrow to a point at the tip. There are 4–5 white bracts fringed with green margins that surround the flower bases, hiding the sepals. The fruit is a tapered, ½–1"-long capsule.

Bloom Season: February to April

Habitat/Range: Occurs on steep, rocky banks, slopes, and washes below 4,000' in creosote bush scrub in the southern, eastern, and northern Mojave Desert to southern Nevada and north-eastern Arizona. In the western Mojave, it is only known from areas around Red Rock Canyon State Park. It is widespread in the Sonoran Desert to Baja California and Sonora, Mexico.

Comments: Like all members of the loasa family, the foliage of this plant has minutely barbed hairs that cling to clothing like Velcro. The plant is pollinated by oligolectic bees (specialists on a genus or narrow group of plants), including *Perdita koebelei* and *Xeralictus bicuspidariae*, and occasionally by hawk moths.

ADONIS BLAZING STAR

Mentzelia longiloba J. Darl. var. *longiloba*
Loasa Family (Loasaceae)

Description: This branched, often hairless biennial to short-lived perennial has erect stems up to 3' tall. The dark-green leaves in the basal rosette are shallowly pinnately scalloped or lobed, and those along the stem are alternate, sessile, pinnately lobed, and sometimes toothed. The flowers, which open in late afternoon, have 5 green sepals and 5 separate, up-to-1"-long, golden-yellow petals with rounded tips. The stamens are unusual in that the filament width grades from narrow in the center to the outer ones being wider and nearly petal-like. The fruit is a short, cylindrical capsule containing flattened seeds with wide, white wings.

Bloom Season: March to June

Habitat/Range: Found on fine-sandy soils and dunes below 3,200' within creosote bush scrub from the central Mojave Desert to Arizona, Utah, Colorado, and Texas. Its range extends to the Sonoran and Chihuahuan Deserts of northern Mexico and northern Baja California, Mexico.

Comments: This genus was named for Christian Mentzel (1622–1701), a German physician, botanist, and student of Chinese history and culture. Over 20 of the 95 known species of *Mentzelia* occur in the Mojave Desert.

SHINING BLAZING STAR
Mentzelia nitens Greene
Loasa Family (Loasaceae)

Description: This annual is decumbent to erect with spreading branches, and it can grow up to 13" tall. The basal rosette leaves are somewhat narrow with short, rounded lobes, while the upper leaves are alternate and mostly entire, although some might have a few sharp lobes. The flowers, which open in the morning, have sessile, green bracts below and 5 green sepals less than ¼" long. The obovate petals, which are up to ⅔" long, are bright-yellow with orange at the base, and they often have a hint of a crinkly texture and a mucronate tip. The fruit is a curved, ½–1"-long capsule with irregular-shaped, bumpy, mottled, tan seeds that have a conspicuous flap over the attachment scar.

Bloom Season: April to June

Habitat/Range: Occurs on roadsides and flats from 1,500 to 7,000' in creosote bush scrub and Joshua tree woodland in both the Mojave and Sonoran Deserts to western Nevada. Its range barely extends into the Great Basin Desert in the upper Owens Valley. It often grows up through other shrubs.

Comments: Reported ethnobotanical uses of *Mentzelia* species include eating the seeds and using the roots for arthritis, fever, stomachache, bruises and swellings, and thirst prevention.

CREAMY BLAZING STAR
Mentzelia tridentata (Davidson) H. J. Thomps. & J. E. Roberts
Loasa Family (Loasaceae)

Description: This erect, up-to-6"-tall annual has lanceolate, wavy-margined, or toothed leaves in a basal rosette and along the stem. The flowers, which open in the morning, are surrounded by 4–5 wide, sessile, toothed, green bracts that hide the short sepals. The broad, ovate petals are light-yellow to cream-colored, and they narrow abruptly to a point at the tip. The stamens are so beautiful with their flattened, tri-colored filaments! They are 3-lobed at the tip, the middle bearing the anther. The fruit is a tapered, ½–1"-long capsule.

Bloom Season: April to May

Habitat/Range: Found on talus slopes in creosote bush scrub below 4,000'. It is endemic to the central Mojave Desert, especially around Barstow and extending to Red Rock Canyon State Park, Ridgecrest, and into the lower Owens Valley near Olancha.

Comments: This species was originally described in 1910 by Dr. Anstruther Davidson (1860–1932), a Scottish-born medical doctor who emigrated to the United States and practiced dermatology in Los Angeles. He published papers in medicine, botany, and natural history, and authored the 1923 *Flora of Southern California* with George L. Moxley.

ROUGH MENODORA, BROOM TWINBERRY

Menodora scabra var. *glabrescens* A. Gray
Olive Family (Oleaceae)

Description: This broom-like subshrub has bright-green, erect, wand-like stems that bear simple, alternate, linear to narrowly lanceolate leaves that are up to 1" long, usually longer toward the base of the plant. The showy, ¾–1"-wide yellow flowers are in a terminal panicle, each with 4–6 spreading petals that are fused only near the base. There are two stamens, typical for the olive family, and 5–8 linear calyx lobes that remain attached in fruit. The fruit is a yellowish to pinkish, 2-lobed, circumscissile capsule with 2 seeds in each cell.

Bloom Season: June to July

Habitat/Range: Found in sandy or rocky soils in desert scrub and pinyon-juniper woodland in the eastern and southern Mojave Desert, along the foothills of the peninsular ranges in the western Sonoran Desert to Baja California, Mexico, and east through Arizona and into Sonora, Mexico.

Comments: This species is popular in desert gardening. The genus name, *Menodora*, is derived from the Greek *menos*, for "force" or "courage," and *doron* for "gift," in reference to the force or strength it gives to animals. This genus is found in three widely spaced geographic areas: the southwestern United States and Mexico, southern South America, and South Africa.

MOJAVE SUN CUP, FIELD PRIMROSE

Camissonia campestris (E. Greene) Raven
Evening Primrose Family (Onagraceae)

Description: This branched annual has very slender and somewhat curving, hairless stems with white, peeling epidermis. The alternate, 1"-long leaves are linear to narrowly elliptic with fine-toothed margins. The yellow flowers have 4 separate petals, each with 1–2 red dots at the base, and the 4 sepals are reflexed in pairs. The stigma is positioned above the anthers, and the linear fruits are ¾–1½" long.

Bloom Season: March to May

Habitat/Range: Found in open, sandy areas below 3,000' in creosote bush scrub in the Mojave Desert and in interior southern California to San Diego County.

Comments: This genus was named in honor of Adelbert Ludwig von Chamisso (1781–1838), a botanist on the 1815–1818 expedition aboard the Russian ship, the *Rurik*, which visited California in the early 1800s. He named the California poppy (*Eschscholzia californica*) in honor of his good friend, Dr. Johann Friedrich Gustav von Eschscholtz.

GOLDEN EVENING PRIMROSE

Chylismia brevipes (A. Gray) Small subsp. *brevipes*
Evening Primrose Family (Onagraceae)

Description: This annual produces 1–2'-tall stems from a basal rosette. The 2–6"-long, pinnate leaves have conspicuous red veins on the undersurfaces. Smaller, bract-like leaves may be found up the stem. Yellow, 4-parted flowers with ¼–¾"-long petals are produced in nodding clusters; these open in the morning. The cylindrical, ¾–4"-long, slender fruits contain 2 rows of tiny seeds in each compartment.

Bloom Season: March to May

Habitat/Range: Occurs in washes and on dry slopes below 5,000' in creosote bush scrub and Joshua tree woodland in both the Mojave and Sonoran Deserts to Inyo County, California.

Comments: Golden evening primrose has been known to hybridize occasionally with brown-eyed primrose, a white-petaled species with flowers that open in the evening. The hybrids resemble brown-eyed primrose in size, shape, and habit, but the petals are yellowish. Golden evening primrose has been used to study the effects of increased temperature and carbon dioxide on the photosynthetic rates of desert plants.

YELLOW EVENING PRIMROSE, SPRING EVENING PRIMROSE

Oenothera primiveris A. Gray
Evening Primrose Family (Onagraceae)

Description: This stemless, glandular annual grows from a deep taproot. The entire plant has coarse hairs, sometimes with blistered bases. The ½–5"-long, pinnately lobed or toothed leaves are in a strong basal rosette, and they have petioles about the same length as the blades. Each 4-parted flower has ¼–1½"-long, bright-yellow petals, which fade to an orange or purplish color as they age. The ovate capsules are ½–1" long, square in cross section, and have tiny, wrinkled seeds. Last year's plants remain standing as a stout, 6–10" tall, woody stem.

Bloom Season: March to May

Habitat/Range: Found in dry, sandy areas below 5,000' in creosote bush scrub, Joshua tree woodland, and pinyon-juniper woodland in both the Mojave and Sonoran Deserts to Texas and Sonora, Mexico.

Comments: Plants with grayish-green leaves and 1–1½" petals were previously recognized as subsp. *bufonis*; these cannot self-pollinate. Those with green leaves and ¼–1"-long petals were recognized as the self-pollinated subsp. *primiveris*. Subspecies are no longer recognized in this taxon.

TETRAPTERON, PALMER PRIMROSE

Tetrapteron palmeri (S. Watson) W. L. Wagner & Hoch

Evening Primrose Family (Onagraceae)

Description: A tuft of minutely serrated, up-to-4¼"-long basal leaves arise from the strong taproot of this annual. The short stems have peeling epidermis, and the outer leaves dry up and get crispy early. The yellow, 4-petaled flowers, which open in the early morning, arise singly in axils of the basal rosette. The unusual, somewhat leathery, 4-winged fruits seem too large for the plant.

Bloom Season: April to May

Habitat/Range: Found in open, flat areas in the Mojave Desert and other areas of California to Oregon and Nevada.

Comments: This species was formerly in the genus *Camissonia*, which has now been split into numerous genera, including *Tetrapteron, Chylismia, Eremothera, Camissonia,* and *Camissoniopsis. Tetrapteron* is distinguished by having a very short, if any, stem and winged, 4-angled fruits. *Chylismia* species have pedicelled fruits with 2 rows of seeds per chamber, basal leaves, and conspicuous brown oil cells on the leaves. The genera *Eremothera, Camissonia,* and *Cammisoniopsis* all have sessile fruits with only 1 row of seeds per chamber, but are separated by flower color (*Eremothera* is white, and others, yellow) and by fruit shape (cylindrical fruits in *Camissonia,* and 4-angled fruits in *Camissoniopsis*).

DESERT GOLD-POPPY

Eschscholzia glyptosperma E. Greene

Poppy Family (Papaveraceae)

Description: This slender, 8–12"-tall annual has several leafless stems that grow from a basal rosette of dissected leaves with pointed lobes. Yellow-gold flowers with 4 separate, ½–1"-long petals open from erect buds, and the sepals fall off when the flowers open. The receptacles lack spreading rims. The 1½–2¾"-long, cylindrical capsules have numerous tiny, round, pitted seeds.

Bloom Season: March to May

Habitat/Range: Desert gold-poppy occurs on open flats and slopes below 5,000' in creosote bush scrub and Joshua tree woodland in the Mojave Desert and in the Sonoran Desert.

Comments: Edward L. Greene (1843–1915), who described over 4,400 species of the American West, described this species in 1885 as "a most peculiar species, collected in 1884, by Mrs. Curran [1844–1920], on the Mohave Desert. The seeds are remarkably unlike those of any other known *Eschscholtzia.*"

237

PARISH'S POPPY

Eschscholzia parishii E. Greene
Poppy Family (Papaveraceae)

Description: This slender, hairless, 8–14"-tall annual has leaves dissected into linear lobes with blunt tips. Most leaves are basal, but some are reduced in size up the stem. The yellow flowers, which open from nodding buds, have 4 separate, ½–1¼"-long petals and 24 stamens; the sepals fall off when the flowers open. The receptacles lack spreading rims. The 2–2¾"-long capsules have numerous tiny, tan to brown seeds.

Bloom Season: March to April

Habitat/Range: Found on desert slopes below 4,000' in creosote bush scrub and Joshua tree woodland in the southern Mojave Desert, excluding the desert mountains, and in the Sonoran Desert to northwestern Mexico.

Comments: Five similar taxa include three subspecies of *E. minutiflora*: the widespread Coville's poppy (*E. minutiflora* subsp. *covillei*) with petals to just over ½"; the widespread little gold poppy (*E. minutiflora* subsp. *minutiflora*) with petals up to ¼"; and Red Rock poppy (*E. minutiflora* subsp. *twisselmannii*) with dark filament bases, only found in the El Paso and Rand Mountains. Joshua tree poppy (*E. androuxii*), which has reddish filament bases, is found around Joshua Tree National Park. The cryptic desert poppy (*E. papastillii*) has an expanded, cone-shaped receptacle with a small rim. It occurs from the southern Mojave National Preserve south through Joshua Tree National Park to central Imperial County.

GHOST-FLOWER

Antirrhinum confertiflorum Benth. ex A. DC.
Plantain Family (Plantaginaceae)

Description: This hairy, erect, 4–16"-tall annual has alternate, lanceolate, ½–2½"-long leaves on short stalks. The showy, cream-colored flowers are over 1" long and are sessile in upper leaf axils. They are 2-lipped with a swollen base and constricted throat, and the lower lip has maroon spots. The fruit is a rounded, ½" capsule with dark, tiny seeds.

Bloom Season: March to April

Habitat/Range: Ghost-flower grows in washes and in gravelly and sandy areas below 3,000' in creosote bush scrub. It is primarily a Sonoran Desert species, but it occurs in the southern Mojave Desert at Sheephole Pass, the Bristol Mountains, Rattlesnake Canyon, and near Cleghorn Pass and also in the eastern Mojave.

Comments: There are striking similarities in color, size, and growth form between this species and sand blazing star (*Mentzelia involucrata*), and to a lesser degree, rock nettle (*Eucnide urens*). This is possibly an example of convergent evolution where similar features were favored as plants evolved in the same environment.

TWINING SNAPDRAGON
Antirrhinum filipes A. Gray
Plantain Family (Plantaginaceae)

Description: This hairless annual has very slender, twining stems with opposite, narrow, 1–2"-long leaves. The bright-yellow, 2-lipped, ½"-long flowers with dark-red spots on the lower lip are produced on 1–4"-long, twisted stalks. The thin walls of the 2-chambered fruits rupture to release numerous seeds with 4–6 thick, parallel ridges.

Bloom Season: March to May

Habitat/Range: Twining snapdragon grows through and over small shrubs in sandy soil below 5,000' in creosote bush scrub and Joshua tree woodland in the Mojave Desert to Inyo County, Nevada, and Utah, and in the Sonoran Desert to Sonora, Mexico.

Comments: The type specimen was collected by John S. Newberry (1822–1892) along the bank of the Colorado River, while he served as the expedition physician and geologist for the Colorado River Expedition of 1857–1858. The expedition was commanded by Lt. Joseph Christmas Ives (1829–1868). Ives designed and built a 54'-long steamboat for this trip. He sent it in disassembled form to Robinson's Landing, which was located near the mouth of the Colorado; he later reassembled the boat on-site!

GOLDEN DESERT SNAPDRAGON
Antirrhinum mohavea D. J. Keil
Plantain Family (Plantaginaceae)

Description: This erect, glandular, 2–8"-tall annual has alternate, ovate leaves on short stalks. The deep-yellow flowers have upper and lower flaring, fan-shaped lips and maroon spots on the swollen bases of the lower lip. The corolla encloses 2 fertile stamens, each with 1 anther sac and 2 sterile staminodes. The dry, ovate fruits are ¼–½" long.

Bloom Season: March to April

Habitat/Range: Occurs on sandy and gravelly hillsides and washes below 2,500' in creosote bush scrub in the Mojave Desert east of Daggett and the Ord Mountains to the Sonoran Desert and Baja California, Mexico.

Comments: These flowers look much like cultivated snapdragons (genus *Antirrhinum*), to which they are closely related. However, cultivated snapdragons have 4 stamens, each with 2 anther sacs.

SNAPDRAGON PENSTEMON, YELLOW KECKIELLA

Keckiella antirrhinoides Straw var. *microphylla* (A. Gray) N. Holmgren
Plantain Family (Plantaginaceae)

Description: This erect, 2–8'-tall shrub has spreading branches. The grayish-green, inversely lanceolate, ¼–¾"-long leaves are opposite and often in bundles, due to the development of the axillary buds. The yellow flowers are produced in loose, branched clusters. Each 2-lipped, ½–1"-long flower has an inflated throat and a densely hairy, protruding staminode. The dry, ovate, 2-chambered fruits cling to the plant for a long time after splitting to release the seeds.

Bloom Season: April to June

Habitat/Range: Snapdragon penstemon occurs in rocky soils below 5,000' in mixed creosote scrub, Joshua tree woodland, and pinyon-juniper woodland in the southern and eastern Mojave Desert and the western Sonoran Desert to central Arizona and Baja California, Mexico.

Comments: Snapdragon penstemon is the food plant for the desert mountain checkerspot butterfly (*Euphydryas chalcedona kingstonensis*). These can be seen patrolling canyons in the eastern Mojave Desert in April and sometimes after summer rain. The related Rothrock's keckiella (*K. rothrockii*) is a shorter shrub (to 2' tall) with ¼–½" flowers that occurs in the mountains of the northern and eastern Mojave Desert.

GOLDEN LINANTHUS

Leptosiphon chrysanthus J. M. Porter & R. Patt. subsp. *chrysanthus*
Phlox Family (Polemoniaceae)

Description: The very slender, graceful stems of this 2–6"-tall annual bear sparse, opposite leaves with 3–7 palmately arranged, linear lobes up to ¼" long. The flowers occur singly on slender peduncles. The calyx is deeply cleft into 5 segments that are connected by membrane for around ⅔ of their length. The yellow, funnel-shaped corolla has 5 spreading lobes, an orange or brownish throat, and a hairy ring at the top of the short tube. The hairless stamens are attached above the hairy throat ring, and they have orange pollen. The stigma is 3-parted, and it protrudes from the flower tube.

Bloom Season: March to June

Habitat/Range: Golden linanthus can be locally abundant below 6,000' from desert flats in creosote bush scrub to Joshua tree woodland and pinyon-juniper woodland in both the Mojave and Sonoran Deserts. It is especially abundant on the north slopes of the Transverse Ranges in the western Mojave Desert and into the Los Padres National Forest. It ranges to Utah, New Mexico, and Baja California, Mexico.

Comments: White desert trumpets (*Leptosiphon chrysanthus* var. *decorus*) are similar, but they have white to cream-colored flowers, which may occasionally be lavender-tinged. They occupy some of the range of golden linanthus, but they are absent from the western Mojave Desert.

THORNY MILKWORT
Rhinotropis acanthoclada (A. Gray) J. R. Abbott
Milkwort Family (Polygalaceae)

Description: This spiny, rigid, highly branched, up-to-40"-tall, grayish shrub has twigs covered in short, white, spreading hairs. The alternate, hairy, oblanceolate, ¼–1"-long leaves are on short petioles. The bilaterally symmetrical, nearly ¼"-long flowers superficially resemble pea flowers, with side wings formed by 2 large, yellowish sepals that resemble petals; there are 3 other sepals that are not showy. The 2 upper petals form a yellowish, banner-like structure that is rounded and purplish at the top, and a third petal forms a yellow, boat-shaped structure at the bottom (the keel) that encloses 8 stamens.

Bloom Season: May to August

Habitat/Range: Occurs in the southern Mojave Desert in the Lucerne Valley area and in the eastern Mojave in the Eagle and New York Mountain Ranges to southern Utah and Arizona.

Comments: *Polygala*, the genus to which this plant was formerly assigned, is rich in triterpene saponins, which are being evaluated as potential anti-inflammatory, antidepressant, immunoadjuvant, and anticancer drugs. Some of the isolated compounds hold promise for treatment of neurodegenerative diseases such as Alzheimer's disease.

BRITTLE SPINEFLOWER
Chorizanthe brevicornu Torrey var. *brevicornu*
Buckwheat Family (Polygonaceae)

Description: This erect, 2–20"-tall annual has a forked branching pattern. The lower stems are often reddish, while upper stems, branches, and flower stalks are yellowish-green. When dried, the stems become very brittle. The linear, ¾–3"-long basal rosette leaves wither and crumble early, leaving the plant leafless except for the leaf-like, opposite bracts at the branching points on the stems. In each branch axil, whorls of 6 fused bracts form cylindrical but somewhat ribbed involucres, each with a very tiny flower with yellowish sepals barely protruding from the top.

Bloom Season: March to June

Habitat/Range: Brittle spineflower is found on rocky slopes and gravelly flats below 5,000' in creosote bush scrub and Joshua tree woodland. It occurs in deserts from Mono County to Baja California, Mexico.

Comments: *Chorizanthe brevicornu* var. *spathulata* grows from 5,000 to 7,000' in the desert mountains. Its calyx is not as ribbed, its stems are more reddish, and its leaves are broader than those of var. *brevicornu*. The involucral bracts have curved, sharp teeth that can attach to the fur or skin of small mammals, thus facilitating seed dispersal of this low-to-the-ground plant. Animal dispersal of seeds is called epizoochory.

241

SPINY-HERB
Chorizanthe rigida (Torrey) Torrey & A. Gray
Buckwheat Family (Polygonaceae)

Description: This erect annual grows 1–6" tall. The stalked, broadly elliptic, ¼–1¼"-long leaves occur in a basal rosette as well as on the stems, and they have woolly hairs on the undersurface. As the plant matures, narrow secondary leaves develop into a dense clump of hard thorns. Scattered between thorns are 3-angled tubes (the involucres), with 3 spine-tipped teeth, housing the tiny, yellowish, 6-parted flowers. The thorny, dark-brown, dried plant bodies often remain intact through the following growth season.

Bloom Season: March to May

Habitat/Range: Spiny-herb is common on rocky and gravelly soils below 6,000' in creosote bush scrub in deserts from Baja California, Mexico, north to the Owens Valley. It seems to occupy the most barren habitats and is especially prevalent on desert pavement.

Comments: Fossilized pack-rat midden data record this species in the Marble Mountains between 4,000 and 9,000 years ago, and in the Eureka Valley between 1,500 and 4,000 years ago. Dead spiny-herb can retain its seeds for long periods of time in its dried, hardened involucres; these can then be released gradually when rainfall is sufficient for germination. This condition of delaying seed dispersal is called serotiny. At least 30 serotinous species have been identified from the Mojave and Sonoran Deserts, collectively.

DESERT TRUMPET
Eriogonum inflatum Torrey & Frémont var. *inflatum*
Buckwheat Family (Polygonaceae)

Description: This unique, 4–60"-tall perennial has stout, bluish-green stems that are inflated at the nodes. The upper stems have a forked branching pattern, forming a leafless and hairless, canopied flower cluster. Each small clump of flowers has a cup-shaped whorl of fused bracts below, called the involucre, and each involucre has 5 teeth and its own thin stalk connecting it to the stem. Each tiny flower has 6 yellow sepals with white hairs.

Bloom Season: March to July, and also September to October following summer rain

Habitat/Range: Desert trumpet is very common on gravelly flats and in sandy washes below 6,000' in creosote bush scrub, Joshua tree woodland, blackbush scrub, sagebrush scrub, and pinyon-juniper woodland. It is found in the Mojave and Colorado Deserts and throughout much of the southwestern United States.

Comments: Native Americans used the hollow, inflated stems as pipes. It has been postulated that since the inflated stems hold very high levels of carbon dioxide, they may function to increase photosynthesis rates; however, research has shown that the plant uses this trapped gas 6–10 times slower than it uses carbon dioxide from the external atmosphere. So why are the stems inflated? It appears that the stem is less sensitive to high temperatures and low water availability than leaf tissue, and the stem shape somehow facilitates light reaching the shaded side, so it may be important in maintaining adequate photosynthesis in the late part of the season when water availability is very low and the leaves have withered.

YELLOW TURBANS

Eriogonum pusillum Torr. & A. Gray
Buckwheat Family (Polygonaceae)

Description: The erect, hairless stem of this annual is up to 12" tall. The round to oblong leaves are all basal, with blades up to 1¼" long on petioles of approximately the same length. The undersurfaces are white-woolly, while the upper surfaces may be hairy to nearly hairless. The 2–10"-long inflorescence has hairless branches and erect peduncles, which bear tiny, inverted, cone-shaped involucres with several glandular, yellow, 6-parted flowers.

Bloom Season: March to June

Habitat/Range: Yellow turbans are found up to 10,000' in the Mojave, Sonoran, and Great Basin Deserts.

Comments: The similar kidney-leaf buckwheat (*E. reniformae*) can easily be distinguished by its hairless involucres. Thomas's buckwheat (*E. thomasii*) also has hairless involucres, but it differs from kidney-leaf buckwheat by having heart-shaped leaves and outer perianth lobes that are sac-like at the bases. It also tends to change from yellow to whitish or rose-colored with age. All three have similar ranges as they occur over most of the Mojave Desert, and all are common in sandy soil.

GOLDEN CARPET
Gilmania luteola (Cov.) Cov.
Buckwheat Family (Polygonaceae)

Description: This low, branched annual forms loose, horizontal mats up to 8" in diameter. The round, hairless, ¼" leaf blades are on stalks up to ¾" long, in a rosette at the base of the plant. There are also clusters of narrow, leaf-like, bristle-tipped bracts at branching points along the stem where the flower stalks arise. Several tiny, yellow, 6-lobed flowers are produced in each 5-parted involucre.

Bloom Season: March to April

Habitat/Range: Golden carpet is known from only 5 occurrences on barren alkali slopes in Death Valley National Park, especially at Artists Palette and the surrounding hills.

Comments: This species is in the California Native Plant Society's Inventory of Rare and Endangered Vascular Plants of California. Its entire range is within Death Valley National Park. It is especially known from Artists Palette, where there is a lot of foot traffic that may trample plants.

BLACKBUSH
Coleogyne ramosissima Torrey
Rose Family (Rosaceae)

Description: This summer deciduous, highly branched, somewhat spiny, 1–6'-tall shrub has gray bark that turns black with age or moisture, giving the plant its common name. The linear, entire, ¼–½"-long leaves are in opposite clusters along the stems. The yellow flowers, which occur singly on the tips of branches, have 4 sepals and no petals. The small, crescent-shaped, brown, hairless fruits cling to the shrub throughout the year.

Bloom Season: April to June

Habitat/Range: Occurs on dry, north-facing slopes below 5,000' in creosote bush scrub, Joshua tree woodland, and pinyon-juniper woodland in the San Bernardino Mountains and mountains of the eastern Mojave to northwestern Arizona, southern Nevada, Utah, and Colorado. It is also found in Death Valley National Park and north along the foothills of the eastern Sierra Nevada Range to the Mammoth area.

Comments: Blackbush has a shallow root system, as few of its roots can penetrate the caliche soil on which it commonly grows. It is primarily wind-pollinated, but there are very few seedlings; they are usually killed during the summer heat and drought. The dense stands carry fire easily, but since they do not resprout or seed readily, they are often replaced by turpentine broom (*Thamnosma montana*), bitterbrush (*Purshia glandulosa*), desert almond (*Prunus fasciculata*), or other species.

PANAMINT BUTTERFLY BUSH

Buddleja utahensis Cov.
Figwort Family (Scrophulariaceae)

Description: This 1–2'-tall, grayish-green, densely branched shrub is covered with branched and stellate hairs. The thick, linear, ½–1¼"-long leaves have wavy, rolled-under margins. The male and female flowers are produced on separate plants in dense, rounded clusters in leaf axils on upper stems. Each creamy yellowish, 4-lobed flower is less than ¼" long.

Bloom Season: May to October

Habitat/Range: Found on rocky, carbonate soils from 2,500 to 4,500' in the eastern Mojave Desert to Nevada and Utah. It is relatively rare in California, occurring in few places, including the Panamint Mountains, the Kingston Range, and the Grapevine Mountains.

Comments: The Panamint butterfly bush was considered for listing as threatened or endangered, but it was rejected when found to be too common. This is one of the few Mojave Desert plants that have remained in the figwort family after molecular research divided it into separate families of monkeyflowers, penstemons, paintbrushes, and others.

THICK-LEAVED GROUND-CHERRY

Physalis crassifolia Benth.
Nightshade Family (Solanaceae)

Description: Thick-leaved ground-cherry is a sticky, 8–20"-tall perennial with ridged stems that are often branched in a zigzag pattern. The alternate, ovate, ½–1¼"-long leaf blades have entire or wavy margins, and they are on petioles equally as long. The yellow, 5-parted, ½–¾", widely bell-shaped flowers are produced singly in leaf axils. The calyx dries and expands to nearly 1" long, enclosing the green, fleshy berry as it develops.

Bloom Season: March to May

Habitat/Range: This species is found in sandy, gravelly, and rocky areas below 4,000' in creosote bush scrub in both the Mojave and Sonoran Deserts to Nevada, Arizona, and New Mexico.

Comments: Withanolide chemicals extracted from aeroponically grown *P. crassifolia* show strong, selective activity against prostate cancer cells. Other species of this genus are cultivated as ornamentals, such as the Chinese lantern (*P. alkekengi*), and some are edible, such as tomatillo (*P. philadelphica*).

WARTY CALTROP

Kallstroemia parviflora Norton
Caltrop Family (Zygophyllaceae)

Description: This hairy, prostrate to decumbent, summer annual is less than 3' tall. The pinnately compound leaves have 6–10 leaflets, and the stipules subtending each leaf are very apparent. The flowers are produced in leaf axils on pedicels that are longer than the subtending leaf. It has 5 separate, hairy, green sepals, 5 bright-yellow to gold petals, 5 stamens with yellow pollen, and a superior ovary. The fruit is around ¼" wide with a roundish, ridged, and bumpy body extending into a very long style. The bristly, hairy sepals, which are persistent in fruit, are about the same length as the fruit body.

Bloom Season: August to October

Habitat/Range: Occurs in the eastern Mojave Desert, and also around Warner Springs in San Diego County. Its range extends to the central United States and central Mexico.

Comments: *Kallstroemia* is the largest genus of the caltrop family in the New World. It is in the same tribe of the nasty puncture weed (also called goat-heads), *Tribulus terrestris*, from Africa. The similar *Kallstoemia californica* has smaller flowers and the sepals are deciduous in fruit.

CREOSOTE BUSH
Larrea tridentata DC. (Cov.)
Caltrop Family (Zygophyllaceae)

Description: This erect, 2–7'-tall evergreen shrub has spreading, brittle, gray branches with gummy, black, horizontal bands. The opposite, dark-green, sticky leaves have 2 fused, triangular leaflets, giving the appearance of a simple leaf with a butterfly shape. The 5-parted, ½–¾" flowers with yellow, clawed petals are produced singly in leaf axils, followed by spherical, nearly ¼" fruits that are covered with white or rust-colored hairs.

Bloom Season: November to May

Habitat/Range: Creosote bush is the dominant species across the Mojave, Sonoran, and Chihuahuan Deserts. It has different chromosome numbers in the different deserts. In the Mojave, plants have 6 sets of chromosomes, Sonoran Desert plants have 4 sets, and in the Chihuahuan Desert, plants have 2 sets of chromosomes.

Comments: Look for the leafy balls of tissue the plant produces when the creosote leafy gall midge (*Asphondylia* species) deposits its eggs in the branchlets. You may also find the tapered cases of creosote bagworm moth (*Thyridopteryx meadi*) stuck to branches. The lac scale insect (*Tachardiella larrea*) is responsible for blackish stem exudates called lac, which was used as adhesive and a coating for making tools, weapons, pottery, toys, and instruments; other lac scale species produce commercially available shellac. Creosote tea was used to cure urinary tract infections, colds, and skin problems. However, creosote has a lignan that causes liver toxicity, and some people get contact dermatitis from creosote.

GREEN AND BROWN FLOWERS

Many green and brown flowers do not attract animal pollinators but instead rely on wind or water to transfer pollen. Since the pollen grains are scattered by chance, the plants often produce massive amounts to increase the chances of pollen landing on a receptive stigma. The stigma surfaces are often feathery or very sticky, to increase the chances of catching the pollen; this is especially seen in the grasses.

HONEYSWEET

Tidestromia suffruticosa (Torr.) Standl. var.
oblongifolia (S. Watson) Sánch.Pino & Flores Olv.
Pigweed Family (Amaranthaceae)

Description: This rounded, 6–36"-tall perennial
has grayish-white, ovate, ½–1¼"-long leaves with
wedge-shaped bases and a distinctive vein pattern. The tiny, inconspicuous flowers are in small
clusters in leaf axils and are enclosed by bract-like
leaves.

Bloom Season: April to December

Habitat/Range: Honeysweet is common in washes
and on rocky hillsides in the eastern Mojave
Desert to the Sonoran Desert, Texas, and northern
Baja California, Mexico.

Comments: Honeysweet, a C4 plant adapted to
heat, has one of the highest rates of photosynthesis ever recorded. This genus was named for Ivar
Tidestrom (1854–1956), a Swedish emigrant who
earned a PhD in botany and then worked for the
US Forest Service, the Smithsonian Institute, and
the Bureau of Plant Industry. He authored *Flora of
Utah and Nevada* in 1925.

SPEARLEAF

Matelea parvifolia (Torr.) Woodson
Dogbane Family (Apocynaceae)

Description: The twining stems of this herbaceous, milky-sapped perennial are covered in hairs
and bear opposite, petiolate, narrowly heart-
shaped leaves less than ½" long. The open corolla
has 5 triangular, greenish to purplish lobes with
hairs on the top surfaces, and 5 smaller projections that point outward between the lobes. The
5-sided, star-like structure in the center is made
up of stamens with fused anthers wrapped around
and united to the flat pistil head. The pendant pod
is nearly 3" long with fine grooves along its length
and hairy-tufted seeds inside.

Bloom Season: March to May

Habitat/Range: Occurs in dry, rocky places from
2,300 to 3,300' in Joshua Tree National Park and
the eastern Mojave Desert to Nevada, Texas, and
Baja California, Mexico.

Comments: Flowers in the milkweed section
of the dogbane family transfer pollen from one
flower to another in the form of a pollinarium,
which consists of 2 waxy sacs of pollen grains
(the pollinia), each attached to a slender thread
(the translator arm) and joined together to form a
wishbone-shaped structure. When an insect lands
on the flower, its leg may slip into an area where
the pollinarium hooks onto a hair on the insect's
leg. If the insect is too small, it cannot escape and
will likely die in the flower; however, large insects
can free themselves, and the pollinarium may
remain attached to their leg to be transferred to
another flower.

WHITE BUR-SAGE, BURROBUSH
Ambrosia dumosa (A. Gray) Payne
Sunflower Family (Asteraceae)

Description: This 8–36"-tall, drought-deciduous shrub has crowded, ¼–1½"-long, pinnately divided leaves with white, woolly hairs. Separate male and female flowers occur on the same plant. The ¼" male flower heads are oriented downward so that pollen will dust the 2-flowered female heads below. The fruit is a ¼", spherical bur with 30–40 flattened spines.

Bloom Season: March to June, and September to November following summer rain

Habitat/Range: White bur-sage is found in creosote bush scrub below 5,000' throughout the Mojave and Sonoran Deserts to northwestern Mexico.

Comments: The roots secrete a compound that inhibits the root growth of neighboring white bur-sage and creosote bushes, and they also inhibit root growth of neighboring white bur-sage by root-to-root contact; these mechanisms limit competition in creosote bush scrub. Its shallow root system allows it to occupy desert pavement or caliche, areas where creosote roots cannot penetrate deep enough to get adequate water. Repeat photography shows individual white bur-sage plants often live more than 75 years. Fossilized pack-rat midden data show that this species spread across the Mojave between 9,000 and 5,000 years ago.

CHEESEBUSH, WINGED RAGWEED
Ambrosia salsola (Torr. & A. Gray) Strother & B. G. Baldw.
Sunflower Family (Asteraceae)

Description: This yellowish-green, resinous, scraggly, 2–3½'-tall shrub has linear, ¾–2"-long leaves that are mostly entire above, but may have lobes below. Crushed leaves and stem tips yield a foul, cheesy odor. Numerous small, cup-like male flower heads are in spike-like clusters above the female heads, which are in leaf axils. The female heads have single flowers and winged, papery bracts that spread open as the ¼"-long, spindle-shaped fruits develop.

Bloom Season: March to June

Habitat/Range: Cheesebush is very common on sandy flats, washes, and disturbed sites in creosote bush scrub, shadscale scrub, Joshua tree woodland, and pinyon-juniper woodland from Inyo County, California, to northwestern Mexico.

Comments: The highest rates of photosynthesis in cheesebush take place in April, when plants are in full leaf. The stems also contribute significantly to photosynthesis, but by the end of summer, the net photosynthesis rate drops to nearly zero, when they lose about half of their leaves and some of their twigs. Although native, this species has many weedy characteristics, including a high rate of seed production, a short life span, and the ability to rapidly establish in disturbed areas and resprout after burning. It may prove to be useful in revegetation efforts. Hybrids between cheesebush and white bur-sage (*A. dumosa*) have been documented.

BUDSAGE

Artemisia spinescens D.C. Eaton
Sunflower Family (Asteraceae)

Description: This stout, compact, aromatic, up to 2'-tall shrub has white-woolly young stems that persist as they age, developing into thorns. The leaves, which appear as early as February or March, fall from the plant by the heat of mid-summer. They are alternate, densely hairy, less than 1" long, and palmately divided into 2 to 5 narrowly spoon-shaped segments. The inconspicuous flowers appear in green, ball-like heads subtended by 5 to 8 widely ovate, densely soft-hairy phyllaries. Each head has disk flowers only, the central staminate (male), and the outer ones functionally pistillate (female). There are no rays present.

Bloom Season: April to June

Habitat/Range: Budsage is found on clay or gravelly, somewhat alkali soils in saltbush scrub below 6,000 feet in the Mojave and Great Basin Deserts to Oregon, Montana, and New Mexico.

Comments: Budsage is an important winter browse plant for wildlife and livestock in winter. This is the only *Artemisia* species that blooms in spring. It is also distinguished by having spinescent branchlets, and the arrangement of florets in the head is unique for a member of this genus. It has previously been placed in its own monotypic genus, *Picrothamnus*.

BIG SAGEBRUSH, GREAT BASIN SAGEBRUSH
Artemisia tridentata Nutt. subsp. *tridentata*
Sunflower Family (Asteraceae)

Description: This aromatic, 3–9'-tall, evergreen shrub has a short, thick trunk with hairy, gray bark. The narrow, wedge-shaped, ½–1½"-long leaves have 3 lobes at the tip. Numerous ¹⁄₁₀" flower heads with hairy phyllaries are produced in spreading, branched, 12"-long clusters, followed by tiny, glandular or hairy fruits.

Bloom Season: August to October

Habitat/Range: Occurs in dry, sandy soils and desert washes from 1,000 to 10,000' in mountains in the western, northern, and eastern Mojave Desert and on north-facing slopes of the Transverse Ranges. Its range extends throughout the western states.

Comments: Woolly bladder galls made by the sagebrush gall midge (*Asplondylia artemisiae*) are often quite obvious on the stems and leaves. Native Americans chewed leaves or made them into a tea for colds, headaches, stomachaches, and to get rid of worms. The smoke from burning branches was used to disinfect the air at funerals, ceremonials, and sickbeds, and the wood was used for fuel and textiles. Seeds were eaten only in time of great need, since they are distasteful. This genus is named for the Greek goddess, Artemis, who was supposedly cured by a related species.

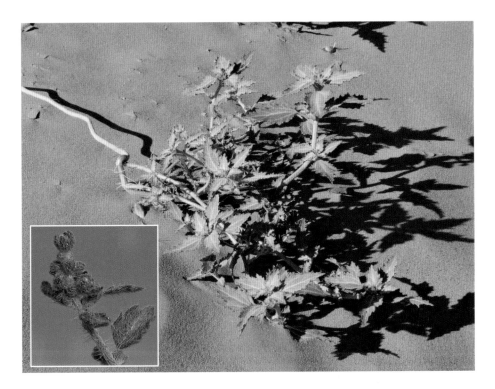

BUGSEED, DESERT TWINBUGS
Dicoria canescens A. Gray
Sunflower Family (Asteraceae)

Description: The stiff, white hairs of this 1–3'-tall, widely branching annual bear opposite, lanceolate, toothed, 3-veined, 1–2"-long lower leaves in early spring. Newer growth from later in the season will appear on the upper parts of the plant; these leaves are alternate and smaller, with a more rounded appearance; they are shown in the photo inset. Each flower head has several tiny male flowers with greenish corollas and 1–2 female flowers without corollas. The heads are subtended by 4–7 green, lanceolate outer phyllaries and up to 4 (but usually 2) fuzzy, persistent, hood-like inner phyllaries that enclose the female flowers. The flattened, ovate, ¼"-long fruit with toothed wings resembles a bug.

Bloom Season: September to January

Habitat/Range: Found in open areas on very sandy soils below 4,000' in creosote bush scrub and Joshua tree woodland in the Mojave Desert. It also occurs from the Colorado Desert to Sonora, Mexico.

Comments: The akenes resemble bugs, hence the common name, bugseed. Fruits of this species were found in a Native American basket found in the Last Chance Mountains, indicating that they were likely used as a winter food source. Surprisingly, a study of Eureka Dunes plants showed that *Dicoria canescens*, which does C3 photosynthesis, had summer photosynthetic rates well exceeding that of the dune endemic grass, *Swallenia alexandrae*, which has heat-efficient C4 photosynthesis.

SILVER CHOLLA

Cylindropuntia echinocarpa (Engelm. & J. M. Bigelow) F. M. Knuth
Cactus Family (Cactaceae)

Description: This 2–4'-tall cactus has a short trunk below, branching above into a dense crown. The detachable, cylindrical joints have conspicuous bumps with 3–10, ¾–1¼"-long spines. Each spine is enclosed in a silvery-gray, papery sheath, which gives the plant a silver cast and its common name. The greenish-yellow flowers are produced on branch tips, followed by ¾"-long, dry, angular, spiny, and malodorous fruits with white seeds. Very few fruits reach maturity, and immature fruits are often found in profusion littering the ground beneath the plant.

Bloom Season: April to May

Habitat/Range: Common in dry washes and flats below 6,000' in creosote bush scrub, Joshua tree woodland, and pinyon-juniper woodland in the Mojave, Sonoran, and Great Basin Deserts to central Nevada, southwestern Utah, western Arizona, and northwestern Sonora and Baja California, Mexico.

Comments: Some individuals have spines with straw-colored sheaths, giving these plants a golden cast and the common name of golden cholla. A study of golden cholla at the Granite Mountains Reserve in the eastern Mojave Desert showed that plant health and size decreases when it is surrounded by smaller plants. However, the plants are larger when there is higher rock coverage, and the presence of soil crusts had no effect on its health or size. This was surprising, since soil crusts are known to help many other species by preventing evaporation from the soil surface.

IODINE BUSH

Allenrolfea occidentalis (S. Watson) Kuntze
Goosefoot Family (Chenopodiaceae)

Description: This unusual, dark-green shrub with succulent, jointed stems and alternate branches is usually less than 2' tall. The triangular, minute, scale-like leaves extend down the stem below their attachment points. The tiny flowers are arranged in a spiral pattern in the axils of bracts on the upper, fleshy stem tips, forming ¼–1" spikes.

Bloom Season: June to August

Habitat/Range: Found at alkali seeps and edges of alkali dry lakes in very salty soils in the Great Basin, Mojave, and Sonoran Deserts to Oregon and northern Mexico.

Comments: Iodine bush tolerates very salty conditions by storing salt in its stem tissues and absorbing water to dilute the salt. It can live in soil with over 6 percent salt, which is very high compared to the 2 percent limit of most salt-tolerant species. By the end of the summer, the terminal joints of stems have such a high salt concentration that they turn pink and fall off. This genus was named for Robert Allen Rolfe (1855–1921), who wrote the first book on orchid taxonomy.

FOUR-WING SALTBUSH (A. canescens)

SHADSCALE (A. confertifolia)

SALTBUSH
Atriplex species
Goosefoot Family (Chenopodiaceae)

Genus Description: The saltbushes are the dominant species in saltbush scrub communities and sometimes in alkali sinks. The mostly alternate leaves appear scaley due to dense, multicellular hairs with inflated "bladder cell" tips that store and shed excess salt. Many have leaves oriented vertically to minimize solar radiation. Most have heat-efficient C4 photosynthesis with internal Kranz anatomy, which can be seen as dark veins after leaf hairs are rubbed off. Most have separate male and female plants, with flowers produced in clusters in leaf axils and on branch tips. Male flowers consist of 3–5 calyx lobes and 3–5 stamens. The female flowers mature into a flattened fruit with 2 surrounding bracts; these are important in species identification. There are 7 shrubby *Atriplex* taxa in the Mojave Desert.

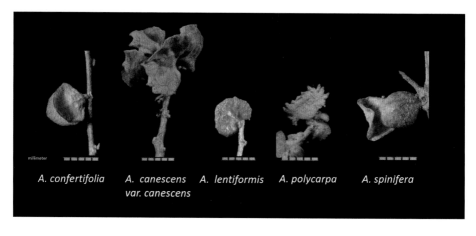

millimeter

A. confertifolia   *A. canescens*   *A. lentiformis*   *A. polycarpa*   *A. spinifera*
                       var. *canescens*

DESERT HOLLY (*A. hymenelytra*)

PARRY'S SALTBUSH (*A. parryi*)

ALL-SCALE (*A. polycarpa*)

SPINY SALTBUSH (*A. spinifera*)

WHEEL-SCALE, MECCA ORACH
Atriplex elegans (Moq.) D. Dietr. var. *fasciculata* (S. Watson) M. E. Jones
Goosefoot Family (Chenopodiaceae)

Description: The stems of this annual are branched from the base and lie mostly flat, but the tips may curve upward, achieving heights of 4"–2' tall. The leaves are up to 1" long with entire margins, tapering bases, and dense, white scales on the undersurface. The male flowers, with stamens only, occur in clusters in leaf axils. The female flowers have 2 flat, circular bracts that are almost completely fused around an ovary with 2 style branches. In fruit these bracts appear smooth or with 1 bump, and there are minute teeth around the edges.

Bloom Season: March to July

Habitat/Range: Found in playas and other saline and alkali places in the Mojave and Sonoran Deserts to Nevada, Arizona, and northern Mexico.

Comments: *Atriplex elegans* var. *elegans* differs from var. *fasciculata* in that the fruit bracts have deeper teeth on the margins and leaves may have teeth on the edges. The Pima used tender shoots as greens.

HOP-SAGE
Grayia spinosa (Hook.) Moq.
Goosefoot Family (Chenopodiaceae)

Description: This deciduous, 1–3'-tall shrub has gray, striped bark with twigs that harden into spines. The alternate, oblong, mealy-textured leaves are ½–1½" long, somewhat fleshy, and often gray at the tip. Male and female flowers are produced in dense clusters on separate plants, the female on branch tips and the male in leaf axils and on branch tips. Each female flower is surrounded by 2 round, green, ¼–½" bracts, which turn red and very showy with age.

Bloom Season: March to June

Habitat/Range: Hop-sage is common in creosote bush scrub, Joshua tree woodland, shadscale scrub, and pinyon-juniper woodland in the Mojave Desert to eastern Washington and Wyoming.

Comments: The leaves of hop-sage, winter fat, and saltbush species have been shown to be the preferred food plants for the Mojave ground squirrel (*Xerospermophilus mohavensis*), a rodent listed as threatened by the US Fish and Wildlife Service. Its range is restricted to the western Mojave Desert, where it has low abundance and patchy distribution. They are active aboveground from February through July, and after reproduction, and if conditions are favorable, they will double their body size in preparation for hibernation during the other months.

WINTER FAT

Krascheninnikovia lanata (Pursh) A. D. J. Meeuse
& Smit
Goosefoot Family (Chenopodiaceae)

Description: Winter fat is a 1–2½'-high shrub with slender, entire, ½–2"-long leaves in alternating bundles along erect stems. The plant is covered with white or rust-colored, stellate hairs with occasional, interspersed, longer, simple hairs. Numerous tiny male flowers with protruding stamens occur in spike-like clusters at the tops of stems, and the ¼"-long female flowers are in clusters in leaf axils below. Bracts under both female and male flowers have dense tufts of hair, giving the upper half of the plant a woolly appearance.

Bloom Season: April to August

Habitat/Range: Winter fat is common on rocky and gravelly flats above 2,000' in creosote bush scrub, Joshua tree woodland, blackbush scrub, shadscale scrub, and pinyon-juniper woodland in the Mojave Desert. It is widespread in the western states to the Rocky Mountains.

Comments: Wildlife and livestock derive much nutrition from this evergreen during winter months, hence the common name. Because of its importance as forage, this plant has been widely used for research, including studies of how invasive species affect its nutrient content, how regrowth is affected by grazing, and how parent material should be chosen for restoration. This genus was named for Stephan P. Krascheninnikov (1713–1755), a Russian botanist.

ARROW-SCALE, COVILLE'S ORACH

Stutzia covillei (Standl.) E. H. Zacharias
Goosefoot Family (Chenopodiaceae)

Description: This fleshy, branched, 4–16"-tall annual has alternate, ½–1¾"-long leaves that are triangular with outward-projecting lobes at the base, and they are green on both the upper and lower surfaces. Tiny, sessile, green flowers are produced in dense clusters at branch tips and in upper leaf axils.

Bloom Season: April to August

Habitat/Range: Arrow-scale is found in alkaline soils and sinks below 5,000' in creosote bush scrub, shadscale scrub, and sagebrush scrub in the Mojave Desert to the eastern Sierra Nevada. Its range extends to the San Joaquin Valley, Oregon, and Utah.

Comments: The species may be confused with the somewhat similar Nuttall's poverty weed (*Mono-lepis nuttalliana*), which has flowers in axillary but not terminal clusters. The leaves tend to be narrower and not as triangular or fleshy as those of arrow-scale.

BUSH SEEPWEED, INK-BLITE
Suaeda nigra (Raf.) J. F. Macbr.
Goosefoot Family (Chenopodiaceae)

Description: This muddy-looking, sparsely leafy, 1–4'-tall subshrub has yellowish young stems that brown with age. The dark-green, linear lower leaves are up to 1½" long, while upper leaves are shorter, lighter green, and succulent. Clusters of tiny, greenish, 5-parted flowers are produced near the top of the plant. The flowers may have male or female parts or both. The stems of the flower cluster turn a dark-reddish-brown color when dried.

Bloom Season: May to September

Habitat/Range: Occurs in alkaline soils below 5,000' in creosote bush scrub and alkali sink communities in the Mojave, Sonoran, and Great Basin Deserts to Canada, Texas, and Mexico.

Comments: Salts collect in the leaves during the growing season and are eliminated when the leaves fall off. This progressively increases soil salts, making the area uninhabitable by all but the most salt-tolerant species. Bush seepweed produces 2 types of seeds, hard black and soft brown; the soft brown are better at germinating at high levels of salinity and are one of the most tolerant of all seeds to saline conditions. Native Americans extracted a black dye from the stems that was used in basketry, giving the plant the common name of ink-blite.

CALIFORNIA CROTON
Croton californicus Muell.
Spurge Family (Euphorbiaceae)

Description: This 1–3'-tall, light-olive-green subshrub is covered with short, stellate hairs. The alternate, entire, elliptic leaves are 1–2" long on ½–1½" stalks. Male and female flowers most often occur on separate plants. The deciduous male flowers consist of around 10–15 stamens in a small, hairy, cup-like calyx. The female flowers have 5 sepals and no petals. The green, 3-lobed fruit is around ¼" long with 3 persistent styles that are split twice.

Bloom Season: March to October

Habitat/Range: Found in sandy soil at low elevations in the Mojave Desert, as at Kelso Dunes, where it forms hummocks and stabilizes soil. It is widespread throughout southern California to Baja California, Mexico.

Comments: Most California croton plants are usually either male or female, but some populations have up to 18 percent of the plants with both male and female flowers. A plant can also change gender within or between flowering seasons.

LINEAR-LEAVED STILLINGIA

Stillingia linearifolia S. Watson
Spurge Family (Euphorbiaceae)

Description: This erect, branched, 1–2'-tall peren-nial with alternate, narrow, entire leaves bears separate male and female flowers in terminal spikes on the same plant. The male flowers have a 2-lobed calyx and 2 stamens, while female flowers have ovaries with 3 compartments and styles.

Bloom Season: March to May

Habitat/Range: Linear-leaved stillingia occurs in open, dry sites below 4,500' in creosote bush scrub in the central and eastern Mojave Desert. In the Sonoran Desert it occurs the length of the Baja California peninsula and along coastal Sonora, Mexico.

Comments: A very similar species, tooth-leaf (*S. paucidentata*) differs from linear-leaved stillingia in that it has teeth on the leaf margin near the base. It seems to replace linear-leaved stillingia in areas west of Barstow, California. A fluid extracted from the root of *S. sylvatica* of the southeastern United States has been used as an alternative medicine treatment for syphilis and liver disorders. Controlled studies are needed.

ANNUAL STILLINGIA

Stillingia spinulosa Torr.
Spurge Family (Euphorbiaceae)

Description: This 2–18"-tall, densely clumped, milky-sapped plant has alternate, spiny-toothed, 1"-long leaves with 3 veins emerging from the base. The tiny male flowers with 2 stamens each are produced in ¼–½"-long spikes in leaf axils, with 1–2 female flowers below. The 3-lobed fruit has 3 styles and is less than ¼" long.

Bloom Season: March to May

Habitat/Range: Annual stillingia grows in sandy soils and dunes below 3,000' in creosote bush scrub in the eastern and southern Mojave Desert to southern Nevada and in the Sonoran Desert to western Arizona, northwestern Sonora, and northern Baja California, Mexico.

Comments: This genus was named for the English naturalist B. Stillingfleet (1702–1771), an educated Englishman who was rejected for a college posi-tion but instead spent years tutoring a relative who went on to earn academic awards. He studied botany and music in his later years. His publica-tions include a text on the Linnaean classification system and a book about plant phenology.

NOSEBURN

Tragia ramosa Torrey
Spurge Family (Euphorbiaceae)

Description: This 4–12"-tall, stiff-hairy, clear-sapped perennial grows from a woody base. The branched and sometimes twining stems bear ½–¾"-long, alternate, sharp-toothed leaves with tiny stipules. Each flower cluster contains 2–4 male flowers and 1 female flower. The male flowers have 4–5 recurved sepals and 3–6 stamens. The female flowers have 4–8 sepals and a 3-parted ovary with a style that is split into 3 parts from near the base.

Bloom Season: April to May

Habitat/Range: Noseburn is found on roadsides and in dry, rocky places from 3,000 to 5,500' in the mountains of the eastern Mojave Desert to the central United States and Mexico.

Comments: The leaves of this innocent-looking plant can deliver a nasty sting that can raise welts and blisters. This involves injection of calcium oxalate crystals under the skin by means of stiff hairs on the leaf surface. A demographic study of numerous forbes in Kansas grasslands showed that the expected life span for *T. ramosa* there is 2 years, but that it can live as long as 25 years! It is not known whether it can survive that long in the Mojave Desert. Numerous *Tragia* species from Africa and India are used traditionally for a variety of ailments, and *T. involucrata* from India has been shown to have antitumor activity.

MOJAVE PAINTBRUSH

Castilleja plagiotoma A. Gray
Broom-Rape Family (Orobanchaceae)

Description: The erect, 1–2'-tall stems of this grayish-green perennial often grow up through low shrubs. The foliage has sparse, branched hairs. The linear, 1–2"-long lower leaves grade into 3-lobed leaves and green, white-hairy bracts higher up the stem, and the bilateral flowers are enclosed in green, 3-lobed flower bracts. The ½"-long, split calyx has straight lobes, and the hairy, tubular, greenish-yellow corolla is nearly 1" long. The fruit is a 2-chambered capsule.

Bloom Season: April to June

Habitat/Range: Occurs from 1,000 to 7,500' in Joshua tree woodland, sagebrush scrub, and pinyon-juniper woodland on desert slopes of the Transverse Ranges and in scattered locations in Los Angeles, Kern, and San Luis Obispo Counties in California.

Comments: This plant is on the California Native Plant Society's watch list. Like other *Castilleja* species, it is a root hemiparasite. Its host plant is usually California buckwheat (*Eriogonum fasciculatum* var. *polifolium*), but it has also been observed on matchweed (*Gutierrezia microcephala*), big sagebrush (*Artemisia tridentata*), and short-stemmed bastard-sage (*Eriogonum wrightii* var. *subscaposum*). Mojave paintbrush is a host plant for the larvae of Erlich's checkerspot butterfly (*Euphydryas editha erlichii*), which flies from late March to early May.

DESERT NEEDLEGRASS (*Stipa speciosa*)

SALTGRASS (*Distichlis spicata*)

MOJAVE DESERT GRASSES
of various genera and species

Grass Family (Poaceae)

Genus Description: The grasses, with their hollow stems (except at the nodes), sheathed leaves, and tiny, green flowers grouped into clusters called spikelets, are not always the most noticed of desert plants. However, there are over 120 grass species that occur in the California portion of the Mojave alone. Many are annuals, some of which germinate in winter and early spring, and some that germinate after summer rain. Many of the late summer to fall bloomers have C4 photosynthesis, which enables them to grow in the heat of summer. Perennial grasses may survive harsh conditions by dying back and resprouting later from stored root reserves. Some of the perennial bunchgrasses (*Hilaria rigida*, *Muhlenbergia porteri*) die back only to the nodes, thereby getting a head start on growth when conditions become favorable.

The grasses pictured here are among the most common native species. Over 40 of the grass taxa found in the Mojave are nonnatives from Eurasia, South America, and even Australia and India. Some of these cause increased fire frequency and other ecological problems that are discussed in the introduction.

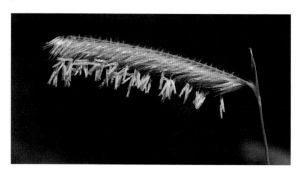

BLUE GRAMMA (*Bouteloua gracilis*)

SIX-WEEKS GRAMMA
(*Bouteloua barbata*)

SAND RICEGRASS (*Stipa hymenoides*)

DESERT FLUFFGRASS
(*Dasyochloa pulchella*)

PORTER'S MUHLY
(*Muhlenbergia porteri*)

PURPLE THREE-AWN (*Aristida purpurea*)

BIG GALLETA (*Hilaria rigida*)

LINEAR-LEAVED CAMBESS
Oligomeris linifolia (M. Vahl) J. F. Macbr.
Mignonette Family (Resedaceae)

Description: This somewhat erect, fleshy, branching, 4–12"-tall annual has entire, linear, sessile, ½–1½"-long leaves in alternate bundles. The flowers are produced in 1–4"-long spikes on the upper stems. Each tiny flower has 4 sepals, 2 greenish-white petals, and a triangular bract below.

Bloom Season: March to July

Habitat/Range: This species occurs in alkali flats and creosote bush scrub in deserts and on sea bluffs throughout the American Southwest to California's Channel Islands and Baja California, Mexico. It is also found in some areas of the Middle East, India, southern Europe, and northern Africa.

Comments: Linear-leaved cambess is often common in areas with desert varnish. The genus name literally means "few parts" in Greek, referring to the flower structure. This plant has been used for pain and inflammation in traditional medicine, and a recent study in rats provides preliminary evidence that root extracts may be effective in pain reduction.

PARRY'S NOLINA, PARRY'S BEARGRASS
Nolina parryi S. Watson
Butcher's-Broom Family (Ruscaceae)

Description: Parry's nolina is somewhat shrub-like, with 65–200 long, concave, grayish-green, sawtooth-margined leaves in dense rosettes atop a 12–16"-thick, 3–6'-tall trunk. Masses of cream-colored, 6-parted flowers are produced in dense, branched, 4–12'-tall clusters on erect stalks, followed by ½"-long, ½"-wide capsules with 3 compartments.

Bloom Season: April to June

Habitat/Range: Occurs from 3,500 to 6,000' in Joshua tree woodland and pinyon-juniper woodland on desert slopes of the eastern San Bernardino Mountains and also in the Kingston, Eagle, and Little San Bernardino Mountain Ranges in the Mojave Desert. It is also found in the Sonoran Desert.

Comments: The genus *Nolina* was named for Pierre Charles Nolin (1717–1795), a French agricultural writer in the mid-1700s. Bigelow's nolina (*N. bigelovii*), a trunkless species with flat, rigid leaves and brown fibers peeling from the margins, is found in dry canyons below 3,000' in the Sheephole and Eagle Mountains in the Mojave Desert.

CRUCIFIXION THORN
Castela emoryi (A. Gray) Moran & Felger
Quassia Family (Simaroubaceae)

Description: This thorny, densely branched shrub can be up to 3' tall and spreading, or 6–12' and erect. Juvenile plants have ½"-long, scale-like leaves, but these drop early, leaving the older plants leafless. Male and female flowers are produced on separate plants. Each inconspicuous flower develops into a fruit with a spreading whorl of 5–6, ¼"-long, 1-seeded parts, which often completely dry on the plant and cling on for 5–7 years.

Bloom Season: June to July

Habitat/Range: Found in gravelly soils in creosote bush scrub and dry playas below 2,000' from the central Mojave south and east into the Sonoran Desert in Arizona and western Sonora, Mexico.

Comments: Crucifixion thorn is considered to be a serotinous species, because it can retain and protect its seeds for long periods of time before dispersing them during a favorable year. This species is protected at Crucifixion Thorn Natural Area, a Bureau of Land Management–administered area in Imperial County, California. This genus was named for Rene R. L. Castel (1759–1832) of France, who was a botanist, editor, and poet.

DESERT MISTLETOE
Phoradendron californicum Nutt.
Mistletoe Family (Viscaceae)

Description: Desert mistletoe has 1–4'-long, rounded, reddish stems, which appear in dense, branched clumps in the canopies of its host plants. It appears to be leafless, although there are small, scale-like leaves present. The tiny, inconspicuous, green flowers develop into a profusion of ⅛" round, bright-reddish-pink berries.

Bloom Season: January to March

Habitat/Range: This species is found in the Mojave, Sonoran, and Great Basin Deserts to Baja California, Mexico. Its distribution depends on the availability of pea family host plants, including catclaw (*Senegallia greggi*) and honey mesquite (*Neltuma odorata*) in the Mojave Desert. In the Colorado Desert, hosts also include palo verde (*Parkinsonia* sp.) and ironwood (*Olneya tesota*). Desert mistletoe has also been observed on creosote bush (*Larrea tridentata*).

Comments: The fruits are a favored food item of the Phainopepla, a shiny, crested, black bird with red eyes and white underwing patches. The birds are effective seed dispersal agents, as the seeds pass through their digestive tract and are deposited on other plants with guano. The sticky seeds readily attach to the new host plant where they germinate to form a seedling, which can then invade xylem and phloem tissues. This plant's genus name literally means "tree thief" in Greek, referring to its parasitic habit.

GLOSSARY

alternate: Placed singly along a stem, one after another, usually each successive item on a different side of the stem from previous. As one traces the orientation from one item to the next above, a spiral is drawn around the stem. Usually used in reference to arrangement of leaves on a stem (see **opposite** and **whorled** for comparison).

annual: A plant that completes its life cycle, from seed germination to production of new seeds, within a year, then dies (see **perennial** and **biennial** for comparison).

anther: A sac at the tip of the stamen where the pollen is formed.

axil: The region in the angle formed by the upper side of the leaf, or leaf stalk, where it joins the stem.

banner: The upper petal in many of the flowers of the bean family (see **"pea" flower**), often bent upward or even backward, usually broader than the other petals, and always covering them in the bud; also called the standard or flag petal.

basal: At the base or bottom of; generally used in reference to leaves located at the base of the stem, at ground level.

beak: A conic projection or abruptly tapering end of a fruit.

biennial: A plant completing its life cycle in two years and normally not producing flowers during the first year (see **annual** and **perennial** for comparison).

bilateral: In reference to the shape of a flower as viewed "face on," a shortened term for "bilaterally symmetrical" and substitution for the technical term "zygomorphic." A bilateral flower is one that can be divided into mirror images in only one plane through the center of the flower. Mammals, fish, birds, and insects, for example, are bilaterally symmetrical (see **radial** for comparison).

blade: The broad, flat part of a structure, usually in reference to leaves or petals, often contrasting with the stalk of the structure.

bract: Reduced or modified leaf, often associated with flowers. May or may not be green, sometimes scale-like.

bristle: A stiff hair, usually erect or curving away from its attachment point.

bulb: Underground plant part that is a short, swollen stem covered by fleshy, modified, food-storing, scale-like leaves that are usually nongreen (an example is the onion).

calyx: A collective term for the outer set of flower parts, composed of sepals, which may be separate or joined to one another; usually green. If there is only one set of parts outside the stamens or pistil, it is by definition the calyx, even though it may resemble a corolla (see **corolla** and **petal-like parts** for comparison).

capsule: A dry fruit that releases seeds through splits or holes; as used in this guide, usually not elongate (see **pod** for comparison).

catkin: A spike of male or female flowers that falls off the plant as a single unit after flowering or fruiting. Willows, oaks, and other wind-pollinated plants often bear catkins.

clasping: Surrounding or partially wrapping around a stem or branch.

cluster: Any grouping or close arrangement of individual flowers; "flower cluster" is used as a substitute for the commonly used but more technical term "inflorescence."

compound leaf: A leaf that is divided to its midrib or stalk into two to many leaflets, each of which resembles a complete leaf. A leaf will have a bud in its axil, whereas leaflets do not (see **palmately compound leaf**, **pinnately compound leaf**, and **simple leaf** for comparison).

corm: A fleshy, enlarged, underground stem base with scales.

corolla: Collective term for the set of flower parts interior to the calyx and exterior to the stamens (if present), composed of petals, which may be free or united; often white or brightly colored, rarely green (see **calyx** and **petal-like parts** for comparison).

cotyledon: A fleshy leaf in the embryo of a seed that stores food for the eventual seed germination process.

deciduous: A term referring to the more or less synchronized shedding of structures, usually leaves. Shrubs and trees that drop all their leaves at the end of the growing season are "deciduous," or leaves may be said to be "deciduous." Many desert plants are evergreen but will shed their leaves during severe drought and then are "drought deciduous" (see **evergreen** for comparison).

disk flower: Small, tubular, usually trumpet-shaped flower in the central portion of the flower head of plants in the sunflower family (Asteraceae) (see illustration p. 48; see **ray flower**, **ligule**, and **strap-shaped flower** for comparison).

elliptical: In reference to the shape of a plane cut obliquely through the axis of a cone, usually in reference to leaf shape (see illustration p. 47).

entire: Usually in reference to a leaf margin that is plain, not lobed or toothed (see illustration p. 46).

erect: Standing more or less perpendicularly to the surface.

evergreen: Plants that bear green leaves throughout the year. Leaves may be shed asynchronously or synchronously, but in either case, new leaves are in place before old ones are shed (see **deciduous** for comparison).

family: A group of related genera, usually easily recognized by sharing similar features (such as floral features, fruit types, stem anatomy, etc.).

fascicle: A cluster or bundle of leaves or flowers.

filament: The usually slender stalk of a stamen, tipped by the anther.

flower head: As used in this guide, a dense and continuous group of flowers, without obvious branches or spaces between them; often mistaken for a single "flower" until structure is understood. The term is used especially in reference to the grouping of flowers in the sunflower family (Asteraceae).

fruit: The mature ovary of a plant, containing ripe seeds; a fruit may be fleshy or hard, large or small, and may consist of other parts of the flower or plant.

genera: See **genus**.

genus: A group of closely related species, sharing many characteristics in common; plural, "genera."

glandular: Bearing glands, which are structures that secrete something. Glands in plants are often borne at tips of hairs, and the exuded substance is usually moist or sticky and sometimes odoriferous. Alternatively, they may be part of the surface layer and appear as darkened spots. Glandular secretions on the surface of plants usually inhibit or repel potential insects or other animals that might eat the plant.

glochids: Bundles of very short, dense spines that may occur on cactus plants.

herbaceous: A term that means "not woody." Such a plant is usually soft and green.

hood: A curved or folded structure, often somewhat scoop-shaped, associated with the corolla. In this guide "hoods" are those scoop-like structures interior to the petals and exterior to the stamens in milkweeds (Asclepiadaceae); since most milkweeds have reflexed petals, the hoods are typically the most prominent feature of the flowers. Species with bilateral flowers also often have the upper lip "hood-like"; that is, much like a deeply cupped visor.

inflorescence: The structure on which flowers are borne, in this guide called the "flower cluster"; various specialized terms describe the form of the inflorescence.

inrolled: Margins of leaves are rolled under, or revolute.

involucre: A distinct series of bracts or leaves that subtend a flower or a flower cluster. Often used in the description of the flower head of the sunflower family (Asteraceae), where in this guide "whorl of bracts" is substituted.

keel: Referring especially to the two joined petals forming the lower part of the flower in the bean family (Fabaceae), which resembles the prow of a boat (see illustration p. 48); any structure that is a sharp, narrow ridge.

lanceolate: Narrow and pointed at both ends, usually broader just below the middle, much like the tip of a lance. When describing a structure that is basically lanceolate, but broader above the middle, in this guide the term "inversely lanceolate" is used interchangeably with the more technical term, "oblanceolate."

leaf: The flattened, usually photosynthetic and therefore "food-producing" organ of the plant, attached to the stem.

leaf blade: The broadened, flattened part of the leaf, in contrast to the leaf stalk.

leaflet: A distinct leaf-like segment of a compound leaf.

leaf stalk: The slender portion of a leaf, distinguished from the blade, continuous with the midrib, and attaching the leaf to the stem; technically the "petiole."

limb: The flared or expanded part of the corolla above the throat or tube.

linear: Long and very narrow, with parallel or nearly parallel sides (see illustration p. 47).

lobe: A segment of an incompletely divided plant part, typically rounded at tip; often used in reference to the partial segmentation of the leaf blade.

margin: The edge of a leaf or other plant part.

midrib: The central or main vein of a leaf.

nectar guides: Markings on the flower of a contrasting color or that reflect ultraviolet light, to direct the pollinating animal to the center of the flower.

nectar spur: A tubular extension of a petal or sepal that secretes nectar.

node: The region of the stem where one or more leaves are attached. Buds are commonly borne at nodes, in axils of leaves.

nutlet: A term for a small, hard, one-seeded fruit or segment of a fruit.

oblong: A shape with more or less parallel sides, longer in one direction than the other, as used here, with rounded ends; commonly used with leaf shape (see illustration p. 47).

opposite: Paired directly across from each other along a stem or axis (see **alternate** and **whorled** for comparison).

ovary: The portion of the flower where seeds develop, usually a swollen area below the style (if present) and stigma; develops into the fruit.

ovate: More or less egg-shaped in outline, often bluntly pointed at tip.

pads: Used here in reference to flattened stem-joints of *Opuntia*. The pads are part of the stem, the spine clusters (technically areoles) derived from branch systems, the needles modified from leaves.

palmate: Referring to an arrangement where segments attach to a common point, much like fingers attach to the palm of a hand. Used commonly to describe lobing of a leaf (palmately lobed) or compound leaves (palmately compound). A palmately compound leaf is one that has three or more leaflets attached at the tip of the leaf stalk; an example is the leaves of lupines in the bean family (Fabaceae) (see illustration p. 46).

pappus: In the sunflower family (Asteraceae) the modified calyx, consisting of a crown of scales, bristles, or soft hairs at the top of the seedlike fruit.

parallel: Side by side, about the same distance apart for the entire length; often used in reference to veins or edges of leaves.

parasitic plant: A plant that lives on another plant, robbing it of nourishment.

"pea" flower: As used in this guide, a reference to the flower shape seen in many of the species in the bean family (Fabaceae); a flower that has a banner, two wings, and a keel (see illustration p. 48).

perennial: A plant that normally lives for more than one year (see **annual** and **biennial** for comparison).

petal: A unit of the corolla, usually flattened and brightly colored.

petal-like parts: Referring to parts of a flower that resemble petals but technically are not petals, or where the distinction between petals and sepals is not immediately evident; in technical works the term "tepals" may be used. In this guide "petal-like parts" is used in the cactus family (Cactaceae), where sepals are thoroughly intergradient with petals; in the lily family (Liliaceae), where sepals may be brightly colored like the petals; and in the four o'clock family (Nyctaginaceae), where there are no petals, and the calyx is brightly colored and fragile, resembling a corolla.

photosynthesis: The process by which plants use energy in light to rearrange and join molecules of carbon dioxide from the air, all to store the sun's energy in molecules of sugar built from the carbon dioxide and water; the plant's "food." Except for rare instances (such as around deep-sea vents), all life on Earth depends on this process.

phyllaries: A series of bracts below the flower heads of sunflower family (Asteraceae) plants.

pinna: The primary division of a compound leaf (plural, "pinnae"), often equivalent to a leaflet (as in *Astragalus* and *Lupinus*). In the case of a twice-compound leaf, this guide uses "segment" in place of pinna, the leaflets being the small leaf-like structures resulting from division of the pinna.

pinnate: Referring to an arrangement where parts are aligned along opposite sides of an axis, much like the barbs of a feather are aligned along each side of the common central axis. Used commonly to describe lobing of a leaf (pinnately lobed) or compound leaves (pinnately compound). A pinnately compound leaf is one that has two or more leaflets arranged along opposite sides of a common axis; the leaves of many members of the bean family (Fabaceae) are an example of this (see illustration p. 46).

pistil: The female part of the flower, consisting of ovary, style, and stigma; a flower may have one pistil or several pistils.

pod: As used in this guide, a dry, elongate fruit that splits open upon maturity to release seeds (see **capsule** for comparison).

pollen: Tiny, often powdery male reproductive cells formed in the anther, ultimately producing the sperm prior to fertilization of the egg within the ovary of the plant.

pollination: The transfer of pollen from the anther of one flower to the stigma of another.

prostrate: Growing flat on the ground.

pulvinus: A swelling at the base of a leaf stalk (petiole) or at the base of a leaflet, which often aids in the movement of leaves or leaflets.

rachis: The main stem or axis of a pinnately compound leaf.

radial: In reference to the shape of a flower as viewed "face on," a shortened term for "radially symmetrical," and substitution for the technical term "actinomorphic." A radial flower is one that can be divided into mirror images by several planes through the center of the flower. A starfish is radially symmetrical (see **bilateral** for comparison).

ray flower: A flower at the periphery of the head of the sunflower family (Asteraceae), the corolla extended far to one side, flattened and shaped like a single petal; a flower head may have one, several, or many ray flowers, or it may have none; when several or many are present they usually extend outward like the rays of a star (see illustration p. 48; see **disk flower** and **strap-shaped flower** for comparison).

receptacle: The expanded portion of a stalk where flower parts are attached.

recurved: Bent backward.

reflexed: Abruptly bent backward.

rhizome: A horizontal, underground stem.

rosette: A dense cluster of leaves very closely spaced around the stem, often at ground level, but in members of the agave family (Agavaceae), sometimes at the top of a stout trunk.

scale: Any thin, membranous, usually translucent structure that somewhat resembles scales of fish or reptiles.

scarification: The breaking of the seed coat prior to germination.

seedlike: Resembling a seed; in this guide, used to refer to the fruits of various plants, especially members of the sunflower family (Asteraceae), where the "seed" (as in the sunflower "seed") is technically a one-seeded fruit, the outer covering consisting of ovary wall joined to the bases of other flower parts, the true seed contained inside.

sepal: A unit of the calyx, typically flattened and green, but occasionally brightly colored (see **petal-like parts** for comparison).

serrate: Saw-toothed, with teeth pointing toward the tip or front.

shrub: A multistemmed woody plant of moderate to low height with stems arising at ground or near level.

simple leaf: A leaf that is not compound. A simple leaf may have a plain (entire) margin, or the margin may be toothed or deeply lobed. As long as clefts between the lobes do not extend to the midrib, the leaf is simple. A deeply lobed oak leaf, for example, is "simple."

spatulate: Referring to a shape broader in the upper half, round at the tip (see illustration p. 47).

species: A group of very similar individuals that use their environment in a similar manner and that are capable of mating with one another to produce viable offspring. Because many plants reproduce asexually (e.g., dandelion, *Taraxacum*) or tend to self-pollinate and self-fertilize (e.g., some suncups, *Camissonia*), the definition is more difficult to apply in plants than in many animal groups. Species are internationally referred to by a scientific name, a binomial, such as *Taraxacum officinale*, where the first name is the genus name, and the second is the specific epithet, which modifies the genus name.

specific epithet: See **species**.

spike: An elongate, unbranched, often dense cluster of stalkless or nearly stalkless flowers.

spikelet: The basic flower cluster unit of grass family plants. Each spikelet has two bracts called glumes at the base, with sessile flowers called florets above.

stalk: As used in this guide, a stem-like structure supporting a leaf, flower, or flower cluster (technically "petiole," "pedicel," and "peduncle," respectively).

stalkless: Lacking a stalk; when stalkless, a leaf blade or a flower is directly attached to the stem.

stamen: The male part of the flower, consisting of the slender, stalk-like filament and the sac-like anther, in which pollen forms.

staminode: A stamen that lacks an anther and is therefore sterile. Staminodes in the figwort family are often hairy.

standard: See **banner**.

stellate hairs: A star-like pattern of hair growth, with several slender hairs radiating from a common point of attachment at their bases.

stigma: Portion of the pistil receptive to pollen; usually at the top of the style, and often appearing fuzzy or sticky.

stipules: A pair of attachments at the base of a leaf, often connected to each other. Leaves may or may not have stipules.

stolon: An aboveground horizontal stem or runner.

style: The portion of the pistil between the ovary and the stigma, often slender; each pollen grain will produce a tube that traverses the style, delivering sperm to the eggs within the ovary.

strap-shaped flower: In reference to the type of flowers found in the heads of dandelions (*Taraxacum*) and their relatives in the sunflower family (Asteraceae). The flowers throughout the head are strap-shaped, the corolla extended conspicuously toward the periphery of the head, the flowers in the center smaller than those near the edge of the head. Usually each corolla has five tiny teeth at the tip. These are contrasted with ray flowers, which are similar, but which are found only at the periphery of the flower head surrounding the disk flowers.

subshrub: Plants with a shrubby appearance but with woody tissue only near the base and soft, green stems above.

subspecies: A group of individuals within a species that have a distinct range, habitat, and structure; in plants usually not conceptually different from variety, but both terms remain in use due to historical reasons.

subtend: Situated below or beneath, often encasing or enclosing something.

succulent: Thickened, fleshy, and juicy.

tendril: A slender, coiling structure that may be part of a stem or leaf. The tendrils of vines and climbing plants wind around other plants or objects for support.

toothed: Bearing teeth or sharply angled projections along an edge.

tubercle: A small, rounded or conical projection.

umbel: A flower cluster where each of the individual flower stalks attach at a common point at the tip of the main stalk of the flower cluster, much like the ribs of an umbrella attach at the top of the umbrella.

variety: A group of individuals within a species that have a distinct range, habitat, and structure; in plants usually not conceptually different from subspecies, but both terms remain in use due to historical reasons.

veins: Bundles of small tubes, some of which carry water and minerals, others of which carry a sugar solution. Water and sugar solutions may move in opposite directions through different series of cells in the same vein.

whorled: Three or more parts attached at the same point around a stem or axis (see **alternate** and **opposite** for comparison).

wings: A flat, thin, extended portion; in the bean family (Fabaceae), specifically referring to the two side petals of the flower, flanking the keel.

INDEX OF SYNONYMS

As explained in the introduction, there have been numerous recent changes in the scientific names of many Mojave Desert plant taxa. In earlier floras and plant identification manuals, plants were classified and named based mainly on their morphology, or outward appearance, and sometimes on their chemistry as well. Recent name changes reflect new information about relationships among taxa as elucidated by molecular genetic studies. It is important for floras and identification manuals alike to provide previous plant names. This allows the professional and the layman alike the means to track these name changes, to see how our understanding of plant relationships has changed over time. It can also eliminate confusion, since many readers may know plants by their former scientific names, but they are not familiar with the new nomenclature. This index of synonyms was provided so that you can look up a plant by its previous scientific name, as it appeared in the second edition (2013) of *Mojave Desert Wildflowers*, and find out the new, accepted scientific name, according to The Jepson Flora Project, Jepson eFlora (2023).

2nd EDITION MDWF	3rd EDITION MDWF
Atriplex covillei	*Stutzia covillei*
Chamaesyce albomarginata	*Euphorbia albomarginata*
Chamaesyce setiloba	*Euphorbia setiloba*
Coryphantha chlorantha	*Escobaria chlorantha*
Cryptantha angustifolia	*Johnstonella angustifolia*
Cryptantha circumscissa	*Greeneocharis circumscissa*
Cryptantha costata	*Johnstonella costata*
Cryptantha micrantha var. lepida	*Eremocarya lepida*
Cryptantha nevadensis var. nevadensis	*Cryptantha nevadensis*
Cryptantha nevadensis var. rigida	*Cryptantha juniperensis*
Dichelostemma capitata	*Dipterostemon capitatus*
Hyptis emoryi	*Condea emoryi*
Mimulus bigelovii	*Diplacus bigelovii*
Mimulus mohavensis	*Diplacus mohavensis*
Mimulus rupicola	*Diplacus rupicola*
Mohavea breviflora	*Antirrhinum mohavea*

2nd EDITION MDWF	*3rd EDITION MDWF*
Mohavea confertiflora	Antirrhinum confertiflorum
Oenothera californica	Oenothera avita subsp. californica
Orobanche cooperi	Aphyllon cooperi
Oxytheca perfoliata	Mucronea perfoliata
Peritome arborea	Cleomella arborea
Prosopis glandulosa var. torreyana	Neltuma odorata
Prosopis pubescens	Strombocarpa pubescens

In addition to changes in the scientific names, some taxa now belong to a plant family that differs from the family into which it was placed in the second edition. Those changes, according to The Jepson Flora Project, Jepson eFlora (2023), include the following:

Scientific name	*Previous family in 2nd edition*	*Family recognized in this edition*
Eriodictyon trichocalyx	Boraginaceae	Namaceae
Heliotropium curassavicum	Boraginaceae	Heliotropiaceae
Nama demissa	Boraginaceae	Namaceae
Phacelia campanularia	Boraginaceae	Hydrophyllaceae
Phacelia crenulata	Boraginaceae	Hydrophyllaceae
Phacelia distans	Boraginaceae	Hydrophyllaceae
Phacelia fremontii	Boraginaceae	Hydrophyllaceae
Phacelia ivesiana	Boraginaceae	Hydrophyllaceae
Phacelia neglecta	Boraginaceae	Hydrophyllaceae
Phacelia parishii	Boraginaceae	Hydrophyllaceae
Phacelia pedicillata	Boraginaceae	Hydrophyllaceae
Phacelia rotundifolia	Boraginaceae	Hydrophyllaceae
Phacelia vallis-mortae	Boraginaceae	Hydrophyllaceae
Pholisma arenarium	Boraginaceae	Lennoaceae
Tiquilia plicata	Boraginaceae	Ehretiaceae

FOR FURTHER READING

Mojave Desert vegetation, plant identification, and taxonomy:

Baldwin, Bruce G., Douglas H. Goldman, David J. Keil, Robert Patterson, Thomas J. Rosatti, and Dieter H. Wilken, eds. *The Jepson Manual: Vascular Plants of California*, 2nd edition. Berkeley: University of California Press, 2012.

Benson, Lyman. *The Native Cacti of California*. Palo Alto, CA: Stanford University Press, 1969.

Benson, Lyman, and Robert A. Darrow. *The Trees and Shrubs of the Southwestern Deserts*. Tucson: The University of Arizona Press, 1954.

Bowers, J. E. *Flowers and Shrubs of the Mojave Desert*. Tucson, AZ: Southwest Parks and Monuments Association, 1999.

DeDecker, Mary. *Flora of the Northern Mojave Desert*. Berkeley: California Native Plant Society, Special Publication Number 7, 1984.

Epple, Anne Orth. *A Field Guide to the Plants of Arizona*. Mesa, AZ: LewAnn Publishing Company, 1995.

Ingram, Stephen. *Cacti, Agaves, and Yuccas of California and Nevada*. Solvang, CA: Cachuma Press, 2008.

Jaeger, Edmund C. *Desert Wild Flowers*. Palo Alto, CA: Stanford University Press, 1941.

Jepson Flora Project (eds.) 2023, Jepson eFlora, https://ucjeps.berkeley.edu/eflora/.

Kearney, Thomas H., and Robert H. Peebles. *Arizona Flora*. Berkeley: University of California Press, 1964.

Knute, Adrienne. *Plants of the East Mojave*. Cima, CA: Wide Horizons Press, 1991.

McMinn, Howard E. *An Illustrated Manual of California Shrubs*. Berkeley: University of California Press, 1939.

Munz, Philip A. *California Desert Wildflowers*. Berkeley: University of California Press, 1969.

———. *A Flora of Southern California*. Berkeley: University of California Press, 1974.

Pavlik, Bruce M. "Sand Dune Flora of the Great Basin and Mojave Deserts of California, Nevada, and Oregon." *Madroño* 32 (4): 197–213 (1985).

Stewart, Jon M. *Mojave Desert Wildflowers*. Albuquerque, NM: Jon Stewart Photography, 1998.

Taylor, Ronald J. *Desert Wildflowers of North America*. Missoula, MT: Mountain Press Publishing Company, 1998.

Turner, Raymond M., Janice E. Bowers, and Tony L. Burgess. 1995. *Sonoran Desert Plants: An Ecological Atlas.* Tucson: The University of Arizona Press, 1995.

Twisselmann, Ernest C. *A Flora of Kern County.* San Francisco: University of San Francisco, 1967.

Wallace, Gary D. "Plantae Coulterianae: Thomas Coulter's California Exsiccata." *Aliso* 37 (1): 73 (2019).

Welsh, S. L., N. D. Atwood, S. Goodrich, and L. C. Higgins, eds. *A Utah Flora.* Provo, UT: Brigham Young University, 1993.

Plant names and herbarium collection:

Bailey, L. H. *How Plants Get Their Names.* New York: Dover Publications, 1963.

Coombes, Allen J. *Dictionary of Plant Names.* Portland, OR: Timber Press, 1997.

Nilsson, Karen B. *A Wildflower by Any Other Name.* Yosemite Association, Yosemite National Park, California, 1994.

Ross, Timothy S. "Herbarium Specimens as Documents: Purposes and General Collecting Techniques." *Crossosoma* 22 (1): 3–39 (1996).

Desert ecosystems, ecology, natural history, and conservation:

Belnap, J., and D. A. Gillette. "Vulnerability of Desert Biological Crusts to Wind Erosion: The Influences of Crust Development, Soil Texture, and Disturbance." *Journal of Arid Environments* 39 (2): 133–42 (1998).

Bossard, Carla C., J. M. Randall, and Marc C. Hoshovsky, eds. *Invasive Plants of California's Wildlands.* Berkeley: University of California Press, 2000.

Brooks, M. L. "Competition between Alien Annual Grasses and Native Annual Plants in the Mojave Desert." *The American Midland Naturalist* 144 (1): 92–108 (2000).

Eldridge, David. "Ecology and Management of Biological Soil Crusts: Recent Developments and Future Challengers." *The Bryologist* 103 (4): 742–47.

Hall Jr., Clarence A., and Victoria Doyle-Jones, eds. *Plant Biology of Eastern California.* Bishop, CA: University of California, White Mountain Research Station, 1988.

Historic Indian Territories Map. http://mojavedesert.net/mojave-desert-indians/map.html.

Hohmann, M. G., and W. A. Hall. "A Framework for Prioritizing Conservation of Listed and At-Risk Species across Taxa and Installations: A Demonstration Using the Plant Biodiversity and DoD Hotspot of California." US Army Corps of Engineers, Engineer Research and Development Center, Construction Engineering Research Laboratory Project 16-829.

Jaeger, Edmund C. *The California Deserts*, 4th ed. Palo Alto, CA: Stanford University Press, 1965.

―――. *The North American Deserts*. Palo Alto, CA: Stanford University Press, 1957.

Lauer, A. "How 'Green Energy' Is Threatening Biodiversity, Human Health, and Environmental Justice: An Example from the Mojave Desert, California." *Sustainable Environment* 9 (1) (2023). doi.org/10.1080/27658511.

Lovich, J. E., and D. Bainbridge. "Anthropogenic Degradation of the Southern California Desert Ecosystem and Prospects for Natural Recovery and Restoration." *Environmental Management* 24 (3): 309–26 (1999).

Martinez-Berdeja, A., E. Ezcurra, and A. C. Sanders. "Delayed Seed Dispersal in California Deserts." *Madroño* 62 (1): 21–32 (2015).

Miller, L. M., and D. W. Keith. "Observation-Based Solar and Wind Power Capacity Factors and Power Densities." *Environmental Research Letters* (October 2018). doi.org/10.1088/1748-9326/aae102.

Osmond, C. B., S. D. Smith, B. Gui-Ying, et al. "Stem Photosynthesis in a Desert Ephemeral, *Eriogonum inflatum*." *Oecologia* 72: 542–49 (1987). doi.org/10.1007/BF00378980.

Parker, S. S., et al. "Conservation of Mojave Desert Springs and Associated Biota: Status, Threats, and Policy Opportunities." *Biodiversity and Conservation* 30: 311–27 (2021).

Pavlik, Bruce M. *The California Deserts: An Ecological Rediscovery*. Berkeley and Los Angeles, CA: University of California Press, 2008.

Phillips, Steven J., and Patricia W. Comus, eds. *A Natural History of the Sonoran Desert*. Tucson, AZ: Arizona-Sonora Desert Museum, 2000.

Rundel, Philip W., Robert J. Gustafson, and Michael E. Kaufman. *California Desert Plants: Sonoran-Mojave-Great Basin*. Backcountry Press, 2022.

Schoenherr, Allan A. *A Natural History of California*. Berkeley: University of California Press, 1992.

Historical information, ethnobotany, and medicinal uses of plants:

Bean, Lowell J., and Katherine S. Saubel. *Temalpakh: Cahuilla Indian Knowledge and Usage of Plants*. Banning, CA: Malki Museum Press, 1972.

Fowler, Catherine S., and Willards Z. Park. *Ethnographic Notes on the Northern Paiute of Western Nevada 1933–1940*. Salt Lake City: University of Utah Press, 1989.

Hodge, F. W., ed. *Handbook of the American Indians North of Mexico*, Part 2. Smithsonian Institution, Bureau of American Ethnology, Bulletin 30 (1912).

Irwin, C. N., ed. *The Shoshoni Indians of Inyo County, California: The Kerr Manuscript.* Independence, CA: Eastern California Museum, 1980.

Johnston, Frank. *The Serrano Indians of Southern California.* Banning, CA: Malki Museum Press, 1965.

Kroeber, A. L. *Handbook of the Indians of California.* 1925; Reprint, New York: Dover Publications, 1976.

Laird, Carobeth. *The Chemehuevis.* Banning, CA: Malki Museum Press, 1976.

Moore, Michael. *Medicinal Plants of the Pacific West.* Santa Fe, NM: Red Crane Books, 1993.

Murphey, Edith Van Allen. *Indian Uses of Native Plants.* Glenwood, IL: Meyerbooks, 1959.

Rhode, David. *Native Plants of Southern Nevada: An Ethnobotany.* Salt Lake City: University of Utah Press, 2002.

"The Serrano Indians, Early Inhabitants of Victor Valley." *San Bernardino Museum Quarterly* (Winter 1962).

Smith, Gerald A., and Ruth D. Simpson. *Basket Makers of San Bernardino County.* Redlands, CA: San Bernardino County Museum, 1964.

Stickel, E. G., and L. J. Weinman-Roberts. *An Overview of the Cultural Resources of the Western Mojave Desert.* A Special Report Prepared at the Request of the US Department of Interior, Bureau of Land Management, 1980.

Sturtevant, W. C., ed. *Handbook of North American Indians, Volume 10: Southwest.* Washington, DC: Smithsonian Institution, 1983.

———. *Handbook of North American Indians, Volume 11: Great Basin.* Washington, DC: Smithsonian Institution, 1986.

Walker, Clifford J. *Back Door to California: The Story of the Mojave River Trail.* Barstow, CA: Mojave River Valley Museum Association, 1986.

Insects:

Emmel, Thomas C., and John F. Emmel. "The Butterflies of Southern California." Natural History Museum of Los Angeles County, Science Series 26 (1973).

Holland, W. J. *The Moth Book: A Guide to the Moths of North America.* New York: Dover Publications, 1968.

Pellmyr, Olle. "Yuccas, Yucca Moths, and Coevolution: A Review." *Annals of the Missouri Botanic Garden* 90 (1) (2002).

Powell, Jerry A., and Charles L. Hogue. *California Insects*. Berkeley: University of California Press, 1979.

Pratt, G. F., D. Walker, J. Zarki, and J. F. Emmel. *The Butterflies and Skippers of Joshua Tree National Park*. Mojave Desert Land Trust, 2023.

Scott, James A. *The Butterflies of North America: A Natural History and Field Guide*. Palo Alto, CA: Stanford University Press, 1986.

Stewart, Bob. *Common Butterflies of California*. Point Reyes Station, CA: West Coast Lady Press, 1997.

Geology and pack-rat middens:

Betancourt, Julio L., Thomas R. Van Devender, and Paul S. Martin, eds. *Packrat Middens*. Tucson: The University of Arizona Press, 1990.

Hunt, Charles B. *Death Valley: Geology, Ecology, Archaeology*. Berkeley: University of California Press, 1975.

INDEX